MYTHS OF MIGHTY WOMEN

MYTHS OF MIGHTY WOMEN

Their Application in Psychoanalytic Psychotherapy

edited by

*Arlene Kramer Richards
and Lucille Spira*

A volume in the Psychoanalysis & Women Series
for the Committee on Women and Psychoanalysis
of the International Psychoanalytical Association

KARNAC

First published in 2015 by
Karnac Books Ltd
118 Finchley Road, London NW3 5HT

British Library Cataloguing in Publication Data

A C.I.P. for this book is available from the British Library

ISBN 978 1 78220 304 9

Edited, designed and produced by The Studio Publishing Services Ltd
www.publishingservicesuk.co.uk
e-mail: studio@publishingservicesuk.co.uk

www.karnacbooks.com

CONTENTS

PART III: THE POWER OF MOTHERS
AND THE GODDESSES WITHIN

PART IV: THE POWER OF WOMEN'S SEXUALITY

PART V: THE FATHER'S CONTRIBUTION
TO WOMEN'S POWER

PART VI

ACKNOWLEDGEMENTS

Chapters One, Two, Five, Seven, Nine, Sixteen, and Seventeen are versions of papers that were presented at a COWAP Conference, "Myths of the Mighty Woman: What Makes a Woman?", held in New York City, 11–12 October 2014. We thank all those who participated in that conference, which became the basis for this work:

(Presenters): Cecile Bassen, Irmgard Dettbarn, Giselle Galdi, Philip Matyszak, Alicia Ostriker, Arlene Kramer Richards, John Munder Ross, Ellen Sinkman, Frances Thomson-Salo, and Arthur A. Lynch who moderated the programme.

(Discussion Group Leaders): Sandra Buechler, Paula Ellman, Deborah Green, Judith Logue, Margery Quackenbush, Lucille Spira, and Patsy Turrini.

There are many others to thank for their help and support: The International Psychoanalytical Association for their support throughout; Frances Thomson-Salo of the IPA Committee on Women and Psychoanalysis for her overall guidance, substantive help, and support; Tamar and Larry Schwartz and Steve Thierman for their help throughout the conference; Dr Kenneth Winarick of the Karen Horney Center for his support of the event.

Rod Tweedy, our Karnac editor, and Cecily Blench, who patiently responded to all our concerns, deserve special thanks, along with Merle Molofsky, colleague and friend, for her generous and delicate editorial help. We would also like to thank the team at The Studio, who produced the book. The wonderful psychoanalysts, literary scholars, and classicists who so generously contributed their work to create *Myths of Mighty Women: Their Application in Psychoanalytic Psychotherapy* cannot be thanked enough.

This book is dedicated to Helen Meyers—an esteemed educator and enthusiastic exponent of psychoanalytic theory. She supported many women on their paths to becoming psychoanalysts, and she was a strong advocate for COWAP. We are grateful to Donald Meyers and Andrew Meyers for giving us permission for this dedication and for their beautiful tribute to her in this work.

Arlene Kramer Richards

I appreciate the inspiration and teaching of my friends, colleagues, family, and patients. My husband Arnold Richards has been my support, my audience and my muse. He helps me to feel powerful and appreciated. My children Tamar, Rebecca, and Stephen have given me the gift of time and space to do my own work from the dark days of writing a dissertation to the present. My daughter-in-law Carol has been a dear friend and my grandsons Joshua and Justin a source of joy. I would never have arrived where I am without all of them.

My colleague and friend Lucille Spira has worked loyally and fruitfully on the conference that gave rise to this book. From concept to detail, from the technical to the social she has been a true partner. I have felt lucky beyond my desserts all my life, but never as much as I feel now.

Lucille Spira

I am pleased to be part of a book dedicated to Dr Helen Meyers. Dr Meyers was the Medical Director of Riverdale Mental Health Association where I began my career as a psychotherapist. She was Riverdale's psychoanalytic mighty woman, admired by all. Stimulating and sometimes intimidating, her teaching, derived from a broad range of psychoanalytic theory, was always to the point. She was her own person, an accomplished woman in all spheres. Furthermore, she drove a Jaguar, a clue that she had an Artemis side.

Without Arlene Kramer Richards, a special kind of mighty woman, who inspires all of those who know her, this book would not have happened. To many, she is the psychoanalyst, consultant, or friend who "gets it". Athena is always at her side. I thank her so much for bringing me along on this project.

My patients, every day, as they say what is on their mind, teach me not only about themselves, but also about the vicissitudes of life. The NYSPP Board, led by Ed Fancher and Miriam Pierce, deserve recognition for helping to keep psychoanalytic psychotherapy in the forefront. I thank the NYSPP Psychoanalytic Socio-Cultural Literary Group members, E. Henschel, M. Razavi, S. Parness, R. Espie, and B. Hertzberg, who make the novels we read more interesting and relevant to our work as psychotherapists.

On a more personal note, I thank Bill Spira for the space and support that he gives me to disappear and pursue my interests. I am grateful to Carol Munter and my other colleagues and friends (Lillian Berman, Lynne Herbst, and Linda Halperin) who were so generous in supporting this effort.

Permissions

We are grateful for permission to reprint the following material:

Lines from *Whatever Happened to Miriam* by Arthur Strimling (published by agreement with the author).

Lines from *The Nakedness of the Fathers* by Alicia Ostriker (published by kind permission of the author).

"Meyers has her say" (interview by Henry Schwartz) is published with permission from the *Bulletin of the Association for Psychoanalytic Medicine* (Columbia University, Spring 2010).

We thank Henry Schwartz for allowing us to include his interview with Helen Meyers, in which she impressively describes how she understands and integrates psychoanalytic theory to the practice of psychoanalysis and psychotherapy.

ABOUT THE EDITORS AND CONTRIBUTORS

Ronnie Ancona, PhD, Professor of Classics at Hunter College and CUNY Graduate Center, is a Latin scholar, and author of *Time and the Erotic in Horace's Odes* (Duke University, 1994), co-editor of *Gendered Dynamics in Latin Love Poetry* (Johns Hopkins University, 2005), and, with Sarah Pomeroy, of the series *Women in Antiquity* (Oxford University Press). She has published works on Latin poetry and pedagogy.

Irmgard Dettbarn, DrPhil, is a psychologist and member of the International Psychoanalytical Association. A former teacher, since 2007 she has been an interim training analyst in Beijing, China. She has published on psychoanalysis and the media, and is in private practice in Berlin.

Elizabeth Haase, MD, trained with Columbia Center for Psychoanalysis and has written and taught in the areas of gender development, sexuality, and shame. She is on the boards of the Association for the Advancement of Psychodynamic Psychiatry, the Helix Center, and the journals of the Association for Psychoanalytic Medicine and the American Academy of Psychoanalysis and Dynamic Psychiatry.

Philip Matyszak, DPhil, has a BA Honours degree from the University of London and a Doctorate in Roman History from Oxford University. He has written extensively on the ancient world, both in the academic sphere and for the general reader. He currently teaches online courses for Madingley Hall, University of Cambridge.

Andrew Meyers, MA, MPhil, is proud to have grown up during what many consider to be the Golden Age of American psychoanalysis as the son of two influential psychoanalysts and teachers, one of whom was, indeed, a "mighty woman". He is also the proud father of two very psychodynamically minded and mighty women. He is currently Director of Interdisciplinary Studies and the City Semester Program at the Ethical Culture Fieldston School.

Donald Meyers, MD, has served the Columbia Psychoanalytic Center for over fifty years in many capacities, including Organizer and First Director of the Child Psychoanalysis Program and as a training analyst and as a clinical professor of psychiatry at the College of Physicians and Surgeons, Columbia University Medical Center NYC. He has also served as Secretary of the American Psychoanalytic Association.

Merle Molofsky, MFA, is a psychoanalyst, poet, and playwright. Recent publications include a novel, *Streets, 1970* (IP Books, 2015), and a chapter in *Living Moments: On the Work of Michael Eigen* (Karnac, 2015). She is a member of the Faculty, National Psychological Association for Psychoanalysis, on the Advisory Board of the Harlem Family Institute and on the Editorial Board of *The Psychoanalytic Review*, and is a member of the Board of Directors, International Forum for Psychoanalytic Education.

Alicia Ostriker, PhD, is a poet and critic and the author of fifteen volumes of poetry, most recently *The Old Woman, the Tulip, and the Dog*. As a critic, she is author of *The Nakedness of the Fathers: Biblical Visions and Revisions* and other books on poetry and the bible. She is Distinguished Professor Emerita of English Literature at Rutgers. Her work won both a Paterson Poetry Award, and a William Carlos Williams Award of the Poetry Society of America, among other honours. She is Chancellor of the Academy of American Poets.

Elina Reenkola, MD, is a training analyst the Finnish Psychoanalytic Society in Helsinki. A former European COWAP co-chair, she has published four books on female psychology in Finnish: *Naisen verhottu sisin* (1997), also published in English, *The Veiled Female Core* (2002), *Intohimoinen nainen* (2008) (Female Desire), *Nainen ja viha* (2012) (Vicissitudes of Female Aggression), and *Nainen ja häpeä* (2014) (Female Shame). She has also written articles on pregnancy, breast-feeding, sister fantasy, and female revenge.

Arlene Kramer Richards, EdD, is a member of the International Psychoanalytical Association and COWAP, a Fellow, training and supervising analyst, IPTAR, and a training analyst at the New York Freudian Society. She is a member of the Faculty of Tonji Medical College, and has published numerous articles and books on topics including gender related issues and women's psychology, loneliness, and on literature and films.

John Munder Ross, PhD, is a training analyst at Columbia, has published eight books and numerous articles, many of them on gender related issues, fathers and children, and applied psycho-analysis. Dr Ross is in private practice in New York. He is a member of the International Psychoanalytical Association and the American Psychoanalytic Association.

Paul Schwaber, PhD, is Professor of Letters Emeritus at Wesleyan University and a psychoanalyst in private practice. He has written on relations of psychoanalysis and imaginative literature, most notably *The Cast of Characters: a Reading of 'Ulysses'* (Yale University Press, 1999). He and his wife, Rosemary Balsam, MD, edit the Book Review section of the *Journal of the American Psychoanalytic Association*.

Henry P. Schwartz, MD, is a former President of the Association for Psychoanalytic Medicine, and the former editor-in-chief of its publication, *The Bulletin*. A child and adolescent psychiatrist and psycho-analyst, he is a member of the Faculty of the Columbia Psychoanalytic Institute and the NYU-Langone School of Medicine. He has a private practice in New York City.

Ellen Sinkman, LCSW, is a training and supervising psychoanalyst and a member of the International Psychoanalytical Association, Contemporary Freudian Society, and the Institute for Psychoanalytic Training and Research. She has a private practice in psychoanalysis and psychotherapy in New York City and Westchester. She is the author of *The Psychology of Beauty: Creation of a Beautiful Self* (2013, Jason Aronson).

Lucille Spira, LCSW/PhD, is a member of the New York School for Psychoanalytic Psychotherapy and Psychoanalysis (NYSPP), and has delivered presentations on loneliness and literary works at NYSPP and the American Psychoanalytic Association, Division 39, etc. She is Co-Chair of the American Psychoanalytic Association's Loneliness Discussion Group, and has published in various psychoanalytic journals. She co-edited with A. K. Richards and A. A. Lynch *Encounters with Loneliness: Only the Lonely* (Best Anthology, Gradiva Award, 2014), and is in private practice in New York.

Frances Thomson-Salo, MD, is a professor trained with the British Psychoanalytical Society, and is immediate past President of the Australian Society, Overall Chair of the IPA Committee of Women and Psychoanalysis, a Board member of the *International Journal of Psychoanalysis*, Honorary Principal Fellow, Department of Psychiatry, University of Melbourne, and Honorary Fellow of the Murdoch Children's Research Institute.

Patsy Turrini, MSW, LCSW, is the co-author of *Separation–Individuation: Theory and Application*, and co-editor of *Inner World of the Mother*. She is a member of the NYSPP Adjunct Faculty and a supervisor on the Advanced Program in Psychoanalysis and Psychotherapy at the Derner Institute, Adelphi University. She has published a number of papers, and is the Originator of the Mothers Center Model: Motherscenters.org.

SERIES EDITOR'S FOREWORD

As the Overall Chair of the International Psychoanalytical Association's Committee on Women and Psychoanalysis (COWAP), I am very pleased to write the foreword for this book, which adds to the ever-growing stable of this series. Otto Kernberg, when he was President of the IPA, set up COWAP in 1998 to explore scientific and political issues about the differences between women and men, and a hallmark of COWAP has always been a willingness to engage with other organisations and ideas, and to benefit from opening up a reciprocal discussion.

The chapters in this book offer a multi-faceted experience of both scientific and creative interest with important results, as well as being fascinating in their range and reach, covering both current and long past worldwide issues.

On behalf of COWAP and its wider community, I would like to say how grateful we are to Arlene Kramer Richards and Lucille Spira for their unstinting and, above all, thoughtful hard work in enabling this book to come to fruition. The chapters' vibrancy indicates that as psychoanalytic thinking and work becomes more complex and we need to deepen our understanding of the analytic process, what comes with that is a greater awareness of shared ground and a clarity with respect to broader ways of understanding the field.

I am struck above all by the combined creativity that emerges with the fields studied and in the ways of studying them, and in that way much that is new has been created in this book.

Frances Thomson-Salo
Overall Chair,
Committee on Women and Psychoanalysis

PREFACE

*Myths of Mighty Women: Their Application in Psychoanalytic Psycho-
therapy* began with a conference sponsored by the Committee on
Women and Psychoanalysis (COWAP) of the International Psychoanalytical Association, held at the Karen Horney Center in New York
City, October 2014.

We started with the premise that psychoanalytic psychotherapists
and psychoanalysts empower women when they help them to connect
with strong female figures who, throughout time, have transcended
limits, barriers, and met challenges boldly. Myths of such mighty
women can inspire both psychotherapists and their patients to persist
in doing what is necessary to successfully fulfil their quests. In that
process, we identify with the might of our ancestors, find strength
within ourselves, and the "grandmothers" have their place at the
table.

Here, through the voices of our esteemed contributors, some of
whom presented at the conference, we present myths from eastern
and western society that illustrate the various images and characteristics that have helped to shape values inherent in women's roles.

As Campbell (2008) says about mythic characters, psychoanalytic
psychotherapists and their patients engage in a journey, often with

some reluctance on the part of the patient, towards a particular end. Here, we show how the myths presented in this work are useful to us and to the patients whom we treat. Towards this end, after each section of our authors' contributions, we discuss how a particular myth, as it resonates with various views within psychoanalysis, can be used to better understand and help our women patients to develop their voices so that they can enrich both their lives and those of others.

References

Campbell, J. (2008). *The Hero With a Thousand Faces*. Novato, CA: New World Library.

Introduction: Mighty Medea, or why female figures from Greco-Roman antiquity matter today

Ronnie Ancona

Whether we are psychoanalysts, patients, classics professors, students, or members of today's culture occupying various other positions (and, of course, these positions can overlap), the pull of the myths of mighty women or of the lives of actual mighty women from the past is strong. Figures like Clytemnestra, Pandora, Helen of Troy, Antigone, Medea, Clodia, and Cleopatra from Greco-Roman antiquity continue to fascinate wide-ranging audiences.

The idea that myth can become incorporated into psychoanalysis is, of course, not new. Many today know of Oedipus primarily because of his appearance in Freud's Oedipus complex, while female figures in classical myth have been appropriated as well, as Elektra was by Jung, and, more recently, Psyche has been by Carol Gilligan (2002). This appropriation, though, can go both ways. I, for example, as a Latin scholar, utilised the psychoanalytic work of Jessica Benjamin (1980) when looking for a model to help explain dominance and separation issues in relation to gender in a first century BCE Latin poem by Horace (Ancona, 1989).

Thus, the fact that real world women's issues may be aided by a turn to images of mighty women from the past is a fascinating and welcome development within an already established nexus of connections between psychoanalysis and the study of classical antiquity. The use of myths about mighty women from classical antiquity, specifically in a therapeutic setting, is, in fact, an exciting extension within the general area of classical reception, which examines how earlier Greco-Roman works are received in later times and how that later reception can, in turn, make us rethink those earlier works. (On classical reception, see Martindale (1993) and *Classical Receptions Journal*.)

These old stories (of mythic figures and real ones as well) are reinterpreted by each generation and by each individual and they take on new lives. Those reinterpretations can then make us see retrospectively the earlier versions anew. Thus, myth can contribute to psychoanalysis, but psychoanalysis then also contributes to the study of myth because the myth becomes new in each of its instantiations, including those in the therapeutic setting addressed in this volume.

I will share with you here a few brief reflections on my experience teaching about the figure of Medea to a group of students at Hunter College who had little or no background in the subject. My course is called "Medea: Ancient and Modern Figure in Literature and the Arts" and is offered in the Thomas Hunter Honors Program. Put briefly, Medea is the princess from Colchis on the Black Sea who helps the Greek hero Jason to get the magical Golden Fleece. After he leaves her to remarry, she kills the children she had with him. Students read the most famous version of Medea, that written by the Greek playwright Euripides in the fifth century BCE, but they experience many other Medeas as well.

While students are not the same as patients, they do share with patients a unique set of issues and interests. Just as a particular feature of a given myth may be useful for addressing a specific issue in therapy with a particular individual, so a given feature of the same myth may capture the imagination of a particular student. Students learn over the course of a term that Medea is a very hard figure to "pin down", as they examine numerous works of literature, dance, film, and opera that contain a version of Medea.

While recognising a core to her myth, students see the great variation in how she is reinterpreted over time and over different genres. The myth contains potentially relatable material, but its appearance in a specific formal context (a given play or poem or film) that establishes boundaries for how we interpret her forces the student to see the version of Medea that is there and not the one he or she might want to see there.

Here are some of the ways in which versions of her story may differ. They might provide varied motivations and justifications for the killing of her children. Some might emphasise her divinity (she is the granddaughter of Helios, the Sun). Others make her quite human. In some, her foreignness (she is not Greek) is emphasised. In others, that feature is less important. In some, the chorus sympathises with her; in others, they do not. For both Jason and Medea, the significance of love or sex can vary, as does that of the heroic code with which each can be associated. Finally, how each of them is depicted as a parent might change depending on the perspective presented in a given work. Thus, the student must really read, or view and respond to, the particular Medea and cannot make generalisations about her that the specific work cannot support.

Her story is so powerful that it almost automatically seems to produce emotional as well as intellectual connections with the students. This is part of why the course is so exciting to teach. The student most taken with Medea's jealousy of Jason's new wife and with her witchy powers to cause destruction might be especially drawn to Martha Graham's modern dance piece from the 1940s, "Cave of the Heart," which does not focus on the issue of infanticide, at least not directly. Another student, interested in the younger, more innocent Medea, might be more drawn to the version of her found in Apollonius of Rhodes' third century BCE Greek epic, *Argonautica*, which focuses on her early relationship with Jason. Another, interested in the feminist potential of Medea's story, would probably be excited by her speech to the chorus on the constraints of marriage for women in Euripides' version as well as by the 1970s depiction of her in the context of feminism found in Jules Dassin's film, *A Dream of Passion*.

Students, of course, must argue for their interpretations in an academic context based on the evidence of the particular work under examination, but that does not preclude divergence of points of view. This produces lively debate in class and provides many opportunities for critical writing. Medea, in the same work, can often be viewed as right or wrong, sympathetic or unsympathetic, caring for her children or not caring for her children, human or god-like, sane or crazy. Finally, as a composite figure, she is potentially all of these things and that is why discussion and interpretation often hinges less on what she did than on why. Students become engaged with her motivation and her power. They are attracted to her fearlessness and her ability to take control of a situation, despite her horrific deed of infanticide.

Whether she is sane or crazy, loves her children or does not, loves Jason or hates him (and these are, in many ways, polarities that good art and literature deny), she is ultimately compelling. It is this compelling quality of Medea—she is something "out there" in the "separate" world of story and myth that almost forces us to react personally—that allows for a rich double experience of relatability and distance. When we teach literature and the arts, we want our students to react with passion as well as with critical acumen. In the clinical context, where brain and emotions are also engaged (and not always in synchronisation), I can imagine how myth might be a potentially liberating tool for clinician and patient alike.

References

Ancona, R. (1989). The subterfuge of reason: Horace, *Odes* 1.23 and the construction of male desire. *Helios, 16*: 49–57

Benjamin, J. (1980). The bonds of love: rational violence and erotic domination. In: H. Eisenstein & A. Jardine (Eds.), *The Future of Difference* (pp. 41–70). New Brunswick, NJ: Rutgers.

Classical Receptions Journal. Oxford: Oxford University Press.

Gilligan, C. (2002). *The Birth of Pleasure: A New Map of Love.* New York: Knopf.

Martindale, C. (1993). *Redeeming the Text: Latin Poetry and the Hermeneutics of Reception.* Cambridge: Cambridge University Press.

Ancona's introduction: implications for psychoanalytic psychotherapists

Arlene Kramer Richards and Lucille Spira

Mighty Medea is an inspiring woman character and a frightening one. Her myth, and especially the way Ronnie Ancona teaches it, can inspire the clinician to:

- explore the patient's ambivalent feeling towards any mythological figure;
- elaborate the feelings about the mythological character at different ages so as to open the possibilities for change and development over time;
- help the patient develop awareness of the point of view of other people towards the mythological figure, to tolerate the differences and to appreciate the widening of her world when these alternative ways of understanding are explored.

PART I

THE POWER OF GODDESSES
AND STRONG WOMEN

CHAPTER ONE

What do women want? Inanna and the might of women

Arlene Kramer Richards

Introduction

Why do psychoanalysts study myths? Arlow (1961) thought,

> The myth is a particular kind of communal experience. It is a special form of shared fantasy, and it serves to bring the individual into relationship with members of his cultural group on the basis of certain common needs. Accordingly, the myth can be studied from the point of view of its function in psychic integration—how it plays a role in warding off feelings of guilt and anxiety, how it constitutes a form of adaptation to reality and to the group in which the individual lives, and how it influences the crystallization of the individual identity and the formation of the superego. (p. 375)

In this formulation, the myth serves the society in allowing forbidden wishes a place in reality but containing these wishes so that they do not disrupt the social order. At the same time, myths serve a purpose for each individual in the society. The myth allows an individual to feel less alone, more like others, and more a part of a reliable environment. It "holds" the individual in the sense of Winnicott (1972) and it provides safety in the sense of Sullivan (1968), while it can link all humans in a sense of common underlying wishes, in Jung's (1981) view, and relate people to one another in the process of telling, listening, reading, or viewing the mythological cosmos (Schlochower, 2013). All of these different analytic theories accord a place of importance to myths.

Many of the myths that have been collected and studied are myths of the hero or the king and his path to sovereignty and his downfall from that position. Campbell (2008) collected and discussed the myths in many cultures of how the kingship is ended by death and the next king is the hero who has displaced the prior one. No one has yet put together a parallel set of myths of womanly power in western and eastern cultures, or attempted to find the common thread of how women are empowered and dethroned. It is such a mythology for women that we are now addressing in this volume. Putting together a work parallel to Campbell's myths of mighty men would take much work and require genius like his. However, as a group, we can start on this project with the hope that others will contribute to it and that someone will be able to synthesise what is collected and be interested in doing so. This work would, I hope, help women to see ourselves as having common wishes, hopes, aspirations, fears, doubts, and ways of dealing with all of the contradictions between them.

Myths of mighty women stretch back as far as the origins of spoken language. The earliest such myth that has come down to us in written form is that of Inanna, Queen of Heaven, from Sumer, which was written two thousand years before the Old Testament, the Hebrew Bible. Ironically, this myth from people who lived in what is now Southern Iraq is a kind of message from the ancients of what was the most advanced civilisation in the world to a contemporary civilisation in which Iraq is a problem, not a solution.

Inanna develops

Inanna has a story. It is set in the time when everything on earth had been made; it is explicit that even bread had been made. So, this is a story of the beginning of agriculture and the time when shepherds and farmers lived together. Her story starts with her nurturing a tree. She waits for it to grow, but a serpent goes to live in its roots, a bird in its branches, and Lillith, the wild woman, lives in its trunk.

Gilgamesh, Inanna's brother, cuts down the tree to make her a throne and a bed, and she uses the top branches to make him a crown. She has the throne, the symbol of worldly power and the bed, the symbol of sexuality and procreation. Then she goes to visit her father, Enki. On the way, she leans against an apple tree and looks at her vulva. She applauds herself, naming herself the Queen of Heaven.

This scene of Inanna looking at her vulva and declaring herself the Queen of Heaven attributes woman's power to the awareness of her vulva and the display of the vulva leads to pride in the self. This view is the opposite of Freud's supposition that a little girl feels deprived when she sees her vulva, thinking it inferior to the little boy's penis. It receives later confirmation in the modern psycho-analytic literature, which describes female development in terms of pride, satisfaction, and disparagement of the penis (Mayer, 1985; Richards, 1995). In this view, the little girl feels the vulva as a source of pleasure and, therefore, sees anything different in the way of geni-tals as alien, threatening, and to be rejected. Freud thought that the little girl was envious of the penis, and that observation was the cause of much misery to the growing girl and the grown woman. I think that penis envy is thus conflated with rejection of a genital different from the vulva.

When she reaches her father, Enki, the God of Wisdom, she is offered butter cake, water, and beer. She eats and then drinks beer with her father. They drink and drink. She makes him drunk. While drunk, he gives her all the holy powers he has, including godship, kingship, priest-ship, priestess-ship, the arts, including the art of pros-titution, the sciences, the emotions, the crafts, agriculture, procreation, judge-ship, and the power of decision making.

Thus, Inanna derives her power from her father. Patriarchy precedes matriarchy. Unlike the story of matriarchy and goddess worship as prior to patriarchy and a male god (Gimbutas, 1989), this myth tells of a daughter grabbing power from her father by making him drunk. It foreshadows the myths of women stealing men's powers in the bible (Ostriker, this volume). It also foreshadows Sara, Delilah, Judith, and other women who use intellectual power to over-come men's physical power.

Inanna celebrates her powers when she brings them to her own city. Now she takes a husband. She wants a farmer, but a shepherd insists that he has more to give her. They argue and:

> The word they had spoken
> was a word of desire.
> From the starting of the quarrel came the lovers' desire.
>> (Wolkstein & Kramer, 1983, p. 34)

This description of the role of aggression in fuelling sexual passion sounds both modern and compelling. It could be advice from a marriage counsellor or a family therapist. It could be a precursor of the psychoanalytic theory proposed by Melanie Klein (1952). The aggression integrated into the tenderness of love fuels desire (Lacan, 1973).

Waiting

Then waiting fuels desire. With her chosen lover at her door,

> Inanna, at her mother's command,
> Bathed and anointed herself with scented oil.
> She covered her body with the royal white robe.
> She readied her dowry.
> She arranged her precious lapis beads around her neck.
> She took her seal in her hand.
>> (Wolkstein & Kramer, p. 35)

Again, this waiting time for the husband is a time for increasing her own desire. Inanna does not rush to open her door. She uses the time to increase her own desire. She chooses to make herself desirable with perfume, clothing, and jewellery, very much like a modern woman. By the time she opens her door to her husband, she is eager and ready.

In the Inanna myth, both the virginity and the elaborate preparations for the marital intercourse are dramatic.

She asks,

> Who will plow my vulva? (p. 37)
> And her husband answers,

> Great lady, the king will plow your vulva.
> I, Dumuzi the King will plow your vulva.
>> (p. 37)

So far, the romance and love-making are explicit and unsurprising except in the frankness of the language. But the tone veers gradually; the lovers start to speak of their love in the past tense.

Inanna says,

> He shaped my loins with his fair hands,
> The shepherd Dumuzi filled my lap with cream and milk,
> He stroked my pubic hair,
> He watered my womb.
> He laid his hands on my holy vulva,
> He smoothed my black boat with cream,
> He quickened my narrow boat with milk,
> He caressed me with milk,
> He caressed me on the bed.
>
> (p. 44)

This frank description of sexual love leads Inanna and Dumuzi to a marriage that produces two sons who grow up in their family. However, the idyll does not last forever.

Waning

Later, Dumuzi her husband says,

> Set me free my sister, set me free.
> You will be a little daughter to my father
> Come, my beloved sister, I would go to the palace.
> Set me free . . .
>
> (p. 48)

The text is explicit. Dumuzi wants to remain in the family, offering the position of little sister rather than wife to Inanna. He wants to get out of the sexual relationship and into a loving but fraternal relationship with Inanna.

The romance is over. Inanna goes to the underworld, where she dies and her corpse is hung on the wall. The aching description of her sadness when the marriage ends shows her in the underworld as a metaphor for how she feels in her heart. She mourns him, weeps for his loss and hers. Yet, she does not stay there forever. Being cared for by people in the middle world, she is rescued by their care. When she is rescued, she must provide someone in her place. First, she considers her female friend and adviser, but rejects that idea because she has been faithful to Inanna in war and peace. Then she considers but rejects sacrificing her elder son, then her younger son, but she agrees to sacrifice her estranged husband, the shepherd Dumuzi. He can mourn endlessly instead of her.

But he has family also. Dumuzi's sister mourns him. She begs Inanna to rescue her brother. This is the perfect retort for Inanna. He wanted her to be a sister to him; she allows his sister to be his partner. Inanna offers him half the year in the underground, half in the middle world. She agrees to have his sister serve the other half of the sentence, going down into the underworld when he comes up, and coming back up when he goes down. The story is over; the yearly cycle of six months of fertility and six months of rest is set. For ancient times, the story is happy as well as just.

What does it tell us for our time? First, it precedes the story of Persephone (Kulish & Holtzman, 2008), who leaves her mother for her lover in the underworld for six months of the year. Psychoanalysts have made much of the ambivalence in the story of the daughter's love for her mother being diminished by her love for her husband. Yet, Inanna's myth is different. Her mother is not even part of the story. Inanna is clear: she can live without her husband but cannot live without her female friend and helper and not without her sons. Her story is the story of a woman who fulfils her own destiny, enjoys her sexuality, her lover, and her husband, but finally chooses her own power and her loyalty to her children over her attachment to her husband. Inanna is a woman who can tolerate separation from her husband. Unlike Persephone, she does not spend any time in the underworld; unlike Persephone, she does not choose loyalty to her mother; unlike Persephone, she does not rely on the offer her husband makes her, she decides her own fate.

The modern woman

In this sense, Inanna is a modern woman. The Inanna story means different things to women at different stages in life. To the teenage girl, the story of her getting power from her father (Katz, 2002) is both meaningful and practical. Rather than wishing for a Prince Charming to make her his mate and settling for the status of a second rate power, she can see herself as trading her child status for young adulthood and achievements of her own. She can, as an older teenager or young adult, see the power of Inanna's sexuality, her taking possession of her own body and her pride in the beauty and power of her vulva as a path she can follow.

The waiting time for marriage in Inanna's story is echoed in modern marriage customs in the USA and in eastern cultures as well. A bride in China takes a day off from her job to buy the perfect shoes for her wedding; an American bride takes her mother to many stores to watch her try on one gown after another; an Indian bride sits patiently while her hands are adorned with henna patterns of great intricacy. All such customs delay the wedding and enhance its importance in the minds of the bridal couple, their families, and their friends. The delay serves as a frame enhancing the import of the event. In the USA, this waiting time and elaborate ritual of choosing the place, choosing the guests, choosing the invitations, planning the seating arrangements for the wedding meal, planning the music and the flowers and the colour schemes, choosing the bridesmaids, choosing what they will wear, choosing the groomsmen and what they will wear, and endless other details of a wedding is such an intricate process that people hire professional wedding planners to see to all the details. The constantly increasing intricacies replace the former emphasis on waiting for the consummation of a marriage by preserving the bride's virginity until the wedding night. When premarital sex became ubiquitous, the substitution of the wedding party ritual has filled the place of premarital chastity as a frame for the importance of the marital commitment.

Implications for treatment

Treating a depressed young woman who felt overwhelmed by her parents' success in their working lives and their wealth and power, I spent several years supporting her in her efforts to develop a life of her own. Her road was bumpy. She did not feel pride in her own small achievements when she compared them to what her parents had achieved. When she pursued a field that was too emotionally difficult for her because it required a self-confidence she did not feel, she became depressed again. Leaving that was difficult for her, but with support from her family and from me she chose another field and went to school to train for that. Again, she felt less than adequate. Her best friend had entered that field. She worried whether her friend would feel that she had intruded on her friend's territory. I connected that to fear that her parents would reject her if she succeeded in becoming anything other than their daughter. We talked a lot about how she wanted to be more powerful than they were. Wanting that was what kept her unable to compete with anyone. She was too terrified of inciting others to feel the murderous envy she felt. I interpreted that to her in the form of "What could happen if your father saw you as doing better than him?" We explored the role of envy in herself making her afraid of the envy of others.

I used the Inanna story for my own understanding of a path out of her paralysing envy. She could use her father's power if he made her a gift of it. She could ask his advice for a career choice. He might become proud of her if she used that advice. Like Inanna, she could accept the cultural understanding that her father could give her. Understanding herself as someone who could make her parents proud of the good start they had given her helped her to allow herself success in a field related to the work her father did. She could see it as a continuation of his power rather than a challenge to it. She still vacillates between fear of success and determination to grow up and be independent. But she has come further in her current field than she ever did in her former one and she is continuing to work hard towards her goal.

Yet, the myth of Inanna does not stop with marriage as "happily ever after". Her story continues into the challenges of adulthood. She chooses the man she will marry; she does not wait to be chosen. She chooses a man who brings gifts, who wants her enough to overcome her reluctance. She gives him kingship rather than becoming queen through her marriage. She is unafraid of her power. She wields power in the world even through the years of motherhood and child rearing. And then her husband asks for his freedom.

Inanna gives her husband the freedom he asks for and she chooses her own freedom. She takes what she wants and what she does not want she leaves.

The myth has a developmental message: the young bride is in love with her husband, but once she recognises that her husband does not want to stay with her, her first loyalty is to her children.

Imagine a modern woman in the same situation: her husband has told her that she is no longer what he wants. She has spent the last twenty-five years bringing up their children in a suburban town. When he married her, she was a successful academic; now she is so long out of her field that she cannot go back. He is no longer interested in her. The children are off at college; he no longer comes home to hear her talk to and about them. Talking with her now is talking trivia. Women at work are much more interesting. She goes into a depression. How can she get out of it? Just when she needs him most, he is not there for her. It would be all too easy to blame her husband for ending the marriage, but the story of Inanna suggests a different outcome.

The story of Inanna helps. The modern woman recognises her own power. She has spent these twenty-five years developing social and managerial skills. At this stage of her life, she can use those to start a business. Her idea is to offer high quality day care to working mothers. She can get other older women to work at this after they have successfully raised their own children. She knows many people in her town, even a person who has a very large old house that could be used for a day care centre. She develops a sideline to her business catering dinners, so that the parents who come to pick up their children can get dinner at the same time. She is doing what she did as a wife, but now, on her own, it is an interesting and satisfying business. She is not making a lot of money, but with the settlement from her divorce she has enough to live on. Like Inanna, she has a domain she can take care of. No longer depressed, she is out of the underworld.

This is just one example of how a myth can be used in therapy. The situation will determine whether the therapist uses the myth to remind herself that placing blame is not the best way to deal with a defunct marriage or chooses to tell her patient about the myth, or simply gives her a book with the myth in it. Some patients might need the moral of the story spelled out for them; others will get it once they read the story.

Coming back to Arlow's (1961) discussion of myth, recall that he attributed several functions to myths. He considered the adaptive functions of integrating the individual into the group and of consolidating individual identity and especially the superego. In this, his view parallels that of Jung (1981) even though the conventions of psychoanalytic references at that time would not permit him to acknowledge the precedent. He also pointed to the defensive functions of protecting the individual from guilt and anxiety. I think the myth can also defend against feelings of shame. The idea of the superego consisting of a part that holds up ideals and a part that enforces punishment for misdeeds would show shame as failure to live up to the ideals and guilt as punishment for misdeeds. Yet, if we think of guilt as related to the conscience and shame as related to what others will think about us, then the myth speaks to what we think others expect of us and the failure to live up to that image as impelling hiding from others or oneself what we believe the people around us would disapprove of, then the needs of the person to feel free of condemnation and punishment are met by the guidance myths can give about what is allowed and what is admired by most people in the society in which we live.

That kind of guidance is found in psychotherapy only in oblique ways. We can listen to patients work out their choices and their conflicts in metaphors, in gossip, in discussions of dreams, jokes, and slips of the tongue. We can hear them in talking about films, plays, novels, poetry, music, art, dance, and any hobbies or interests that they choose to pursue. Listening to all of these ways of exploring the world around them and the relationships with other people of their past and present is useful and so fascinating that I cannot imagine anything more interesting to do.

References

Arlow, J. (1961). Ego psychology and the study of mythology. *Journal of the American Psychoanalytic. Association, 9*: 371–393.

Campbell, J. (2008). *The Hero With a Thousand Faces*. Novato, CA: New World Library.

Gimbutas, M. (1989). *The Language of the Goddess*. New York: Harper & Row.

Jung, C. (1981). *Archetypes and the Collective Unconscious*, R. F. C. Hull (Trans.). Princeton, NJ: Princeton University Press.

Katz, A. (2002). Fathers facing their daughters' emerging sexuality. *Psychoanalytic Study of the Child, 57*: 270–293.

Klein, M. (1952). *Envy and Gratitude*. New York: Basic Books.

Kulish, N., & Holtzman, D. (2008). *A Story of Her Own: The Female Oedipus Complex Re-examined and Renamed*. London: Rowan & Littlefield.

Lacan, J. (1973). *The Four Fundamental Concepts of Psychoanalysis*. New York: Norton.

Mayer, E. (1985). Everybody must be just like me. *International Journal of Psychoanalysis*, *66*: 331–348.

Richards, A. K. (1995). Primary femininity and female genital anxiety. *Journal of the American Psychoanalytic Association*, *44*: 261–281.

Schlochower, J. (2013). *Holding and Psychoanalysis*. London: Routledge.

Sullivan, H. S. (1968). *The Interpersonal Theory of Psychoanalysis*. New York: Norton.

Winnicott, D. W. (1972). *Holding and Interpretation: Fragment of an Analysis*. London: Karnac.

Wolkstein, D., & Kramer, S. (1983). *Inanna: Queen of Heaven and Earth*. New York: Harper & Row.

CHAPTER TWO

Meng Jiangnü: reflections about a Chinese myth

Irmgard Dettbarn

The first encounter with Meng Jiangnü

I first encountered Meng Jiangnü while reading an announcement from a publishing house about a project in which famous writers were invited to retell the old myths of their countries. At that time I had just moved to China to live there for three years and was happy to find a Chinese myth rewritten by Su Tong and titled *Binu and the Great Wall of China* (2008).

The myth stems from the time in which the First Emperor (214 BCE) continued to add to the building of the Great Wall, intended to defend against predatory attacks by nomads. Chinese farmers are recruited from all over the country to build the wall. Thus, farmers from warm regions are ordered to go to the cold North, without proper clothing to protect them from the rain, snow, and wind. A young married farmer is among them. His wife, Meng Jiangnü, worries about him, so she makes him warm clothes and shoes. But she cannot find anyone to take the warm clothes to her husband. No one is willing to do so, as the way there is too far, too unfamiliar, and too dangerous. So Meng Jiangnü takes on this difficult task herself. When she arrives, she hears that her husband has died of exhaustion and is buried in the wall. She goes to the place where his dead body is supposed to be under the wall and she wails and wails and wails. A snowstorm begins and the wall starts to crumble on the spot where her husband lies and his corpse becomes visible. The news of this strange event spreads through the country until the story reaches the Emperor. He wants to meet this remarkable woman. He is amazed by the beauty of the young woman, who wails endlessly, and asks for her hand in marriage. But Meng Jiangnü makes three demands, which the emperor must meet if he is to marry her. Her husband's body should be put in a coffin. He is to be given a state funeral. The emperor and his loyal subjects should mourn for him. In short, she claims a burial according to the rites for men of great nobility. The Emperor agrees. Her conditions are fulfilled. After the funeral, Meng Jiangnü stops wailing. She looks at her husband's grave and then she throws herself off the highest rock to her death.

I found this information on the Internet, and in conversation with Chinese friends.

My interpretation of this story is the following: Meng Jiangnü embodies the ideal of the "moral person", a Chinese ideal figure; faithful and true to her heart, she follows her goals and does not allow anything to divert her. Thanks to the strength of her feelings and her love for her husband, she has incredible power. Her feelings, and her ability to express them, are so strong that even the Emperor, representing the highest power, is compelled to take action by her moral and emotional intensity. He comes to see Meng Jiangnü. Her feelings manage to defeat him. The myth asks us to consider the problem of what the Emperor wanted: did he want to punish her, maybe even by putting her to death, because her tears have begun to destroy the wall that he had ordered to be built?

Apparently, the Emperor cannot resist Meng Jiangnü's power when he meets her in person. On the one hand, Meng Jiangnü's power is expressed in her actions and, on the other hand, in her tears as she mourns the death of her husband. This is apparent in the story. Tears are, in contrast to spoken or verbal expressions, more ambiguous. Thus, the myth is a masterpiece in the both the depiction and the covering up of feelings. Tears can be expressions of grief. They also can be tears of anger: for example, anger about the helplessness one experiences when faced with enforced hopelessness and injustice.

This is not rendered explicitly in the text. Meng Jiangnü's exact feelings are covered up, hidden away, but they can be deduced from the end of the story: her suicide. But before she jumps to her death, at the moment when the emperor believes that he has defeated her, the reader can once again experience Meng Jiangnü's power. She sets conditions for the Emperor—a total reversal of the roles intrinsic to power and subjection. Meng Jiangnü demands a symbolic act in order to rehabilitate her husband after his unnecessary death (from exhaustion) and his subsequent burial without honour underneath the wall. She remains true to her ego ideal. The Emperor probably believes that his marriage proposal can break Meng Jiangnü's faithfulness to her ideal. He most probably experiences this as winning back his power, which he had lost because of the strength of a young, unknown woman's feelings. Perhaps there is a symbiotic wish hidden in his offer; maybe he wants to marry Meng Jiangnü because he would like to share the power of these feelings with her, since he has probably never known such feelings. However, not only were Meng Jiangnü's feelings of love immensely strong, but so were her hidden feelings of hatred and revenge. So strong are the complexity and intensity of her feelings that she kills herself: the final decision, so to speak, to follow her love and her ego ideal. By killing herself, she once again takes away the Emperor's power; she takes her revenge by symbolically killing him, because with her death the emperor loses face.

The different versions of the legend

Later on, I discovered a scientific publication about the myth and realised that there have been several different Meng Jiangnüs, depending on the period and the region where the legend was told or written down. Wilt Idema, author of *Meng Jiangnü Brings Down The Great Wall*, commented on what he found in his research: "Thematizing both absolute devotion and the relation between an all powerful state and a single individual . . . the legend was bound to exert an abiding attraction and to generate multiple retellings and widely divergent interpretations" (Idema, 2008, p. 4).

After reading these different versions I tried to summarise and interpret them and realised that I was finding this very difficult. It seemed like an overwhelming amount of information that made it necessary for me to deal with the cultural heritage I was encountering, the ideas of the soul in ancient China, the different philosophical movements of Confucianism, Taoism, Buddhism . . . I was fascinated by the different versions, but found myself wondering, should I present all of them in detail? Would it be possible to sum them all up in one or two phrases to discover what it was that made Meng Jiangnü's myth so powerful that her story survived more than 2,000 years? Was it possible to grasp this complexity, to explain this phenomenon using psychoanalytic terms? Or was it more than that?

I tried to remember my original motive for choosing this topic: I was trying to find meeting points between Chinese and Western culture, which is the home of psychoanalysis. Meng Jiangnü was to be part of my first public talk in an international congress in China, which might also be attended by analysands and their friends. I wanted to show that in our various cultural backgrounds, we have something in common, and I thought I had found it in this myth.

The different versions of the myth use the most diverse literary genres: ballads, songs, narratives in diverse speech rhythms, and more. To do justice to underlying mythic themes, I will focus on the content here.

The initial story for Meng Jiangnü is a narrative from the sixth century BCE in which the ritual of the expression of condolences is not carried out correctly. The widow of a combatant who died in a fight has authority over the leader of the enemy forces in insisting on the correct performance of the rituals. Observance of the rituals is deemed more important than who won the fight. Once the rituals have been completed in the accepted way, the widow weeps. She weeps so heartbreakingly that everyone else weeps with her; this was the basis for the story of Meng Jiangnü.

The first narratives, which provide a platform for Meng Jiangnü's story, are all about soldiers who die in combat, while in later texts, where we also find Meng Jiangnü's name for the first time, the story is based on the Emperor's order to build the wall. We find some variations in the narratives (sneaky servants, mean superiors), but the main content follows the myth I described first in which the recently married couple is separated by the enforced drudgery of the young husband in helping to build the wall. The young wife goes on a long journey to take her beloved husband food and clothes. However, when she reaches the wall, she learns that he has already died. She starts wailing, the particular wailing to which many legends owe their name. Then follows the encounter with the Emperor. Meng Jiangnü lays down her conditions. The Emperor fulfils them. She throws herself into the sea or into a river.

I quote here one of the wonderful ancient poems about this story:

> Somber clouds rose over the mountains of Long, As the sound of her weeping saddened the wasteland. If you say that man is bereft of the power to move, then why did the Long Wall come tumbling down?

> Over a thousand fathoms the stone wall was torn; The wide world of rivers and mountains turned over. Of course the Wall should never have collapsed, it all occurred because of this single woman! Beyond the border—too bad for words: a shuddering heart does not dare listen. (Idema, 2008, p. 12)

Other texts tell a different story about the initial meeting between Meng Jiangnü and Qi Liang, a conscripted worker who has fled from the construction work of the wall and is hiding in the garden of Meng Jiangnü's parents. Qi Liang and Meng Jiangnü meet unexpectedly there. Meng Jiangnü is, because of some special situation, naked: something, a fan, perhaps, has fallen into the well and she needs to undress in order to retrieve it. She is startled when she realises that she is being observed. Qi Liang is also alarmed when he sees her, because he wants to remain undetected. This scene evokes for me, a western writer, the story of Adam and Eve in the Garden of Eden, when Eve bites into the apple taken from the Tree of Knowledge and both she and Adam become aware of their nudity.

In Meng Jiangnü's story, there is a solution for this shameful situation. A man who sees a woman naked has to marry her, because "A woman's body cannot be seen by a second man, so please don't refuse!" (Idema, 2008, p. 9)—so Meng Jiangnü begs the conscript. In that way she can adhere to the rite, and Qi Liang, an escapee from drudgery, marries her.

The impact of a myth also becomes clear through its rejection:

> During the Cultural Revolution (1966–78), the legend's negative characterization of the First Emperor (beloved by Mao Zedong) resulted in a strident ideological condemnation of the tale as poisonous weed judgment. (Idema, 2008, p. 21)

How this judgement influenced the thinking of a teenager in those days was explained to me by a Chinese friend, who told me,

> "Back then, Meng Jiangnü for me was one of the negative mythological figures because she wept only for her dead husband. I did not feel the slightest bit of compassion for her; she was so weak, such an egoist and so melodramatic. What I had learnt was that the Chinese wall and politics were much more important than feelings, and that feelings were the private suffering of one's own."

All the different versions of the text describe the relationship of a couple, husband and wife, or the separation of the two people of this union due to the premature death of the husband through some external violent impact (war, or forced labour in the construction of the wall, respectively). The lovers in the Meng Jiangnü stories are only allowed to spend a little time together. There are rituals associated with death, and the surviving wife successfully demands their completion from the authorities. What is it that makes rites so meaningful?

Rites

> In completing rites the human being aims at some sort of coherence and continuity that is oriented on nature . . . Rites are based on the principle of strict repetition. In this way the human being adapts to the cyclic structure of natural regeneration processes and takes part in the cosmic life he admires as divine and eternal. (Assmann, 1997, p. 102, translated for this edition)

In Confucianism, rites play a very important role: the positive function of rites as a moral orientation for the completion of one's personality is often emphasized (Liu, 2006, p. 6). On the other hand, the sovereign is not free to reign simply according to his own will, but needs to adhere to norms of behaviour that are manifest in the rites, which means "To rule a state according to the principle of the rites" (Confucius, quoted in Liu, 2006). In this case, the rites function as a political standard, according to which the actions of the sovereign are evaluated. From this point of view, the sovereign is no longer simply the highest authority in person, but is also obliged to adhere to a higher order (Liu, 2006, p. 12).

We can learn from the original story, or the story that Meng Jiangnü's tale was based on, that this thinking already existed in China before Confucius's time: the wife in the sixth century BCE was able to use her demand for the completion of the rite to free herself, at least in part, from an apparently inescapable situation. It becomes very clear in Meng Jiangnü's texts that the rites were considered more important than the Emperor and the secular world, and that he had to comply with them.

Meng Jiangnü succeeds her demand for their fulfilment, which brings order into the world. She becomes a representative of the demands of the superego. Her behaviour is contrary to Freud's idea that most women are capable of developing only a weak superego. In fact, here, in pursuing her ego ideal, she becomes a corporeal representation of the superego for the following centuries. Should we ascribe these contradictions to cultural differences, or do they show a personal Freudian point of view? In connection with Freud's written statements, I would like to point out that his actions were, in fact, paradoxical: by listening to women, he was able to create psychoanalytic theory and therapeutic techniques.

Death rituals

At the heart of the text are death rituals, which were termed guides for the next world (*Jenseitsführer*) by the psychoanalyst Eberhard Haas. They protect the survivors from malign influences which can be experienced from being in the vicinity of death. The living have duties to fulfil for the dead, the first of which is to organise the funeral. "One who does not care for the dead should expect their revenge" (Haas, 1998, p. 451, translated for this edition).

Haas tries to understand rites from a psychoanalytical perspective in the following way:

> Death rituals are some sort of container – analogous to Bion – which contain (take in), transform or transcend the violence (of death) in the living world.

> Death provokes a crisis in the family and in society. This crisis is characterised by the loss of the differences. . . the differences between life and death. (Haas, 1998, p. 453, translated for this edition)

"The rituals and celebrations, which seem laborious and time-consuming are necessary" (Haas, 1998, p. 454, translated for this edition). Through them the old order can be reinstalled, that is, the distinction between life and death. The crisis is most serious for the next of kin. For them "the border to the realm of the death is permeable at this time" (Haas, p. 454, translated for this edition). That comment allows us to understand the practices that have been adopted by some tribes in which it was the custom to kill the next of kin, widows or other significant people (servants, etc.), because they were considered impure, tainted by association with death.

In almost all versions of the myth we are exploring here, Meng Jiangnü dies by suicide. This is an exception to the tradition of Confucianism, which in general does not approve of suicide; the devoted wife voluntarily follows her husband into death. She is not a suicidal person, whose soul is believed to wander around unredeemed and harm the living. She becomes some sort of saint who is honoured by being allowed to enter the temple. In this way, she can even be considered in the context of the role models of those Confucianists who chose suicide rather than submit to an emperor's authority if that authority did not meet their moral standards.

"A (person) with a strong will would never try to save his life at the cost of his convictions. He is even to sacrifice his life for his conviction" (Martin, 1988, p. 177).

Ritual suicide has historically been quite common, particularly as a form of political protest.

> Suicide was also glamorized by popular stories among the people, in which lovers who are unable to be together in life for various reasons, were joined together in death, as found in the famous ancient Chinese literature, such as "Butterfly Lovers" or in "A Dream of Red Mansions". In these stories, death by suicide was the only way that they were able to be together. And the western readers are here reminded of Romeo and Juliet. (Martin, 1988, p. 177)

Death is overcome by the Buddhist idea that life will continue in another world. Meng Jiangnü's actions also are in line with the Daoist concept of life and death: "When life comes you cannot turn away from it, when it goes you cannot hold on to it" (Dschuang Dsi, 2008, p. 208, translated for this edition). "The basic idea, that life after death is merely some sort of continuation of life on earth in a different environment, was still alive in the common burial customs of our century" in China, explains Bauer (Bauer, 1971, p. 587, translated for this edition).

Other rites

How a rite can solve a situation perceived as shameful and can help in making decisions becomes apparent in the text passages where Meng Jiangnü bathes naked in the well and is observed by a stranger. This unexpected encounter becomes de-sexualised by the rite, and, thus, freed from anxiety, which is split off and displaced from sexuality to the task of complying with the rite.

The wailing described in all of the versions, even appearing in the title of some of them, also has a ritual element. One comment about the widow of the warrior mentioned in the story that is the basis of this myth is: "She was good at weeping". Ritual weeping developed further and further over the centuries, so that, as late as in 2002, Liao Yiwu had the opportunity to interview a "professional mourner", who was seventy years old. He reported, "Our weeping sounds more authentic than that of the . . . relatives of the deceased. . . . We can weep as long as is requested" (Yiwu, 2008, p. 3). At the same time, the wailing of the widow is described as an expression of intense grief and desperation: "My heart is wounded by grief, / With you I will seek refuge together" (Idema, 2008, p. 6).

At the beginning of my interpretation I described the diverse forms of weeping, and I wonder if their very diversity could make us doubt the authenticity of the tears. Does the implementation of a ritual emphasise the power of the weeping? Do the tears of grief, anger, fear, and desperation become "unreal" because they have to be regulated by means of a ritual? Or does this observation help us to understand Assmann's sentence: "If the rites are not carried out correctly, the world collapses, and the sky tumbles on to the earth" (Assmann, 1997, p. 87, translated for this edition). Is this the key to the success of Meng Jiangnü's story? Tears, the wall, rites: those are the central themes of her story. Tears are a metaphor for emotions in their full diversity and omnipresence throughout the centuries: "The tears of the world are a constant quantity. For each one who begins to weep somewhere else another stops", wrote Samuel Beckett in *Waiting for Godot* (1956), 2,000 years after the story of Meng Jiangnü. Tears and emotions, respectively, are signs of vitality, opponents of death.

The wall is a metaphor for protection against peril from enemies both internal and external (the feared attacks of the nomads), as a defence utilising the drives and emotions against the fear of violence, the violence of death, the violence of other people: for example, the authority (emperor), the other sex, fear of shameful feelings about nudity, of sexuality, separation anxieties, and fear of grief.

Interpretation

The vitality of a woman who becomes powerful in mythology and the cultural memory for later generations is characterised by the following.

In Meng Jiangnü's case, her power comes from identification with the rituals. If we take the function of the rituals to be that of organising the protection of life, as described above, then we find in Meng Jiangnü a guardian of the living, representing the most noble function of a good superego, which enables her to face the reality of the strange, the path to be taken, the hazards to be faced, of her own gender and the other, to accept all the risks that arise and to take a stand.

Meng Jiangnü faces her emotions. Through showing her feelings, the defensive walls come down; superfluous defences can be replaced by the adequate expression of emotions. This expression of her emotions enables her to endure an almost unbearable tension between the contradictory demands of rituals and the necessity of finding a solution. The death ritual must be completed. This is only possible for her if she complies with the Emperor's wish to marry her.

She finds a solution to this dilemma. By jumping into the water and entering the realm of death after having fulfilled the rituals, she manages to meet all the expectations demanded of a devoted wife, which is to organise the burial of her dead husband and to follow him into death, without complying with the Emperor's wish to marry her.

It seems to me that the high level of motivation among the Chinese analysands has its foundations in the cultural background: for example, in the myth of Meng Jiangnü as described here. This myth has fascinated the people for 2,000 years, which is probably due to the power of the feelings expressed. However, strong or powerful feelings also create fear. Fear, as well anger and revenge, belongs to those feelings not mentioned in the story. This can be taken as a sign for their cultural resistance. Is the starting point—the building of the wall—not a way of dealing with the fear of enemies? It is also fear that prevents all others from taking Meng Jiangnü's gift of warm clothes to her husband: fear of the strange, the unknown, the journey. Meng Jiangnü confronts this fear. In the myth, her character shows that in this culture there are those who are brave, who go their way without being diverted or misled. Thus, she can become a symbol for the analysands, who also attempt to take the path into the unknown, the terrain of their feelings, of which they are afraid. Yet, they find the courage to make this journey into unfamiliar valleys, hills, and ravines. They are more than likely aware of the strong feelings they might have, similar to Meng Jiangnü's. They sense, with hope, that Meng Jiangnü is not alone in the "talking cure". There is the analytical container; now they must follow unknown paths because, over the past 2,000 years, all those unspoken feelings have multiplied.

Personal remark

Now, we could ask the question as to why this myth became so important for me in my situation of living and working in China. It is a challenge to choose to live in another country, wanting to get to know a new life. Isn't this connected to the idea of reliving the world in a whole new way, to find our self in the strange, as is said so often and so easily? I said that the rituals and myths provided by different cultures can help to bring order into the world, to accompany the transition from one world into the other, to structure and to offer support; if, indeed, that is the case, I think that intensely relating to Meng Jiangnü's story has helped me to face the cycle of life in a foreign culture. Because: "The myth is a story being told in order to help us figure ourselves out and orientate us in the world, a truth of higher order . . ." (Assmann, 1997, p. 74, translated for this edition).

References

Assmann, J. (1997). *Das kulturelle Gedächtnis*. Munich: Beck.

Bauer, W. (1971). *China und die Hoffnung auf Glück*. Munich: Hanser.

Beckett, S. (1956). *Waiting for Godot*. London: Faber and Faber.

Dschuang Dsi (2008). *Das wahre Buch vom südlichen Blütenland*. Munich: Hugendubel.

Haas, E. (1998). Rituale des Abschieds: Anthropologische und psychoanalytische Aspekte der Trauerarbeit. *Psyche, 05*: 450–471.

Idema, W. L. (2008). *Meng Jiangnü Brings Down The Great Wall*. Washington, DC: University of Washington Press.

Liu, H. (2006). Konfuzius als Kritiker. In: H. Roetz (Ed.), *Kritik im alten und modernen China* (pp. 1–19). Wiesbaden: Harrassowitz.

Martin, E. (1988). Gender and ideological differences in representations of life and death. In: J. L. Watson & E. S. Rawski (Eds.), *Death Ritual in Late Imperial and Modern China* (pp. 164–179). Berkeley, CA: University of California Press.

Yiwu, L. (2008). *The Corpse Walker*. New York: Anchor Books.

Su, T. (2008). *Bínu and the Great Wall of China*. Edinburgh: Canongate.

CHAPTER THREE

Taiko, Japanese drumming: the light returns, our hearts beat, the body knows

Merle Molofsky

C ultural manifestations reflect psycho-historical and intrapsychic experience and change. We tend to interpret a culture and a culture's deep-seated concerns by looking not only at its politics, its social mores, its laws, and its customs, but, on an even deeper level, at its arts. All cultural manifestations are a product of human minds, and consequently reveal unconscious process. Therefore, intrapsychic experience and intrapsychic conflict are reflected in artistic expression, and artistic expression also may reflect intrapsychic change. As ontology recapitulates phylogeny, intrapsychic change may reflect cultural–historical shifts.

Taiko, an ancient Japanese folk and classical drum tradition, was revived as a performance art in Japan by Daihachi Oguchi in 1951. By the late 1960s, it had become popular on the west coast of the USA, with its large Japanese population. From there, this vigorously athletic drumming style, modernised by Oguchi into ensemble performance, spread across the country. There are over 1,000 taiko groups in the USA today.

Taiko conveys power, aggression, and a dynamic balance of individuality and group ethos. To understand the appeal of taiko, particularly the appeal of playing taiko, with its evident celebration of raw physical prowess, intricate rhythms, athleticism, and exuberant energy, an understanding of the evolution of taiko from festival and religious performance to ensemble artistry is necessary.

As a classical drum tradition, taiko was played as accompaniment to gagaku, a traditional court dance form. As a traditional folk form, taiko was played in temple rituals and at festivals, usually by a solo performer or two or three drummers at most, in rural and small town Japan. In contemporary Japan and the USA, taiko is now an ensemble stand-alone performance art, although it is still played in traditional religious settings as well.

There is a well established and growing involvement of women in taiko, including all-women ensembles on the West Coast, such as Sawagi, Loud!, and RAW (which stands for Raging Asian Women). While very popular with individuals with ethnic Japanese roots, drummers of other ethnic backgrounds are also drawn to taiko. Along with mixed ethnicities, many taiko groups include drummers across a wide age range. In a taiko group you will find five-year-olds, teen-agers, and adults playing together.

Many westerners have an image of Japanese women as docile, domestic, delicate, submissive, graceful, and feminine, arranging flow-ers, pouring tea or sake, subordinate to men, supremely incarnated in the image of the geisha. The company man, the lonely stay-at-home wife, and the geisha are staples of conventional stereotypic Japan-ese gender roles. When women play taiko, there is nothing about their behaviour that suggests this gender stereotype. To repeat, taiko demands strength, power, athleticism, aggression, and intensity. In addition to banging on a drum with full energy, taiko players also shout.

The fully aggressive, high-energy activity in taiko, so opposite to the gentle docile housewife or geisha image, is not a new development. Taiko always has been informed with a manifestation of female energy, from the myth of its origins and the emergence of Japan as a unified nation in the third century CE. Wild and rampaging female energy, both aggressive and libidinal, is and is not an underground manifesta-tion of Japanese culture—it exists at the root and is in full bloom.

The myth of the origin of taiko

Ame no Uzume, the Shinto female deity of dawn and revelry, is the originator of taiko, bringing taiko to Japan, to the gods, and to humans. Uzume is forthright, fearless, fun-loving, sexual, and bold. Amaterasu, the Sun Goddess, the leader of the heavenly pantheon, terrified by the threats made by her violent, brutal brother, Susanoo, hid from him in a cave, plunging Earth into devastating darkness.

When Uzume learned that Amaterasu was hiding, and therefore light was withheld from earth, she decided to draw her out. She set up a big tub at the mouth of the cave, and as she danced she slowly took off all her clothes. The gods gathered around to watch Uzume. They entered into the spirit of her revelry, laughing uproariously. As Uzume danced, the stamping of her feet in her wild, ecstatic, erotic dance, combined with the uninhibited laughter of the gods, attracted Amaterasu's attention and drew her out of her cave. Because of Uzume's rhythmic stamping striptease of a dance, the Sun Goddess emerged, returning sunlight to the world.

Uzume earned the epithets the "Great Persuader" and the "Heavenly Alarming Female". She is revered, and considered the founder of the Sarume order of sacred festival dancers. She encourages ecstatic singing and dancing. Her tub is the prototype of taiko drums, and her dancing is the prototype of taiko rhythms.

Among her many attributes, Uzume is the goddess of good health, and is considered the prototype of shamanic possession and divination in Shinto. She represents the mysterious power of the female. Today, the Shinto tradition of the Miko, shaman women who are followers of Uzume, still persists. Within this tradition, the image of women as powerful, with access to sacred power, continues in an unbroken lineage from preliterate Japan to today.

Among Uzume's earliest followers was Himiko, whose name means princess, a third century CE princess who is considered the founder of the Japanese nation, the figure who unified the feudal states. Himiko also was a devotee of the Sun Goddess, Amaterasu. How much power Himiko actually wielded is open to question, with some thinking she relegated most of her power to the men of her court, and others thinking she was manipulated by Shinto priests. The 1974 film *Himiko*, directed by Masahiro Shinoda, written by Shinoda and his co-writer Taeko Tomioka, is a moving and profound depiction of the role of Himiko in the founding of Japan as a unified nation.

The Japanese myth of Uzume and Amaterasu and the legend of Himiko illustrate an awareness of, and a reverence for, female energy, with female energy being seen as both earthly and heavenly. Eroticism and erotic ecstasy sublimated into song and dance functions as the bridge to heavenly energy. Female energy is seen as unifying, with a mortal princess, Himiko, creating a modern unified nation out of the primal Japanese identity. Thus, there is a passionate and robust female energy that is an underlying heartbeat of Japanese traditional culture, manifesting today in ensemble taiko, which gives women and men equal roles.

The roots of taiko express female power as generative, libidinal, and aggressive. Female energy generates sunlight, and sunlight generates life on earth.

Rediscovery: myth making and feminism in modern Japan

Some of the strongest, overtly feminist films of the twentieth century were made in Japan. They include *When a Woman Ascends the Stairs* (1960), directed by Mikio Naruse; *Sandaken 8* (1974), directed by Kai Kumai; *Himiko* (1974), and *Ballad of Orin* (1977), both directed by Masahiro Shinoda. All the directors are male.

The themes in these films address roles assigned to women by an authoritarian patriarchy. The woman who ascends the stairs is a bar hostess who yearns to open her own bar. She feels emotionally indebted to her family, rescues them with her hard-won earnings, and therefore, unable to fulfil her dream, is eventually sexually subjugated by bullying, uncaring men. The protagonist of *Sandaken 8* is a twelve- or thirteen-year-old girl, sold by her family to serve as a domestic in the Philippines during the Second World War, but actually bought to serve as a *karayuki-san*, a "comfort woman", a prostitute servicing Japanese soldiers occupying the Philippines. Orin is a young blind woman who, female and disabled, is expected to work only in limited capacities—as a singer/entertainer or a masseuse/prostitute. She is subject to rape and abuse. Himiko is seen as a puppet princess manipulated by powerful priests. None of these women has sufficient agency or power; they are subjugated and severely abused. They are presented as stalwart and strong, but overwhelmed by an authoritarian patriarchy none the less.

The creative vision of all these directors is one that is appalled by the abuse of women by men, and admiring of the stamina and endurance of women. What are the forces that led to the development of such a strongly feminist cinema, culminating in films with far more emotional impact and artistic vision than American films such as *Thelma and Louise*? Japanese culture is known for its highly developed aesthetic sense, its aesthetic traditions. Whatever the themes, Japanese film is recognised worldwide as creating works of utmost artistry. Combine a strong aesthetic response with concern about men dominating women in traditional Japanese culture, and it is not in the least surprising that a powerful feminist vision would emerge, enhanced by the submerged but not totally unconscious recognition of female power in Japanese myth and history.

The creative vision of women in taiko resurrects the fount of female energy in a traditional Japanese art form.

Taiko represents a melding of tradition with an overt and frankly stated feminism. It offers a sense of liberation from repression both in Japan and in the USA, while maintaining a sense of heritage.

Emotionality draws on the power of the drives, fuelled by desire kindled and then either fulfilled or thwarted. Civilisation indeed has its discontents, and cultures impose gender ideals that are inhibiting and frustrating. Taiko's raw emotionality, contained by extreme discipline and acquired skill, allows for expression of aggression and eroticism within the constraints of civilisation, offering sublimation and, for women, gender-bending within a feminine identity and a road of return to ongoing feminine power in Japanese spiritual life. In the USA, too, taiko offers connection to what has been described as a highly physical spirituality, a sense of community and individuality entwined.

Spirituality and taiko

Spirituality entails a journey of discovery, of self-discovery and discovery of intrinsic meaning, essential truth. Worldwide, spiritual quests involve practices such as meditation, retreat and isolation, prayer, contemplation, service. Meditative practices may involve stillness and silence, and they also may involve physical activity. Taiko, like so many physical disciplines, is often considered by its practitioners to be essentially spiritual.

The journey of self-discovery in taiko often is described as a discovery of inner and outer freedom, a sense of total physical and spiritual liberation through disciplined, focused action. The journey of discovery of intrinsic and essential meaning in taiko is often described as the creation of a sense of unity, an integration of the physical, intellectual, emotional, and spiritual, both within one's self and with one's self in relation to a community, the taiko class, the taiko ensemble, and in relation to the world.

Lawrence LeShan (1974) notes that there are many types of meditation, and describes four: the path through the intellect, the path through the emotions, the route of the body, and the path of action. Taiko involves all four paths. LeShan understands meditation as a "coming home" to lost parts of one's self, to become fuller human beings. This very well could be a description of the psychoanalytic process. He also identifies a mystical focus of meditation, the experience of being part of the One, what Freud described as oceanic feeling (1930a).

LeShan sees the latter part of life, from the age of sixty onward, as a process of consolidating and valuing the sense of being part of the One. I would describe this as a developmental step, in which connectedness matters. LeShan states,

> The meaning and validity of our lives are given by that part of us that relates to the world of the One. The mechanics and techniques by which we live our lives are given by that part of us that relates to the world of the Many. It is the One that gives meaning to the Many, and the Many that gives form to the One. (p. 185)

He makes explicit the balance and intertwining of identity and relationship.

Taiko is a point of balance between self and group, identity and relationship. It is a personal and group meditative undertaking.

Drumming is heartbeat. Heartbeat is life. The physical experience of drumming increases sensitivity to one's own physical rhythms, particularly heartbeat. Like all intensive and demanding physical activity, it increases sensitivity to physical sensations: muscular, vascular, respiratory, digestive, sensory. Drumming creates synchronous brain activity, integrating right and left sides of the brain and frontal and lower parts of the brain. Vibration affects the cerebral cortex and the entire limbic system.

Many meditation exercises are breathing exercises. Like heartbeat, respiration is immediate to sustaining life, and is rhythmic. Simple breathing meditation exercises involve focus, one-pointed attention, and connect the practitioner to the experience of being alive while in an alpha wave brain state, and, for advanced practitioners, while in a theta and gamma brain wave state as well. Thus, drumming is an integrative meditative activity.

Master Daichi Oguchi, the founder of contemporary taiko, led a taiko drumming and dancing ensemble in a performance during the Nagano 1998 Olympics. At the 26 June 1998 closing ceremonies, he said,

> Your heart is a taiko. All people listen to a taiko rhythm, dontsuko—dontsuko—in their mother's womb. It's instinct to be drawn to taiko drumming. In taiko man becomes the sound. In taiko, you can hear the rhythm through your skin. (Associated Press, June 26, 1998)

Community and unity in movement

Contemporary taiko is a communal ensemble art form. Master Oguchi calls this wa-daiko, harmonious drumming. By harmony, he is referring to the matching among the taiko drummers working together of energy level, intent, awareness of each other and the relationship with the audience, and integration of the parts of the music, both in composition and performance.

Taiko is primarily a musical art form, yet frequently involves expansive movement, not just the physical movements of drumming, but a choreography that involves drummers sharing one drum, drummers moving from drum to drum, drummers changing places with each other. Drummers may stand, squat, sit, leap up, or run around, in a carefully orchestrated movement pattern. In all music ensembles, musicians must listen to each other, be attuned to the music shared within the ensemble, whether the music is strictly notated and followed, or improvisatory. Some musical ensemble performances, such as marching bands, incorporate movement. *Drumline*, a 2002 American film directed by Charles Stone III, is a fascinating look at marching drum corps competitions, an art form popular in colleges that have a student body that is primarily African-American.

Thus, ensemble forms merging music and movement are, by their nature, intrinsically communal, generating a sense of self and a sense of being part of a whole. In taiko, there is a constant awareness of individual action and integrated communal action. Individuality and belonging to a group are interdependent.

Other ecstatic meditative music and movement activities, such as Afro-Cuban Orisha rituals, Sufi dancing and chanting, Chasidic chanting and dancing, similarly create a sense of unity of self and group.

Abraham Maslow (1964) describes "peak experience" as creating a change in the person's perceptual system, an experience that challenges conscious and unconscious assumptions otherwise taken for granted. The self is experienced as integrating with, uniting with, external reality, the environment, the world. The unique individual exists *in relation to*, in a state similar to Buber's description of the I and Thou experience.

Self discovery

In short interviews, several people from various groups in the New York City metropolitan area taiko community described what they found and experienced in taiko.

Anonymous 1 (female) said, "I feel graceful, strong, feminine, aggressive." Anonymous 2 (female) said, "I have always felt some sort of kinship to drumming since childhood. I took the requisite piano lessons, but the piano just never resonated within me. Don't get me wrong . . . I love music in general, and love music played on all instruments. But there was always something very special about the drums. Perhaps it was because my heartbeat would find itself matching the drum beats, becoming part of the music. I was introduced to taiko drumming when I saw a mesmerising performance of Kodo drummers years ago. When the piece started, I saw a drummer and his drum, a man and a musical instrument. By the time the piece ended, I wasn't sure whether the drum was the instrument of the drummer, or if the drummer became the instrument of the drum! That's when I thought to myself . . . I want to do that . . . to learn the techniques that would give me the discipline and the focus to be a voice of the drums. Imagine my delight when I found that there is a taiko drum group close to my home. And so my taiko journey begins."

Betsy said, "I became interested in taiko drumming before I even knew it had a name. Around 1995 there was a Cherry Blossom Festival in the park across the street and I saw these huge drums and I saw this very skinny young woman playing the drum. I really couldn't see anyone else. She was so dancerish and so macha all at the same time. I thought I would really love to do that without really thinking it would be possible.

"Years later, in 2010, I was having coffee with my friend and she told me she would not be continuing with her Japanese drumming because she and her husband liked to go into the city on Sunday and the timing interfered. I immediately signed up for the class. There were many children but only three adults. I was given my set of *bachi* [drumsticks] and with my first bang on the drum I was hooked. No one told me to step away from the drum, no one told me to be quiet. Within minutes I was hooked. I haven't missed a lesson in a year and a half. There is a tremendous feeling of power from you to the drum and the drum gives you back a wonderful sound."

Kyoko said, "I am a psychologist. I think taiko is a therapeutic musical instrument. You hit it! I want to do taiko, music therapy, with kids, ADHD kids. When I observe kids, I think they could focus with taiko. Taiko represents my freedom as a woman. I left Japan because [Japanese] society is repressive to women. Not much better here. America is repressive of women too. I am offended by sexism and anti-feminism. Taiko is traditional. I like it because it is traditional, but offers freedom."

Les said, "It's fun. It's fun to hit the drums, to play the drums, to play music, and it's an accessible form. When I saw it, I knew I could do it, which I later learned was a goal of Master Oguchi. My sensei told me taiko used to be played by temple drummers or special people in their villages. It was taught by fathers to sons, kept secret. I like the meditative quality. It's not quiet. Drums are not quiet. You learn something, and lose yourself in it. You get into a zone, focused. It becomes automatic. Something thrilling about all that power and noise."

Mike said, "I get my frustrations out, with a sense of achievement and of gaining knowledge."

Sandy said, "My mum loved drums. I heard taiko in the summer in LA. I was very little. I heard of a workshop, and attended. Taiko is energy with other people. It's how it makes you feel. Nothing feels better. Therapeutic, healing, after dad died . . . I am in the moment, with others, receiving and giving back energy."

Yoko said, "Not 'percussion'—unique—traditional but modern—muscles and music—spiritual—peaceful."

Yuko said, "[Only] doing taiko for one month when [you] asked. Rhythm—I feel it in my body." [She points to her heart area, then to her *tanden*, the Japanese word for the area in the body between the navel and the top of the pubic bone, where *ki*, the Japanese word for energy, is stored.]

In these responses, certain themes emerge: tradition, modernity, freedom, therapeutic and healing, spiritual and peaceful, aggressive. Concepts that may seem at first glance to be contradictory actually serve an important function, the healing of splits. Taiko offers continuity with community because it is both a traditional Japanese art form and a "modern" form. In its present form, it is an egalitarian ensemble activity, offering equality among practitioners regardless of age, gender, ethnic/racial/religious origin. It offers an experience that encompasses peacefulness and aggression, thus an integrative experience, where aggression is acceptable and harmless. For women, taiko unifies and harmonises grace and strength, femininity and aggression, defying stereotypical gender roles. Both freedom and discipline are integrated. Discipline was not identified as such, but the psychologist talking about the potential for taiko to help ADHD children develop focus essentially is addressing the practice of taiko as encouraging inner discipline.

Self-discovery conceptualised psychoanalytically involves integration. Integration entails the healing of vertical and horizontal splits, such as internal ego–superego–id conflicts, tensions between libidinal and aggressive impulses, gender role stereotypes, and good and bad self and object representations. Healing splits involves making the unconscious conscious, creating a bridge between unconscious fantasies and wishes, and conscious self-actualisation and self-knowledge. Taiko offers a profound experience to its practitioners, allowing them to confront splits and integrate them through an art form that is physical, meditative, individualistic, and communal.

Psychoanalytic conflict theory explores anxieties created when id impulses are disapproved of by the superego, or when the ego determines that pursuing id impulses would be dangerous to the organism. One of Freud's least developed concepts is that of sublimation, in which repudiated impulses, wishes, and fantasies are given new form acceptable to the superego. In discussing the Dora case (1905e), he implies that transferences are a form of sublimation, containing fantasies and impulses originally directed at someone important in early life reformulated and experienced as now directed to the psychoanalyst. In discussing vicissitudes of sexual aims in early childhood (1905d), he postulates sublimation as a diversion of sexual aims beginning in latency when sexual impulses have no means of expression. Later (1910a), in "Five lectures on psychoanalysis", he describes sublimation as occurring when a forbidden wish is rejected, but then is partially accepted, when directed to an unobjectionable aim.

Rose (1990) understands sublimation as evolving within a theory of reality and perception rather than emerging from unconscious motivation and ego defences. He views sublimation as playing an adaptive role, with the ego regulating interplay between primary and secondary processes.

Loewald (1988) postulates that sublimation is not a cover-up, not a totally repressed or denied wish or fantasy, but, rather, an enhancement of the form the wish or fantasy may take. He addresses the person's experience of uncomfortable or forbidden feelings, with sublimation a means of making the feelings acceptable. Thus, he concludes that sublimation of such wishes, fantasies, and feelings into highly developed cultural expression is the highest achievement of the human mind. It is a means of reconciliation, of accepting and internalising separation, so that wholeness is re-established as a differentiated unity.

If we take seriously the concept that all art, all cultural expression, has a sublimatory function, then we can look at taiko through the lens of sublimation. Taiko performers express a great deal of comfort with their physicality, their sexuality, their aggression. Intense emotion is not covered up, repressed, or denied. Women in taiko easily shake off gender roles, without shaking off their sense of their physical body, their innate femaleness.

In taiko, drummers hit drums with sticks, called bachi, often with full force. Oguchi was a jazz drummer before he began studying taiko seriously, and then performing taiko. I spoke to one New York City area taiko sensei who, like Oguchi, also had been a jazz drummer, but who gave up jazz drumming, he said, because after becoming a taiko drummer he had learned to hit the drum so hard that he would destroy standard jazz drums if he drummed with the same intensity.

There are a number of drum sizes in taiko. Most are double-headed, and can be hit on either side. The largest drum, called an odaiko, can weigh over 1,000 pounds and can be three metres in diameter. To hit an odaiko full force, the drummer sometimes uses a two-handed grip, very similar to the two-handed sword grip used by samurai. Practitioners have to develop a high level of physical strength and coordination to play the odaiko. Any taiko drummer who has played the odaiko is highly conscious of the amount of aggression needed to play well, and is highly conscious of the pleasure experienced in the intensity, or possibly even the violence, of the movements and the artistry required to make music, not war.

Is playing taiko a sublimation of violent fantasies and impulses, of forbidden urges? If it is a harmless expression of conscious violent fantasies and impulses, is the sublimation a defence mechanism or, as Loewald (1988) suggests, an act of making the desire acceptable? There is an exultant power in a taiko performance. The focus, mindfulness, and attentive artistic expression revels in the shared experience of expressed aggression, expressed sexuality.

Sublimation as used by Freud involved an analysis of very specific forbidden fantasies and wishes, which, in the analytic process, emerge in the transference. Perhaps each taiko drummer, perhaps each artist, each poet, each novelist, each dancer, each film maker, each actor, each scientist, each expressive and intellectual human being, is expressing unconscious highly specific human feelings and urges. Perhaps they are expressing them for us as well. Perhaps they are not unconscious. The universality of those feelings and urges are highly recognisable.

As a cultural phenomenon, twentieth and twenty-first century ensemble taiko drumming is just beginning to serve as a vehicle for joyous, peaceful, communal, musical, rhythmic communication of the most primal underpinnings of human dreams, wishes, longings, and differentiated unity.

Let the wild rumpus keep beginning.

References

Freud, S. (1905d). *Three Essays on the Theory of Sexuality. S. E.,* 7: 125–245. London: Hogarth.

Freud, S. (1905e). *Fragment of an Analysis of a Case of Hysteria. S. E.,* 7: 1–122. London: Hogarth.

Freud, S. (1910a). Five lectures on psychoanalysis. *S. E.*, *11*: 3–55. London: Hogarth.

Freud, S. (1930a). *Civilization and its Discontents. S. E.*, *21*: 59–145. London: Hogarth.

LeShan, L. (1974). *How to Meditate: A Guide to Self-Discovery.* New York: Back Bay Books, Little, Brown.

Loewald, H. W. (1988). *Inquiries into Theoretical Psychoanalysis.* New Haven, CT: Yale University Press.

Maslow, A. (1964). *Religions, Values and Peak Experiences.* Columbus, OH: Ohio State University Press.

Rose, G. J. (1990). From ego-defense to reality enhancement: updating the analytic perspective on art. *American Imago, 47*: 69–79.

CHAPTER FOUR

Contributions Part I: implications for psychoanalytic psychotherapy

Arlene Kramer Richards and Lucille Spira

This section begins our discussion of how myths are used to help our women patients move beyond the painful situations and conflicts that bring them to therapy. The various contributions here illustrate the many ways a psychoanalytic psychotherapist can understand and use a particular myth.

Inanna

Dr Arlene Kramer Richards' contribution about the myth of Inanna highlights the use of culture to help her patients. Following a patient's presentations, she taps into her own associations, which she weaves with psychoanalytic theory to gain perspective on the situation. Here, she turned to the myth of Inanna that illustrates, among other things, how marital love can lose its power for one or both of the pair even where it begins gloriously. She shows how reason can overcome the conflict between wanting to see oneself as desirable and wanting to see oneself as powerful.

Women patients talk about the pain of being left by their spouses. The rejection destroys their sense of their feminine power and potential. The anger that hides the helplessness that such situations engender needs an outlet. A feeling of hope that the "abandoned" person can move beyond the role of wife is crucial.

The Inanna story is a concrete example of how, through careful thought and weighing of options, a woman finds a solution to assuage the pain of learning that her husband no longer desires her sexually. The issue for the woman is one of handling potentially devastating narcissistic injury. Like Inanna, the modern woman needs to feel her own strength and her own purpose in fostering her children's development and/or her contribution to society so that she can see her own value. In ego psychological terms, ego strength needs to be fostered so that mourning can be tolerated. The mourning of the loss allows new interests to develop.

At times it is enough for the therapist to keep the myth in mind, while at other times relating aspects of the myth, and in different circumstances the therapist might recommend a particular myth or story that is highly relevant to a patient's situation. Such stories can open a conversation between patient and therapist and locate some of the issues that arise today as ones that our ancestors struggled over and in the best circumstances, as with the myth and the case described, positively resolved.

Meng Jiangnü

Meng Jiangnü speaks to generations of Chinese women and her myth changes from one telling to another. In this way, her myth is like those of the Greeks and Romans. The people who tell the same story from generation to generation tell various versions. Each generation tells a version that speaks to its cohort: their conflicts, their wishes, their fears, their moral dilemmas. Myths, like gossip and like history, exist to serve the people who hear them. Irmgard Dettbarn makes this abundantly clear in her iteration of different versions of the myth of Meng Jiangnü. The earliest story tells of the importance of weeping and mourning. Later versions deal with the conflict between personal loyalty and loyalty to the state.

In the version including the courtship of Meng Jiangnü and her husband, the idea of loyalty is tied to exclusivity. Only a husband may see a woman nude. Because he has seen her nude, she must marry him. The exclusivity of relationship is bound into the morality of marriage. Once this is established, the loyalty that impels her to take him warm clothes and good food is the inevitable outcome of her marriage. And the loyalty that compels her to insist on his burial rites is entailed in the beginning of the story as well. The implications for treatment also stem from this premise.

One of the most vexing questions for an analyst or analytic therapist is how much of one's own ethical convictions is appropriate for the patient. If a patient is exposing himself to his daughter by taking showers with her, does the therapist treat this as a symptom to be eliminated? Or a breach of parental responsibility? Or the acting out of a conflict to be suppressed? Or if a mother invites her lover to have sex when her child is at home? Or in the same room? Or in the same bed? Or in the next room where the child can hear?

The story asserts the absolute loyalty to the husband and the absolute exclusivity of marital sexuality as the highest moral good. The emperor, after all, is taking care of the state. He builds the wall to keep out the others: those who do not belong to the state. From the point of view of the state, he asks her to marry him to assert loyalty to the state over loyalty to the dead husband. If she allowed the emperor to marry her, she would be showing her nudity to him; she would be breaching the code of exclusivity.

Bringing these moral choices and conflicts to the young woman who is deciding whether to devote herself to her career or to marry and devote herself to a spouse and a family is ultimately important and valuable. By seeing the choices from her point of view rather than the analytic therapist's own, she can help the young woman to work out her own moral code and create her own future. Alternatively, if the young woman chooses a ready-made moral code in an established religion, the analytic therapist can help her to see what she gains and what she loses by that.

Taiko drumming

Life begins with the heartbeat. Once the foetus in the womb can register anything, it can register the mother's heartbeat. Once the mother can detect the foetal heartbeat, she understands the foetus to be a baby. The sound profoundly changes everything. Drumming makes the drummer a powerful person. Filling the air with sound, she dominates the motions of her own body, choosing her speed, her alternations of faster and slower, her mind and her emotions, her body and her sense of connection to others. That this is a form of meditation is another way of thinking about meditation as integrative. In psychoanalytic treatment, the body is mostly immobilised and the heartbeat is not heard. Focusing on the expression of feeling in words, the patient relies on emotion and intellect to communicate to another person: the analyst. Similarly, mostly immobile, the analyst concentrates on listening to the patient's words and connecting them to the emotions of which the patient is not fully aware. By excluding motion, the analyst tries to intensify the expression in words. Rather than encouraging the relief of expressing feelings in bodily motion, the analytic process enhances the possibility of understanding the adult patient as a person attempting to cope with unpleasant and even painful feelings. In an analytic therapy, the patient uses sound to evoke feeling. The drummer, like all musicians, uses sound to evoke, as well as express, feelings. By listening as the mother listens to the foetus's heartbeat and the foetus listens to the mother's heartbeat, the analyst evokes love from the patient. By producing the sounds of his or her speech, the sounds of feeling, the patient evokes love from the analyst. A mutual understanding develops in an emotional climate of love. To express this love in a mature way, the patient and analyst restrict their interaction to rational discourse. That discipline is what eventuates in what we call ego strength or superego moderation.

Molofsky shows us another path. Taiko drumming differs from analytic treatment in the obvious way that it encourages and requires physical expression that combines aggressive energy with loving connection to the other musicians and the audience. This is sublimation as contrasted with analytic understanding and mastery of the self. For women who have not had the experience of expressing their emotions through action that connects them to the world, and for women who have not experienced their bodies as powerful, using one's body to express one's feelings in this way can be a useful adjunct to psychoanalysis.

PART II

THE POWER OF VICTIMS, AVENGERS, AND TRICKSTERS

CHAPTER FIVE

Three archetypes in myth: the goddess, the witch, and the mortal

Philip Matyszak

Hecate: the goddess

From earliest times the Greeks and Romans met with new peoples with their own gods. Their religion was basically animistic, in that it assigned semi-human identity and personality to natural forces. Since weather and human emotions are pretty standard, it proved easy enough to syncretise most new deities into the Graeco-Roman belief system. However, sometimes a deity was too different to fit into the standard divine template, yet too popular to ignore. One such deity is the goddess who eventually became the goddess of demons, witchcraft, and magic. This is Hecate, whose name means "she who works from afar".

The mother of the goddess was Asteria, "the starry one", a member of the race of proto-gods called Titans. Zeus once tried to seduce (and for seduce read "rape") Asteria, and pursued her until she fled Olympus. Asteria hid beneath the sea and so came to the attention of Zeus's brother, the equally rapacious Poseidon. Unable to find shelter from air and sea, Asteria transformed herself into an island, to remain forever between the pair. This is now the sacred isle of Delos, in the Cyclades archipelago.

The father of Hecate was Perses, "the destroyer". Perses was more solidly grounded than most Titans, being the ruler of Colchis and points east, for which reason a part of the lands he ruled became known as "Persia". The connection with Colchis is significant for his daughter, Hecate, for we can often trace the origin of particular Greek deities to their original "birthplace". Thus, Zeus was probably imported to mainland Greece from his alleged birthplace of Crete, and worship of Dionysus, god of wine comes from Asia Minor, to where the god was supposedly exiled while young. Thus, it is fair to assume that Hecate was originally a deity from Thrace, or possibly the wild lands of Scythia which lay beyond (Berg, 1974).

However, the ancient poet Bacchylides is having none of this. For him, Hecate is a child of night, more specifically the primordial deity Nyx, a being from the dawn of time who also gave rise to death, Nemesis, Old Age, and the Fates. One can see where Bacchylides is coming from, because Hecate has much in common with Night's scary brood. For example, Hecate more resembles the dread Nemesis than she does her mother Asteria. Like Nemesis, Hecate wears the short (for a contemporary Greek) knee-length tunic of a maiden. Also like Nemesis, Hecate is one of those deities whom no one, not even randy Zeus, thinks of laying a finger upon. Hecate is distant, unknowable, and untouchable. If she had a colleague among the gods, it was Hermes Psychopompus, the god of boundaries, who leads the spirits of the dying from the land of the living to the dead—a suitable companion indeed for the uncanny Hecate.

An ancient goddess, Hecate was present in the war of the Titans, the literally titanic struggle by which Zeus overthrew the elder generation of gods and established his rule in heaven. Or, to be prosaic, worship of Hecate was common among those who identified with the new god Zeus, who supplanted worship of the older divinities of pre-archaic Greece. Hecate herself replaced the Titan Klytios, whom she slew with fire. This is something else that Hecate has in common with Nemesis, Athena, and other virgin goddesses—she is inviolate because she is very good at defending herself. Also, as one of the foremost supporters of Zeus, she had the king of the gods as a powerful protector.

"Hekate whom Zeus the son of Kronos honours above all others. He gave her splendid gifts, a share of the earth and the barren sea. She receives honour also in starry heaven, and is greatly honoured by the immortal gods" (Hesiod, *Theogony*, 411–415, translated for this edition). So says the poet, and anyone familiar with the misogynistic tone of his *Theogony* will know it is rare indeed for the poet to bestow such fulsome praise on a female. But then, Hecate is not a female to gratuitously offend, even with faint praise.

As an example of Hecate's extraordinary inviolability, let us turn to one of the few occasions when Hecate becomes involved with the classical myths. This is when Persephone was abducted by Hades and taken to the underworld. This was not a random kidnapping, for Hades had consulted beforehand with Zeus, Persephone's father. Zeus recommended a kidnapping because he knew that Persephone's mother, Demeter, would never consent. The brothers Zeus and Hades were, together with their older brother Poseidon, the three most powerful gods in the ancient pantheon. Consequently, when Demeter went searching for her daughter, she did so without help from the Olympian gods. In fact, Poseidon compounded the injury by raping Demeter while she searched. The only deity who aided Demeter was Hecate, who eventually coerced Helios, the Sun God, into admitting that he had seen the abduction. While the other gods refused to get involved, and even Demeter suffered for having the temerity to search for her daughter, Hecate remained unadmonished and unpunished for her role in locating Persephone. When a custody agreement was reached, and Persephone consented to spend part of the year with her infernal husband, it was Hecate who thereafter guided Persephone to the underworld and back, for which reason the goddess is often depicted with two flaming torches.

When we look at Hecate's identifying animals (all gods have these, such as the owl of Athena and the eagle of Zeus), we see that same mixture of compassion and the uncanny. Hecate's familiars are a polecat and a black dog. The polecat was notorious in antiquity for its frequent indulgence in a supposedly bizarre sex life. Being turned into one was the punishment inflicted on the nurse who assisted the birth of Heracles against Hera's wishes. "They [the Fates] turned her [the nurse] into a deceitful weasel … Hekate felt sorry for this transformation and made her a sacred servant to herself" (Antoninus Liberalis, *Metamorphoses* 29, translated for this edition). (The general rule among ancient gods was that no god could reverse the punishment inflicted by another, but could mitigate or compensate for that punishment if they were so inclined.)

The other familiar, the black dog, was originally Hecuba, the wife of King Priam of Troy. Hers, too, is a tragic story. She sent a son to a Thracian king for safety but that king treacherously slew that son (and a daughter too, by some accounts). Although by then a captive concubine of Odysseus, Hecuba tricked her way to the treacherous king, blinded him with her fingernails, and killed his children. Surrounded and stoned by the king's outraged subjects, Hecuba turned on the mob, snarling and foaming at the mouth. Acting like a maddened hound, she was transformed into one. At this point Hecate stepped in and made Hecuba a member of her retinue. We note again the connection with Thrace, and the fact that from here on, Hecate has a special connection with dogs.

Although she is described as one of the most ancient of goddesses, worship of Hecate came late to the Greek peninsula from Asia Minor. So, Hecate found her traditional roles already filled. Artemis was the goddess of the moon, Hera and Hestia were goddesses of childbearing (a role Hecate played in Asia Minor), and Zeus himself was god of judgement (Hecate was invoked before trials in places such as Caria.) However, Hecate had a strong following among the common people, who often placed her image above their doorways to ward off evil spirits. So began Hecate's connection with the supernatural.

Since the pantheon of gods was limited to the sacred number of twelve, there was no place for Hecate on Mount Olympus. She became one of the cthonous gods, a denizen of the underworld along with Nemesis, Hermes, Hades, and, indeed, Persephone. The gods of the underworld were familiar with demons and the dark, so it was not long before those wishing ill of others evoked the powers of such spirits. Witness this tablet from ancient Athens.

> Let Pherenicus be bound before Hermes Cthonios and Hecate Cthonia. And Galene, who associates herself with Pherenicus, she I bind before Hermes Cthonios and Hecate Cthonia. And just as lead is thought cold and worthless, so may Pherenicus and all to do with him be cold and useless, and also everything which the allies of Pherenicus say and plot against me. (Price, 1999)

Such lead tablets have been found in wells, buried in walls (curses were more effective if installed in the home of the cursee), or in fresh-dug graves. This particular tablet was probably accompanied by a little doll bound and transfixed in the manner invoked in the curse, rather as some curse tablets actually bear scratched portraits showing the target so bound and transfixed. Oddly enough, the identification of Hecate with curses and the supernatural did not destroy the image of Hecate as a generally benevolent goddess. She might associate with nightmarish and malevolent entities, but if your cause was just, she was on your side.

Hecate became the goddess of the crossroads, for in most cultures, crossroads are liminal places—neither one thing nor the other, but a bit of each. Here, different realms touch, and demons prowl. Who better to guard such places than Hecate, benevolent but familiar with the creatures of the night? To the ancients, a crossroads was more often than not what we today would call a T-junction. An interesting bit of trivia was that this conjunction of three roads led to the Roman name for Hecate, which was Trivia. Hecate was often portrayed as a triple-bodied goddess, one facing each direction of the crossroads, warding the traveller from malign forces.

Predictably, Christianity later took exception to a tripartite deity who associated with demons of the underworld. As Christianity spread through the Roman world, Hecate's image became ever more ghastly, with snakes in her hair, or in animal form. Saints and holy men warned converts not to perform rites at the crossroads, and the medieval church prescribed special punishments for women who took their babies to the crossroads to ask for a blessing—perhaps the final echoes of Hecate's original role as a goddess of child-bearing (Johnston, 1991).

In Shakespeare's *Macbeth*, Hecate is totally malevolent, telling the witches she is "the mistress of your charms, the close contriver of all harms". However, with growing interest in myth and classical religion, Hecate is being rehabilitated once more. She features prominently on neo-pagan websites and has appeared in a number of supernatural-themed television programmes. The world is not yet done with the goddess who works from afar.

Medea: the witch

You probably know of the most extreme case of zoophilia in mythology—the lust of Pasiphae for the bull that fathered the Minotaur. You probably also know of Circe, the witch who turned men into swine. You probably do not know that these two were sisters, or that they had a brother called Aeetes, king of Colchis on the Black Sea. Aeetes was as ordinary as a king could get, given his family, and he fathered a daughter off an ocean nymph, which also was not an extraordinary activity in those early days.

This daughter was Medea, sometimes called the daughter of Hecate because she became a fanatical student of dark magic even while young. While in her teens, Medea developed a crush on a handsome stranger. Strangers were rare in Colchis, because a prophecy had foretold that a stranger would cost Aeetes his throne. Therefore, Aeetes treated strangers with lethal cruelty, hoping in this way to scare off visitors.

But this visitor was Jason, in search of the Golden Fleece, of which Aeetes was the guardian. Aeetes did not want to give up the fleece and set Jason a series of impossible tasks before he would surrender the thing. Jason was equal to the challenge, mainly because he was advised at every turn by Medea (just as, some fifteen years later, Medea's relative Ariadne would help Theseus through the labyrinth to kill her stepbrother, the Minotaur).

When Medea's magic had procured the fleece for the Argonauts, Medea fled Colchis aboard Jason's ship. Medea took her young brother with her, not out of sisterly affection, but because she knew her father had ships capable of catching Jason's boat, the *Argo*. By cutting her brother into calculated segments, and dropping the bits overboard at intervals, Medea forced her father to slow down and collect the fragments of his son for burial. This casual attitude to killing became Medea's hallmark. Medea did not charm, negotiate, or threaten. In a crisis, murder was her first resort.

Next to die was Talos, the invulnerable man of Crete, who threatened the Argonauts and, therefore, the happiness of Medea. Realising that a man who could not be wounded also could not heal, Medea pulled out a nail and watched the life drain from her victim.

Then it was off home to the king who had sent Jason on his suicide mission in the first place. To show her ability, Medea restored the youth of Jason's aged father. Then she offered to do the same for the king, whose intentions toward Jason remained malign. The king's daughters were persuaded to chop their father into meat cubes and boil the bits in a pot from which his rejuvenated majesty would arise.

When the king remained soup, his outraged son and successor wisely decided to do no more than exile Medea and her husband.

And so to Corinth, where Medea and Jason lived unhappily for ten years and had two young children. Finally, Jason found the strong character and homicidal tendencies of Medea too hard on his nerves. He informed Medea that he was divorcing her—in its own way a feat as heroic as getting the Golden Fleece. Medea did not take the news well.

What happened next has been the subject of numerous theatrical treatments, including one each by the Athenian playwright Euripides and the later Roman writer and philosopher Seneca. The most accepted version of the tale is as follows. After her initial anger, Medea appeared to accept her rejection. She even sent a wedding gift of a robe to the princess who was to replace her. Rather naïvely, the princess wore the gift at her wedding and discovered her mistake when the poison-saturated robe caught fire. (Overkill was never a problem for Medea.) The princess's father flung himself on his daughter to douse the flames and both were killed when the maddened girl threw herself down a well.

Jason found that Medea had then taken refuge with her children in the temple of Hera. This temple was a calculated choice, for Hera was the protector of marriage. In that temple, Medea killed her children—in Seneca's account before their father's horrified gaze—before summoning a dragon-drawn chariot on which she fled.

Euripides shows Medea tormented by her actions, killing her children because she could not imagine their lives without her protection (in the ancient world, the father automatically got custody). Her pain and shock at the divorce are a protest against the injustice of marriage for all contemporary Greek women.

> First, we need a husband, someone we get
> for an excessive dowry. He then becomes
> the ruler of our bodies. . . .
> Then comes the crucial struggle: this husband
> we've selected, is he good or bad?
> For a divorce loses women all respect . . .
> (Euripides *Medea*, 230ff, translated for this edition)

The more cynical Seneca, veteran of the Roman imperial court, shows another Medea—a murderous witch coldly rejoicing in a revenge, calculating her every move to cause the greatest pain to her husband.

In which she succeeded, by the way—Jason died a broken man (Guastella, 2001).

Medea found sanctuary in Athens by using her magic to get a son for the aged king. With her position secure, she was disturbed by the arrival of another hero, Theseus. Theseus was another son of the king, the unknown product of a casual liaison now arrived to claim his patrimony. Medea saw only a problem to be disposed of. She persuaded Theseus to undertake the risky job of killing the bull that had fathered the Minotaur, been subsequently captured by Heracles, and released in Marathon, where it had become a public menace. When Theseus demonstrated his heroic credentials by killing the bull Medea persuaded the Athenian king that the youth was a threat. (Which he was—he later caused his father's death.) She came within an ace of poisoning Theseus, but the king recognised his son at the last moment and slapped the deadly chalice from his hands.

Exiled once more, Medea returned home to Colchis, where she found her father in sad straits. As foretold, he had lost his kingdom due to the stranger, Jason. Father and daughter were reconciled, and a quick bout of Medean murder created a vacancy that allowed Aeetes to reclaim his throne. Thereafter, in that faraway land, it appears that Medea lived happily ever after.

The mystique of Medea lies in her defiance of taboo. Infanticide, fratricide, and casual murder are means to an end. Medea is shocking both in her ruthlessness and in that she gets away with it. No one would want Medea close to them, but there is something fascinating about her predatory single-mindedness. In our moments of weakness, Medea is not whom we should be, but perhaps—and this is the disturbing thing about her—she is the person that we could be (Georgia Nugent, 1993).

Psyche: the mortal

Psyche is a hero. This is the important aspect of the story of Cupid and Psyche. The heroic quest in Greek mythology has something of a standard format. Whether our protagonist is Perseus, Heracles, Jason, Theseus, or Psyche, the story is basically the same.

The protagonist has a manifest and generally malign destiny. The protagonist falls into the power of someone powerful and malevolent.

This malevolent personage assigns our hero a quest, or a series of quests, in which the game is rigged for the hero to fail. However, the hero finds an unexpected helper who gives him (or her) an unexpected edge. The hero triumphs and returns home, usually piling up supplementary corpses *en route*. It is a tried and trusted formula that has worked for millennia (Matyszak, 2010)

The story of Cupid and Psyche was known in Greece in the fourth century BC, but the complete tale as we know it today survived antiquity embedded in a novel by a writer of the second century AD called Apuleius. This means we have two important considerations: the story is arguably the last addition to the formal corpus of myth, and it is written as a satire. It is a love story, but tongue-in-cheek and more relevant to contemporary Romans than Olympian gods.

In a nutshell, the story is as follows. Psyche—the name means "butterfly" and, therefore, in a pleasing Greek analogy, "soul"—who is born with unnatural beauty. This arouses the envy of Venus, who sends her son Cupid to do Psyche harm. Instead, Cupid falls in love with Psyche, and spirits her away. They make love every night but Psyche never sees her husband. (The Romans regarded sex with the lights on as a taboo activity.) Her sisters urge Psyche to see whether she has been impregnated by a man or a monster, and encourage her to take a peek at him in bed. So, as Cupid lies sleeping, Psyche furtively lights a lamp. She is so startled by what she sees that she spills burning oil over Cupid, and he, wounded, flies off and abandons her.

Psyche then goes in search of her beloved and so falls into the power of Venus, who sets her four impossible tasks: to sort a mass of mixed grain and poppy seeds into separate piles; to collect golden wool from homicidal sheep; to fill a flask of water from the Styx; to get a box of beauty potion from Persephone, the Queen of the Underworld. Each time Psyche is full of despair at the impossibility of her task and several times attempts suicide. But each time an unexpected helper either guides Psyche through the task or does it for her.

Finally, Cupid recovers from his wounds and finds Psyche. She is in a deep coma, because, despite warnings to the contrary, she took a peek to see what the ointment of Persephone was like. Cupid's kiss revives the hapless girl, and then Cupid appeals to Jupiter. The king of the gods reproaches Cupid for not coming to him earlier, and formalises the relationship with Psyche. Venus is forcibly reconciled and dances at the wedding, where Vulcan oversees the barbecue. All ends happily ever after . . . but.

The notable thing about Psyche is that she is a brain-dead wimp. Her only redeeming feature is her beauty. She repeatedly ignores advice from well-meaning males (don't look at Cupid, don't try the ointment) and her standard solution to getting into a fix is to try to kill herself—and she cannot even manage that. The message of the story is "be decorative and hope that some nearby male will sort things out for you". Thus, Apuleius has taken the standard heroic epic and totally subverted it. Instead of the hero being a highly proactive alpha male, the hero is a passive female. Instead of the standard heroic tasks—usually killing something with lots of teeth—Psyche is set to sorting grain, gathering wool, and fetching water.

We note the degeneration of the female role as the chronology of myth progresses. Hecate is one of the early gods—participant in battles with the giants and familiar with Zeus before he became ruler of Olympus. By the time we get to Medea, we find her struggling within the confines of a male-dominated society. She remains independent, but the cost is high, albeit mostly paid by the people around her. With Psyche (whose story, like many in myth, has had multiple interpretations by different psychoanalysts—cf. Glenn, 1977), we have not a goddess, or a superhuman, but an ordinary woman fully subscribed to the standards of her day. She does not complain about a forced marriage (even though she thought she was getting a dragon), and she responds to her husband's orders and initiative, while her own initiatives—though mostly inspired by others—go disastrously wrong. One finds it hard to imagine what Hecate or Medea would do in Psyche's situation, because they would not have got into it in the first place. But had they done so, things would probably not have gone as well for either Venus or Cupid. Neither Medea nor Hecate was a ready-made victim such as the pair found in meek little Psyche.

It is significant that the story of Psyche comes late, both in the internal chronology of mythology and in the history of the telling. Neither society nor myth had any more place for a powerful woman such as Hecate or Medea. The new protagonists were Helen of Troy, Psyche, and Dido—not goddesses or witches, but very human and victims of love and circumstance. The mighty woman was no more. She had been tamed.

References

Berg, W. (1974). Hecate: Greek or Anatolian? *Numen, 21*(2): 128–140.

Georgia Nugent, S. (1993). Euripides' Medea: the stranger in the house. *Comparative Drama, 27*(3): 306–327.

Glenn, J. (1977). Psychoanalytic writings on classical mythology and religion: 1909–1960. *The Classical World, 70*(4): 225–247.

Guastella, G. (2001). Virgo, coniunx, mater: the wrath of Seneca's Medea. *Classical Antiquity, 20*(2): 197–220.

Johnston, S. (1991). Crossroads. *Zeitschrift für Papyrologie und Epigraphik, 88*: 217–224.

Matyszak, P. (2010). *The Greek and Roman Myths*. London: Thames & Hudson.

Price, S. (1999). Religions of the Ancient Greeks. In: *Key Themes in Ancient History* (pp. 101–102). Cambridge: Cambridge University Press.

CHAPTER SIX

Helen of Troy knocks 'em dead: a story of kidnapping, rape, revenge, and the aftermath

Lucille Spira

Introduction

"**M**irror, mirror on the wall, Who in this land is the fairest of all?" (Grimm & Grimm, 2014). For centuries, many women have been concerned about how they rate on the beauty scale. Helen of Troy, a fictional Greek Heroic Age Queen, supposedly was the most beautiful woman of her time, perhaps all time. That Helen, at least in western culture, was the gold standard is remarkable given that she was a mythic figure, not a real person. The myth of Helen that suggests physical perfection is both possible and the key to a woman's desirability, while toxic, has persisted through the ages.

Until quite recently, a woman needed a man in order to gain access to economic and political power. For women, beauty was seen as key in being selected to share fully in the benefits of society. Helen became emulated because, for women who needed or wanted to captivate men, she epitomised the fantasy that perfect beauty is possible and attracts all. The idea of becoming beautiful like Helen allowed women the hope of being powerful with men. This pursuit of bodily perfection and beauty at the expense of real skills leads to poor self-esteem

(Wolf, 1991), body image problems, and eating disorders (Hirschmann & Munter, 1995).

The pursuit of beauty has its paradoxes, just as the Helen myth has its paradoxes. Being desired solely for being beautiful stirs aggressive wishes. All of us wish to be loved for ourselves; feeling only that one is an object for a man's pleasure results in the wish to punish the man. Our modern psychoanalytic theory suggests that all of our behaviours gratify both sexual and aggressive wishes. Helen's story well illustrates this intertwining, as her sexual power is believed to be the spark that ignited the Trojan War. Throughout this chapter, the scholarly works of Bettany Hughes (2007), and Ruby Blondell (2013), along with Homer's *Iliad*, were important sources for my understanding the myth of Helen and the Age of Heroes.

Helen's origins

Homer did not have to detail Helen's history, as his audience knew her story (Hughes, 2007). Helen's narrative is filled with contradictions (Spentzou, 2006). One controversy centers on her birth story. A version says that Helen is the daughter of Zeus and Nemesis. There, Zeus is said to have pursued Nemesis, a sea nymph, who attempted to evade him by changing her form. As Nemesis assumes the body of a goose, Zeus disguises himself as a swan and rapes her. The rape results in conception; Nemesis lays an egg from which Helen eventually hatches. The egg was given to Queen Leda, the wife of King Tyndareus, and they became Helen's parents (Graves, 1992).

Another version of Helen's birth story has Leda, queen and wife of Tyndareus, as her mother; there it is Leda who is raped by Zeus (Hughes, 2007). Still another variant of Helen's beginnings has Leda willingly surrendering to Zeus (Graves, 1992).

Although Helen's birth and origins are fantastical, the fact of women being raped was a real occurrence then as it is now. The rape statistics are frightening—in the USA every 6.2 minutes a woman is reported raped (Solnit, 2014). As we know, children also are raped and are conceived from rapes.

Clearly, rape is a theme in Helen's story. As a young teenager, she is kidnapped by Theseus, the hero-king, depicted by Renault (1988) in her novel, *The King Must Die*. Whether or not Theseus actually raped young Helen is questionable. Graves (1992) allows for that possibility (32b) though neither Hamilton (1942), nor Matyszak (2010), in their engaging overviews of Greek mythology, mention that Helen was raped. Matyszak thinks that the rape theory arises from an error in translating Latin to English; "raptus", means stealing away, not rape (personal communication.) With that said, we know that girls who are kidnapped are often raped. After Boko Haram kidnapped the Nigerian schoolgirls, a leader of Boko Haram said that the girls cannot be returned because they are married (Nossiter, 2014). It is unlikely that any of those girls volunteered for the role of wife.

The cycle of violence and revenge

The theme of violence and revenge permeates Homer's *Iliad* and Helen's story. Helen's niece, Iphigeneia, is sacrificed by King Agamemnon to repay a debt for a crime he committed against Artemis, a goddess. This begins a cycle of revenge, with Clytemnestra, Helen's half-sister, playing a key role in his death to avenge her daughter. Orestes, her son, murders Clytemnestra at the urging of his sister Electra. They each have a righteous justification for their particular acts of vengeance. Cook (2006) gives inner life to Iphigeneia and shows that she is proud of her mother because she understands that Clytemnestra will avenge her death.

But, where, however, is Helen's revenge? Does she receive justice? I propose that Helen's revenge is the Trojan War. I shall return later to this idea.

First, drawing upon my clinical experience and knowledge of psychoanalytic developmental theory, I will create a hypothetical example highlighting the impact of rape on a young girl's psyche. My focus on rape of a girl does not negate the fact that boys and men are also raped and sexually assaulted. Ostriker (2014) in her poem— "Anger II: The Rape"—poignantly and succinctly, reminds us that we all have a painful, not easily resolvable, story.

Rape of a fictional young girl

Let us assume a young girl is kidnapped and then raped. A rape and kidnapping would surely impact a real girl's development. Although this vignette is not in Helen's voice, if we heard her inner voice, or saw her in psychotherapy, it might resonate with her experience and that of other young rape victims. On the cusp of puberty, she had begun to feel her new power and sense of self as a strong young woman. Such positive feelings that are gained contribute to a girl becoming a confident woman. But, real encounters, like the fictional one here, typically result in the opposite feelings and diminished esteem. The girl's healthy narcissism is smashed, at least temporarily.

The girl who is raped is filled with feelings, some of them new and dangerous. If she did not feel so before, she deduces that being a female is dangerous. She becomes sad, scared, and angry. Some sexually abused and/or kidnapped girls would struggle to suppress the intensity of feelings that beset them after such assaults. Sadly, perhaps defensively, the assaulted girl wonders if she did something to bring about the rape. If she felt any pleasurable feelings, she then feels guilt. Self-hatred leads to her feeling dirty. Kipnis (2006) asserts that the female genital often is viewed as dirty. Passivity, where it was not so before, may become the girl's stance. It is as if she accepts "this is my lot as a female, my fate". Alternatively, it is possible that she begins to take unnecessary and dangerous risks, counter-phobic behaviour.

Destructive fantasies may be displaced on to other men, as if men are only a category and not individuals. An idea that she will have her revenge some time in the future, no matter how long it takes, might become a source of comfort. Then, she is a "lady-in-waiting", plotting to kill, an identification with her attacker. This idea fits my view of Helen.

Caenis, a granddaughter of a water god, raped by Poseidon, asked to be transformed into a male warrior to avoid being raped again (Matyszak, 2010). A real girl, in the worse case, withdraws into a fantasy world. In the best case, she finds a reasonable compromise for her feelings, one that allows her to move forward in the world. On the day described, as sometimes is the case in life, there were no gods, goddesses, or overseers present to protect this girl.

Later, in an attempt to feel powerful, she might use her beauty and sexuality to gain power over those whom she perceives might want to disempower her; she turns passive into active. Helen's voyage with Paris to Troy can be understood in this way.

Helen as an adult

As the story goes, Helen, before her voyage to Troy, was the Queen of Sparta, mother of Hermione and wife to King Menelaus. To win her hand in marriage, kings and aristocrats competed with gifts and displays of strength, well described in *The Song of Achilles* (Miller, 2012). Once Helen selected Menelaus to be her husband, his competitors and fellow countrymen pledged to defend her choice against any usurpers. Menelaus and Helen's other suitors wanted to wed her because, upon her father's death, she would bestow both wealth and a kingship on her husband (Hughes, 2007). Her society was a matrilineal one. Helen was objectified. She was desired as a rich, beautiful woman, who could make her husband a king, rather than for herself (Hughes, 2007).

Helen and Paris

Paris, a handsome Trojan Prince, sails from the East and stops at the palace of Helen and Menelaus. There, unbeknown to them, he plans to claim his long-ago promised prize, Helen.

Many years before, Aphrodite, Hera, and Athena, three goddesses, pitted themselves against one another. Each wanted to be selected the most beautiful goddess. Paris, then, a young shepherd boy, was the judge. Aphrodite, the Goddess of Love, promised that if he chose her, she would give him beautiful Helen. Paris, like many men before him, wanted Helen, so he chose Aphrodite. Along with Helen and her treasures, came strife.

Why did Helen go to Troy?

How you answer the above question depends upon how you understand Helen. Helen's motivations are not well defined; people identify with the aspect, or characteristic, that fits their own psychology. Characterised as a whore or a victim, she is a container for one's too uncomfortable forbidden and unconscious wishes. She is admired and devalued. To label Helen as a whore is inaccurate. Her behaviour better fits that of an adulteress. Alizade (1999) sees adultery as a way by which some women declare equality and power.

As the Helen myth developed over time, it is not surprising that there are different versions of her story, including why Helen went to

Troy. One idea is that she absconded with Paris because she was under the power of Aphrodite. But, if Helen was sexually attracted to Paris, then she was under the power of Eros. This is not unlike the idea of love at first sight, where the lovers are swept away by transference. Psychoanalytic theory explains this type of love as a displacement from our first love, usually a parent, on to an other. Temporarily, the ego is bypassed and not engaged with reality concerns. This is one way to explain why Helen departed from Sparta without Hermione, her daughter—she was drunk on love.

When fate dictates a person's behaviour, they are thought to be without free will. However, there are ways to resist one's fate. Along with Blondell (2013), I believe that Helen was active rather than passive, leaving willingly with Paris. In this version, subjugated women can vicariously discharge their aggressive fantasies against their male subjugators and can imagine the pleasure of following their wishes. Homer's epic suggests that she understood she had at least one other choice. Helen tells Priam, Paris's father:

> . . . if only death had pleased me then, grim death
> That day I followed your son to Troy, forsaking
> My marriage bed, my kinsmen, my child . . ."
> (Homer, 1990, 3: 209–211, p. 134)

By making the choice to leave with Paris, Helen chose destruction, thus satisfying her unconscious murderous wishes. She knew that Menelaus and his comrades would risk all to recover both her and the Spartan treasure.

Typically, women were not warriors and could not earn heroic status. Helen, however, could ensure heroic immortality by igniting a war.

The battlefield

Rich metaphors and dynamic characters inhabit the setting in which Helen gets her revenge. How much of a role does she play in turning that sea wine-dark?

In the *Iliad*, we hear tales of regal male heroes battling their way to victory and also ones of those who lose. The feats of Achilles,

Odysseus, and even Hector, the Trojan Prince, become models by which to measure future heroes. For some, like Achilles, being under the wings of Athena, the Goddess of War, or some other god or goddess, advanced one's chances for victory. In the war between the Greeks and the Trojans, Athena favours the Greeks, while Aphrodite is on the side of the Trojans.

Although these heroic figures fight for the "gloire", they also covet the material goods of their opponents. The sisters, daughters, and even the mothers of the defeated warriors are distributed as booty among the victors.

At the centre of the conflict between Achilles and Agamemnon is the desire of each of them to keep their particular slave girl. Agamemnon is encouraged by both Achilles and his Council to return Chryseis, his slave girl, to her father to prevent Apollo's wrath. Her father is a priest and she is a priestess in one of Apollo's shrines. After much posturing, Agamemnon agrees to do so. To salve his wound over the loss of Chryseis, he orders Achilles to hand him his slave girl, Briseis. Achilles resists Agamemnon's order. If he submits to Agamemnon, his honour will be compromised. In the Age of Heroes, honour, as they defined it, was paramount (Finley, 2002).

Euripides' *Trojan Women* (1915) sympathetically portrays the anxiety that besets the women on the side of the Trojans. As they try to manage their feelings about the losses they have sustained, they must also come to terms with the bleak future that awaits them. They will be distributed among the victors and transported to unknown lands. Andromache, Hector's widow, will witness the death of her young son as the boy is killed to prevent him later from avenging his father's death. Helen's fate is uncertain. Hecuba, the former Trojan Queen, blames Helen for the war and rails against her. She asks Menelaus to kill Helen. Hughes (2007) suggests that Euripides, through the voice of Hecuba, is unsympathetic to Helen because, as an Athenian, he is naturally biased against the Spartans. Had Spartan Helen not been so desirable, Theseus would not have kidnapped her and then there would not have been a war, centuries later, between Sparta and Athens. Euripides sees Helen as responsible for her actions and the events that ensued from her decision to depart with Paris for Troy. In a discussion of women in war that includes Helen of Troy, O'Gorman asserts that women's role in war, historically, is defined by men (O'Gorman, 2006).

Paris, despite all his winning physical attributes, is not a skilled warrior. On the battlefield, he is inept and somewhat cowardly. Hector, his more skilled and valiant brother, expresses his anger at Paris for being selfish. Paris risked the lives of Trojans and all of Troy by absconding with Helen. He urges Paris to take the honourable course and fight it out one on one with Menelaus—winner take all. Paris responds,

> . . . we'll fight it out for Helen and all her wealth.
> And the one who proves the better man and wins,
> he'll take those treasure fairly, lead the woman home.
>   (Homer, 1990, 3: 86–88, p. 131)

This suggests that Paris had his mind not only on Helen but also on her wealth.

The irony

As the war resulted in the deaths of many men, it can be seen as avenging the wrongs that had been done to Helen, to her mother, and to other women who were enslaved, subjugated by men, and unprotected by the gods and goddesses.

Hecuba, in *The Trojan Women*, tells Menelaus that Helen is not a victim. She says that Helen intentionally put the lives of Greek soldiers at risk. Helen did this when she sang lullabies to the troops who were hiding in the horse sent by the Greeks to the Trojans. If those soldiers had been seduced by Helen's voice and had climbed out of the horse, the Trojans would have slaughtered them.

Helen's ploy failed. As the legend goes, Troy was razed and multitudes of men were killed. Helen returned to Sparta and resumed her reign as Queen and wife of King Menelaus. Now, Athena is the winner over Aphrodite. Helen had her revenge both against men who abuse women and against Aphrodite, her puppet mistress.

In contradiction to Blondell (2013), Finley (2002) casts Helen as a passive victim when he asserts that Athena and Hera were responsible for the fall of Troy.

While Helen was admired for her beauty and the power it gave her with men, I see her real power as an avenger. Her legendary narrative resonated with women. For those who were abused and held murderous wishes towards their abusers, her story provided vicarious gratification for their aggressive wishes. This allowed women who often were denied justice to avenge their hurts.

Later, Helen, back in Sparta with Menelaus, dispenses a potion that makes one forget anger and pain (Homer, 1996). I understand this as her way to escape guilt's torment. Helen knocked men dead, especially those who kidnapped and raped women, but she paid a price. However, those who see her only as a passive victim—powerful only in her beauty—hurt women even more.

Real life, revenge, and beyond

Many women do not see themselves as needing a man to rescue or protect them, but others believe that they cannot stand up for themselves in the world. When those women do not find male protection, they often blame themselves for no longer being beautiful enough, young enough, or virginal.

A woman patient whom I treated many years ago wanted revenge for a rape she had suffered. She felt powerless to defend herself or to receive justice for her righteous complaints. She had been raped by a relative in-law. Fearing that the police would laugh at her, she decided not to report the rape. They would laugh, she said, because she was not young, not pretty, and "no virgin".

The above, expressed by my patient, is an example of how the themes of an ancient myth, like that of Helen of Troy, still permeate our present day culture. When such beliefs are unexamined and taken out of context, women get hurt. Because she felt that she lacked the traits that she idealised—the ones valued in Helen's time—she did not feel she was worthy of respect. She also silenced herself because her rapist was part of the family and identifying him would cause trouble. Sadly, she feared that her family would not believe her. They knew that she had a "nervous condition". Following the assault, she did not go to the hospital for medical assistance or call anyone for support.

My patient reported that after her assailant left, although dazed, she showered to erase any traces of him. As the night passed, she decided she would tell her brother. She wanted him to beat up her assailant. In the neighbourhood where she had grown up, brothers protected their sisters. But, at the time of the episode described here, she was in her forties and her brother in his fifties, so she realised that things might be different. If her brother fought with her rapist something bad might happen, not only to the man but also to her brother. "What if my brother killed him?" she asked.

As an attempt to resolve the conflict caused by her aggressive wishes, she decided not to tell her brother and to suppress her feelings about the rape. As her anxiety became heightened, she had accidents that threatened to put her at risk, that is, she crossed streets against the lights and barely avoided being hit by a car. There were several such episodes. She became both agitated and spaced out. Her actions towards herself had a punitive quality. Her repressed feelings of anger towards her brother, as one who could not protect her, along with her angry feelings toward herself and her rapist, exacerbated the masochistic aspects of her character.

In treatment, my patient and I worked together to help her to connect not only with her anger, but with the sadness it masked. A goal was to help her to use her aggression to move herself forward. She maintained her stance of not telling her family about what had happened to her. We understood this as her feeling somewhat responsible for the rape. What made most sense to my patient was that suffering the rape was her punishment for being twice divorced. To her, being a divorcée was a sin.

As she became less anxious, my patient sought vocational training and became employed for the first time since she was eighteen. Although her job was an entry level one, paying a minimum wage, she was proud of this achievement. Her job was a step toward a new independence bringing her into a world beyond the confines of her apartment. She stepped out of her comfort zone both literally and figuratively. Her new job was located in Manhattan. Prior to our work, she had never, on her own, travelled outside of her home borough. In order to be employed, she overcame her anxiety about leaving her familiar surroundings.

As I think about my former patient's situation, had her brother gone to "war" for her, it would not have helped her in the long run. The pattern of her being cast in the role of a helpless woman had contributed to her life's difficulties. Her thoughts that were rooted in the Helen myth needed dislodging. Ancient Greek goddesses such as

Artemis, skilled in self-defence, and Athena with her ability to strate-gise, would be more appropriate mythological figures than Helen from which to draw strength.

My patient's harsh superego was also a factor in her difficulty. With support, my patient discovered that she had inner resources— the capacity to persevere. Eventually, she used her therapy to connect with her feelings both from before and after the rape. To work through victimhood and trauma, the sufferer needs her pain witnessed (Kaufmann & Kaufmann, 2013). Rogers (2007), drawing upon her experience with young victims of sexual assault, believes that those who are assaulted must be helped to give voice to their emotional pain. Humiliation about how she had allowed herself to be fooled by men was a large issue for my patient. The aggressive feelings towards her self, stirred by the rape, needed to be transformed into behaviours that repair the self. She needed help to meet the challenges of voca-tional training and, later, to negotiate the world of work. While her harsh superego allowed her the compromise of work, she was unable to pursue the more typical leisure activities.

Discussion

Women need more than revenge or fantasies of becoming beautiful, or even being beautiful, to be truly powerful. While beauty gives a woman some advantage in the world, a resilient ego enables her to satisfactorily resolve interpersonal and intrapsychic challenges. Along with practical skills, ultimately ego strength trumps beauty (Sinkman, 2013). Strong women, secure men, and powerful women characters all help women develop their potential. As women become more compe-tent in the world, they are more able to find and assert their voices.

The new role models for women are the "bad" girls (Warner, 1995). The Russian punk group, Pussy Riot, exemplifies Warner's view. Though imprisoned for what was considered blasphemous behaviour, they emerged with their voices intact—they became more powerful advocates for human rights. Their goal is justice rather than revenge.

Adopting a vindictive character style is one way that a person can resolve the angry feelings that result from early humiliations (Horney, 1948). While she understood that recourse as neurotic, Horney focused on what she saw as the adaptive component of revenge: that is, vengeful acts towards others defend against suicidal thoughts. This idea describes the situation of my former patient who endangered herself when she decided not to tell her brother and realised she would not have her revenge.

I agree with Poland (Beattie, 2005) that those who cannot find justice are more likely to seek revenge. But, as an adaptive response, revenge, like beauty, can only go so far. The avenger experiences unconscious guilt even when the vengeful acts seem justified. Innocent people can be hurt by another person's act of vengeance. Helen's use of a mind-altering drug suggests that she needs to escape her inner torturer. With my patient, although her vengeful wishes were not gratified, the punitive "accidents" that followed the rape I understood as being linked to unconscious guilt. Her fear that her brother might kill the man who had assaulted her masked her wish to have the man dead.

I end this chapter with a story of a very brave and strong young girl. Some of you have read about the mullah who raped a ten-year-old girl (Nordland, 2014). When those in her village heard that she was raped, many did not want the crime reported. Some thought she should be killed. With the help of a women's organisation, she was rescued and treated for the injuries that she had sustained. Her case came before a court. The mullah's defence team pleaded for reduced charges allowing the lesser punishment for adultery—lashes—rather than the more stringent one meted out for rape. Since adultery is a two-person act, the child victim would be lashed as well. Fortunately, at least so far, a higher form of justice prevailed and the convicted mullah will serve twenty years in prison.

These strong women who sought justice on behalf of this young girl are the Artemis figures of today. Hopefully, through this experience, this child has learnt that she does not have to be silent, passive, or even vengeful. It is her voice and courage, not physical beauty, that make her truly powerful. She stood up to the powerful mullah. Although Aphrodite won the beauty contest, Athena won the war.

Acknowledgement

Carol Munter (IPTAR), psychoanalyst and femininst, is acknowledged for her contribution to this paper.

References

Alizade, A. M. (1999). *Feminine Sensuality*. London: Karnac.

Beattie, H. J. (2005). Revenge: APsaA Panel. *Journal of the American Psychoanalytic Association, 53*: 513–524.

Blondell, R. (2013). *Helen of Troy: Beauty, Myth, Devastation*. New York: Oxford University Press.

Cook, E. (2006). Iphigeneia's wedding. In: V. Zajko & M. Leonard (Eds.), *Laughing with Medusa: Classical Myth and Feminist Thought* (pp. 355–379). New York: Oxford University Press.

Euripides (1915). *The Trojan Women*, G. Murray (Trans.). Public Domain Book.

Finley, M. I. (2002). *The World of Odysseus*. New York: New York Review of Books.

Graves, R. (1955). *The Greek Myths: Complete Edition*. London: Penguin.

Grimm, W., & Grimm, J. (2014). Little Snow-White. In: *Grimms' Fairy Tales*. www.fairy-ebooks.com.

Hamilton, E. (1942). *Mythology*. New York: The New American Library.

Hirschmann, J. R., & Munter, C. H. (1995). *When Women Stop Hating Their Bodies: Freeing Yourself from Food and Weight Obsession*. New York: Fawcett Books.

Homer (1990). *The Iliad*, R. Fagles (Trans.). New York: Penguin.

Homer (1996). *The Odyssey*, R. Fagles (Trans.). New York: Penguin.

Horney, K. (1948). The value of vindictiveness. *American Journal of Psychoanalysis, 8*: 3–12.

Hughes, B. (2007). *Helen of Troy: The Story behind the Most Beautiful Woman in the World*. New York: Vintage.

Kaufmann, J. K., & Kaufmann, P. (2013). Witnessing: its essentialness in psychoanalytic treatment. In: A. K. Richards, L. Spira, & A. A. Lynch (Eds.), *Encounters with Loneliness: Only the Lonely* (pp. 140–157). NewYork: IP Books.

Kipnis, L. (2006). *The Female Thing: Dirt, Sex, Envy, Vulnerability*. New York: Pantheon Books.

Matyszak, P. (2010). *The Greek and Roman Myths: A Guide to the Classical Stories*. London: Thames & Hudson.

Miller, M. (2012). *The Song of Achilles*. New York: Ecco.

Nordland, R. (2014). Afghan mullah who raped girl in his mosque receives 20-year prison sentence. *New York Times*, October 26, p. A12.

Nossiter, A. (2014). In Nigeria, fragile hopes of Boko Haram freeing schoolgirls are dashed. *New York Times*, October 31, p. A9.

O'Gorman, E. (2006). A woman's history of warfare. In: V. Zajko & M. Leonard (Eds.), *Laughing with Medusa: Classical Myth and Feminist Thought* (pp. 189–207). New York: Oxford University Press.

Ostriker, A. (2014). Anger II: The Rape. In: *The Old Woman, the Tulip, and the Dog* (p. 51). Pittsburgh, PA: University of Pittsburgh Press.

Renault, M. (1988). *The King Must Die*. London: Vintage.

Rogers, A. (2007). *The Unsayable: The Hidden Language of Trauma*. New York: Ballantine Books.

Sinkman, E. (2013). *The Psychology of Beauty: Creation of A Beautiful Self*. New York: Jason Aronson.

Solnit, R. (2014). *Men Explain Things to Me*. Chicago, IL: Haymarket.

Spentzou, E. (2006). Defying history: the legacy of Helen in modern Greek poetry. In: V. Zajko & M. Leonard (Eds.), *Laughing with Medusa: Classical Myth and Feminist Thought* (pp. 399–410). New York: Oxford University Press.

Warner, M. (1995). *Six Myths of our Time*. London: Vintage.

Wolf, N. (1991). *The Beauty Myth: How Images of Beauty Are Used Against Women*. New York: William Morrow.

CHAPTER SEVEN

Miriam the prophetess and others: biblical heroines lost and found

Alicia Ostriker

I thought of calling this a chapter on trickster heroines in the Bible. Then I thought of calling it "Vanishing heroines in the Bible". Although an omnipotent male god dominates Hebrew and Christian scriptures, bolstered by powerful male patriarchs, kings, warriors, judges, prophets, and tough, authoritative, charismatic political leaders, and the New Testament gives us a male Jesus and male disciples, the Hebrew Bible happens to include numerous female figures who are either tricksters or successful manipulators, and who are seen as changing the course of history. Most of these figures then vanish from the narratives in which they appear. A pattern of recurrent appearance-plus-disappearance exists in the Bible, I believe, for a reason that should capture the attention of anyone interested in the intersections of religion and psychology. I wish to propose that the presence and erasure of powerful women in Scripture encodes the erasure of the goddess in ancient middle-eastern culture, that this erasure can be reversed, and that the therapist, like the poet–teacher (such as myself), can make use of midrash (reimagining biblical characters) in encouraging girls and women to bring to light and to action their repressed "might". My references might or might not be familiar to my readers, but I trust that their resonance with the psychoanalytic quest will be clear.

Women tricksters

A prime example of a trickster is Miriam, sister of Moses. Miriam appears at three crucial moments in the biblical books of Exodus and Numbers. As a girl, she assists in the rescue of her baby brother by Pharaoh's daughter. As a young woman, she is called a prophetess, and leads the women of Israel in triumphal song and dance after they cross the Red Sea and the Egyptian army drowns, in a poem that is among the oldest texts in the Bible:

> I will sing to the Lord, for he has triumphed gloriously;
> the horse and his rider he has thrown into the sea,

is her refrain. We are told as well that she "took the timbrel in her hand; and all the women followed her with timbrels and with dances" (Ex 15: 20–21). Finally, as an older woman during the wandering of the children of Israel in the wilderness, she questions the authority of Moses, and is smitten with leprosy (or a skin disease resembling leprosy) making her skin "white as snow" for a week; later she dies (Num 20).

If we look more closely at Miriam's trickster self, we see that it emerges within a cluster of female tricksters. To begin, at the opening of the biblical Book of Exodus, the children of Israel are enslaved in Egypt for 400 years. Pharaoh decides they are growing dangerously numerous, and orders the midwives to kill all boy babies born to Hebrew women. Two midwives, Shifra and Puah, refuse to do this, and when Pharaoh questions them, they say that the Hebrew women "are not like the Egyptian women, for they are lively and give birth" before the midwives get there (Ex 1: 15–19). This is trick number one. The phrase used might be taken as a compliment to the Hebrew women, saying they are so healthy, or as an insult, saying they are subhuman, giving birth like animals. Then Pharaoh orders the Egyptians to throw all Hebrew newborn males into the Nile. When the baby Moses is born, his mother hides him for three months, trick number two, then places him in a basket among the bulrushes by the banks of the Nile. There, he is found by Pharaoh's daughter, who decides to take him in. But Moses' sister Miriam has been watching, and suggests, "Shall I go and call a nurse for you from the Hebrew women, that she may nurse the child for you?" When Pharoah's daughter accepts the offer, Miriam fetches her own mother, who of course is also Moses' mother, and who does nurse Moses until he grows old enough to be given to Pharaoh's daughter (Ex 2: 1–10). This is trick number three.

The story of Moses being brought up by Pharaoh's daughter is well known. But must we not acknowledge that the story's implications are nothing less than revolutionary? A slave girl has fooled a princess. A three- to five-year period of nursing, which would not have been uncommon in the ancient world, would have been time enough for Moses' birth mother to implant some ideas in the young prince about the injustice of slavery. More than that, and this is what I really want to emphasise, the story of Moses' birth is the first account we have on earth of civil disobedience, and the disobedience is enacted by a virtual conspiracy of females—the midwives, Moses' mother, Moses' sister Miriam, and Pharaoh's daughter.

It would be difficult to find a more inspiring model of female might than this conspiracy across boundaries of age, class, and ethnicity, to save the life of a slave child who becomes a future liberator. The only real parallel is Aristophanes' *Lysistrata*, in which the women of Athens and Sparta collaborate in a sexual strike until their husbands agree to make peace and end the Peloponnesian War. Yet, the political dimension of the story is not well known or celebrated in our culture. In fact, as I have indicated, Miriam's story follows a recurrent biblical pattern, in which figures of female power and agency appear at the outset of a story or narrative segment, and are typically made to die or disappear by its ending. What happens to Miriam is that she disappears from the narrative after the crossing of the Red Sea, but during the wandering in the wilderness she suddenly reappears as a questioner of authority. Miriam and her brother Aaron challenge Moses (Num 12): "Has the Lord spoken only through Moses? Has he not spoken through us also?" In other words, are we not prophets also? Are we not leaders too? A grammatical quirk of this passage is that the text "Miriam and Aaron spoke against Moses" puts the verb "spoke" in the feminine singular, suggesting either that Miriam was the chief spokesperson, or that Aaron was spliced in at a later date. As a consequence, in any case, Miriam (but not Aaron) is struck with a skin disease similar to leprosy and is expelled from the camp for a week. We hear nothing more of her until her death and burial, which are mentioned in a single sentence (Num 20.1), although Aaron's death and the thirty-day period of mourning that follows it are recounted at length (Num 20: 22–29). By the end of the Exodus story, the three founding siblings, Moses, Aaron, and Miriam, have died. In what we might call their afterlives as text, scholars attempt to show that the Jahwist and Elohist strands of the biblical text (usually called J and E) derive from traditions associated with Moses and Aaron, respectively. What strands of the biblical text are the heritage of Miriam? None. One song. It is reasonable to suppose that once there must once have been a body of legends around the figure of Miriam. As we have the text now, all such material has been edited out, and Miriam's tale is the tale of a powerful woman disempowered.

A trickster, in folklore around the world, is a figure who disobeys rules and gets away with it. The coyote for Native Americans; the fox for many Europeans; the monkey for the Chinese; Loki (a trickster who can change his shape and sex) in Norse mythology. In the folklore layer of the Bible, which appears to be the source of many of its memorably compelling narratives, tricksters abound. We might begin with Eve, who—tricked by the serpent—goes ahead and manipulates or tricks Adam into eating the fruit of the tree of knowledge, an act of disobedience for which they *do not* die, as God said they would if they ate it. They are expelled from Eden, but their lives continue. So, here there is punishment but no death.

The next woman we meet in the Bible is Sarah, Abraham's barren wife, who gives her slave-woman Hagar to her husband to have a child for her (it is a story of surrogate motherhood)—and then, when she gives birth herself, has her husband banish Hagar, to make sure that her own son Isaac will receive the inheritance (Gen 16–17, Gen 21). We can see this as a sort of bait-and-switch strategy, if not technically a trick. Sarah is the dominant spouse in this story. God tells Abraham "listen to the voice of your wife", and he does. But where is Sarah when God commands Abraham to take Isaac up a mountain and sacrifice him? (Gen 22). Sarah is nowhere. And although the sacrifice is averted, Sarah is both literally and figuratively nowhere.

The episode immediately following the *akedah*, the "binding" of Isaac, recounts her death and burial. In the elaborate chapter narrating Abraham's purchase of a burial site for Sarah in what is now the city of Hebron, Abraham uses language that the King James Version translates as "that I may bury my dead out of my sight".[1] He uses the phrase "out of my sight" twice, emphatically, although the local

Hittites simply say "bury your dead". Why so emphatic? Interestingly, modern translations consistently omit the phrase altogether, perhaps wishing to avoid the implication that the patriarch wants to get rid of the matriarch. Does patriarchy wish to bury the memory of matri-archy, effectively, out of sight, out of mind? We usually understand the story of the binding of Isaac as encoding the historical shift from human sacrifice to animal sacrifice. But it can equally well be under-stood as encoding the historical shift from mother-right to father-right. Who owns a child? Isaac in this story is "bound" to the father and the father's God psychologically as well as physically. Traditional rabbinic midrash highlights the link between the binding of Isaac and the death of Sarah by proposing that Sarah is told of her husband's plans by Satan, and dies of a heart attack.

Eve and Sarah are perhaps not full-fledged tricksters, but merely manipulative or, to put it more crudely, simply bossy. After these events, however, we have Isaac's wife Rebecca, who is a fully con-scious and effective trickster. Mother of the twins Jacob and Esau, she favours Jacob, and instructs him to disguise himself as his brother in order to steal the blessing that their father expects to give Esau. When Jacob objects that he may be unmasked and cursed instead of blessed, Rebecca replies (Gen 27: 13), "Let the curse be on me, my son; just obey my voice and go". Jacob does what he is told, he is blessed by his father, escapes his brother's intent to kill him, ultimately is re-named "Israel", a name implying triumph, and goes on to become the third great patriarch of the Bible—all thanks to his mother's trickery. Years later, when he decides to return home, it is "to go to his father Isaac" (Gen 31: 17), but there is no mention of his mother.

After this we meet Rachel and Leah, sisters, Jacob's future wives. Their father Laban fools Jacob with the bed trick, giving him the older daughter Leah on the wedding night, instead of the beloved Rachel. Years later, Rachel gets her own back. As Jacob and his family and servants and flocks are abandoning the cheater Laban, Rachel steals her father's teraphim, his household gods. What were these figures for? They might have brought good fortune, or protection from the evil eye, or perhaps fertility. What would these idols have looked like? They might have been birds or animals, or they might have been female figurines such as have been found by archaeologists through-out the middle east. (Essentially, all of the Palaeolithic (40,000–10,000 BCE) figurines found in the middle east to date have been females. For millennia, homes might have had shrines for them.) Laban gives chase and threatens death to whoever stole his teraphim—and when he comes to Rachel's tent to search it, Rachel has hidden the teraphim under her camel's saddle, and is sitting on the saddle. Apologising for not rising to greet her father, she says (Gen 31: 35), "Let it not displease my lord that I cannot rise before you, for the manner of women is upon me". In other words, she is (oh, horrors) menstruating. So Laban searches but finds nothing, and the forbidden teraphim remain part of the luggage of Jacob's family.

Numerous other women tricksters inhabit scripture. The daughters of Lot get him drunk and have sex with him in order to have children—one of whom will be an ancestor of King David. Tamar pretends to be a prostitute; her son, too, will be an ancestor of David. Potiphar's wife accuses Joseph of rape and gets him thrown into prison. Jael offers to hide the fleeing Canaanite general Sisera, gives him "milk in a lordly cup", and when he falls asleep she drives a tent peg through his skull (Judg 4–5). Ruth the Moabitess sneaks by night to the threshing floor during harvest, where she coaxes the Hebrew landowner Boaz to marry her (not that he takes much coaxing), then slips away before she is seen by others; she becomes, thereby, the great-grandmother of King David. Michal saves the life of her husband David by trickery when her father tries to kill him. Abigail, disobeying her foolish husband's orders, gives food to the future King David's wandering band of mercenaries—and later becomes another of his wives. Bathsheba, still another of David's wives, manipulates him on his deathbed into naming her son Solomon as his successor.

Delilah betrays her lover, Samson. Queen Esther uses a feast to prevent the genocide of the Jewish people by Ahasuerus and Haman. The beautiful widow Judith visits the warrior general Holofernes, who is besieging her town; for three nights she entertains him with a banquet; on the third night, when he falls asleep drunk, she beheads him with his own sword. Medieval and renaissance artists particularly loved this story, and produced thousands of images of it. Judith's sexuality is commonly a feature of such depictions, which at times veer toward the pornographic. We, too, get the picture. Socially powerless women deploy feminine wiles, sexual or maternal, or both at once, to manipulate men and appropriate their power.

There are numerous male trickster figures as well as female ones in the Bible. But my point is precisely that the role of the trickster is, so to speak, an equal opportunity employer. Women in these stories think and act for themselves, accomplishing their goals, as people of a subject class must do, by using their wits. They are heroines (except for Potiphar's wife and Delilah, and even they involuntarily serve God's purposes) because their acts support the ongoing master narrative of God's covenant with the Hebrew people.

Disappearing women

There is a catch, however, and it is implied by what I just said. Eve and Miriam are not killed, but they are punished. Eve, Sarah, Rebecca, Rachel, Tamar, and Ruth become mothers, the nameless incestuous daughters of Lot become mothers, as it were, right onscreen, and Jael and Judith behave like mothers. In each case, when the female figure has achieved her ends she disappears from the story. This is also the case for other mother-figures such as Hannah and the mother of Samson, with the very elaborate birth narratives that they dominate. It is particularly notable that Samson's future mother receives a complex angelic annunciation which she has to explain to her somewhat befuddled husband (Judg 13: 2–23), but at Samson's death "his brethren and all the house of his father came down, and took him, and brought him up, and buried him . . . in the burying place of his father" (Judg 16: 31).

These numerous female figures are by no means simple parallels of each other. In some cases, they are allies, vessels, or even confidantes of God. In other cases, they are enemies. Some are tricksters, but not all. What they do have in common is what William Blake, millennia later, called, with disgust, "female Will" (Essick, 1991). In all these stories, the woman represents Desire. And in each story the disappearance of the female coordinates or coincides with the establishment (or re-establishment following a rebellion or fall) of the exclusively male covenant that climaxes in the life of King David, and, for Christian readers, ultimately in the life of Jesus, who is born from David's lineage.

As far as I am aware, no biblical critic noticed this startlingly recurrent pattern in biblical narrative before I pointed it out it in the essay "Out of my sight: the buried woman in biblical narrative" in my book *Feminist Revision and the Bible* (1993). I assume that this is because scholars, critics, and clergy, as well as ordinary readers of the Bible, universally *take it for granted* that female power must be submerged in order for the story of male maturity, male leadership, male heroism, and, indeed, male divinity, to succeed. The pattern has promulgated itself so successfully that it has become invisible. Here, I mean "succeed" in two senses. Male dominance succeeds in the sense that it successfully dominates culture and society for three or four thousand years, and it also succeeds in the sense of royal succession: what comes earlier is succeeded by what comes later. So, let us ask: why do figures of female cleverness and female power emerge again and again in biblical narratives, only to disappear and emerge again?

My answer to this question is necessarily an intuitive one; readers must consult their own intuitions as well as historical fact. However, an important fact is that goddesses were worshipped everywhere in the ancient world for millennia before the advent and dominance of male gods and, ultimately, of male monotheism, a transition that took about a thousand years, as the historian Gerda Lerner summarises it:

> The observable pattern is: first, the demotion of the Mother-Goddess figure and the ascendance and later dominance of her male consort/ son; then his merging with a storm-god into a male Creator-God, who heads the pantheon of gods and goddesses. Whenever such changes occur, the power of creation and fertility is transferred from the Goddess to the God. (Lerner, 1986, p. 145)

Judaism's ultimate replacement of indigenous goddesses by the One God of the Israelites required the existence of the goddesses to be denied and their worship forbidden. The God of the Bible is very insistent on being worshipped exclusively—"I the Lord am a jealous God . . ." in tones that we today cannot help but interpret as defensive. For goddess worship in fact continued through the period of the first temple and was only successfully eradicated after the Persian exile with the building of the second temple. Numerous Biblical texts testify to the recurrence of goddess worship and the need to uproot "her groves". So, it appears that what has been encoded in the recurrent appearance and disappearance of powerful female characters in the Bible is the obsessively told and re-told moment of transition from a world in which women were humanly and socially powerful, because divinity was in part female, to a world in which that divinity and power were denied.

The return of the repressed

In *Moses and Monotheism*, Freud speculates that Moses was murdered by his rebellious followers, and that memory of this murder was repressed but not extinguished: "the facts which the so-called official written history purposely tried to suppress were in reality never lost" but constituted "a dormant tradition" (Freud, 1930a, pp. 112–113). For Freud, the repressed memory and the guilt attached to it constitute a source of immense emotional energy within Judaism, as "this repressed material retains its impetus to penetrate into consciousness", spurring Jews' intense devotion to their God, and supporting their survival. In my revision of Freud's formulation, I speculate that the imperfectly repressed memory of the Great Mother's murder is among the most profound sources of energy within Judaism, and perhaps Christianity as well, as the work of Marina Warner on the cult of the Virgin Mary (1976) and Elaine Pagels on the suppression of the Gnostic Gospels (1979) would suggest. Is the ideological and psychic need to repress female divinity and female power a consequence of fear? Fear of the "monster mother", or fear of becoming effeminate? Is the need to repress women triggered by women's capacity to create life? Do misogyny and other societal pathologies arise because nurturing is done primarily by a single gender which then absorbs all the infant's adoration and rage, as argued by Dorothy Dinnerstein (1976)? Is it female maternity, or female sexuality, that is most threatening to male dominance, male narcissism, male self-esteem? Whatever the reason, the repressed keeps returning, and is returning today, as a volume such as this one clearly demonstrates.

Feminist theory and midrash over the last quarter-century has begun to revive images of female power in history and culture, at just the moment when we see women becoming rabbis, cantors, biblical scholars, theologians, ministers, bishops, and midrashists.[2] Noting that "the last thirty years have seen a bold, rapidly accelerating renaissance" in midrash writing in North America, Rivkah Walton (2011) observes that the figure of the resourceful Miriam comes to supplant that of the protest-figure Lilith in the 1990s. Rebecca Schwartz's anthology, *All the Women Followed Her: A Collection of Writings on Miriam the Prophet and the Women of the Exodus* (2001), includes numerous poems and fictions celebrating Miriam. An anthology of Miriam-themed writings collected by Enid Dame was published posthumously by the Jewish feminist journal, *Bridges*. Ellen Frankel's *The Five Books of Miriam: A Women's Commentary of the Torah* (1996), sets Miriam's voice in dialogue with Bible texts and with other biblical females. Seder tables nowadays often place "Miriam's cup" alongside "Elijah's Cup", and songs in Miriam's honour join traditional Passover songs in many families.

Much of this recent work celebrates Miriam's creativity and leadership: "I am the Singer, the Dancer, the Drummer of Israel . . . I prophesy the redemption of our people" (Frankel, 1996, p. xx). Rabbi Jill Hammer, whose website Tel Shemesh explores earth-based traditions within Judaism, gives us a mystical and prophetic Miriam. While Moses climbs Mount Sinai to meet God and receive the Torah, Miriam enters a door at the foot of the mountain. Deep underground she meets an aged female who gives her "all the empty places in the Torah . . . Every place there is no ink, every place there is no word", the "gaps" in which unwritten truth will be found (Hammer, 2001, pp. 129–135). There is also work of a more modern political slant. Building on the allusion to water in Miriam's name (which can be translated as "bitter sea") and in her story, and on widespread traditional legends of "Miriam's well" which is supposed to have followed Miriam underground in the desert, Enid Dame's Miriam is invoked to heal a town suffering from contaminated ground water. Rabbi Lynn Gottlieb, in a suite of Miriam poems, beautifully re-imagines the symbolism of the prophetess's "Song at the Sea,"

> Sing to Yehoyah, whose glory thunders,
> ,All the mighty warriors drown in the sea
> Which gave us birth
> When Miriam died
> She bequeathed her power to find water
> To the women who sang with her at the sea.
>
> (Gottlieb, 1995, p. 113)

Pesha Joyce Gertler's Miriam, during her exile, secretly organises Israelite women, has them practise guerrilla theatre, write poems for their descendants, and anticipate the time that she will descend from Sinai with new commandments mandating female power (2007). Eleanor Wilner's Miriam, appalled at the death of Egypt's firstborn sons on the eve of the exodus, goes "to join the others, to leave one ruler / for another, one Egypt for the next" (Wilner, 1989, p. 8). In my poem "The Songs of Miriam", Miriam has "a voice, to announce liberty". She curses with spiritual drought whoever believes God speaks only through Moses, and promises her ongoing liberating power to those who remember her music if they "*Follow me / follow my drum*" (Ostriker, 1994, pp. 145–147). In Walton's prose poem "The Rock", God's mysterious punishment of Moses for hitting a rock to get water instead of speaking to it (Num 20: 1–3) is explained: the rock is Miriam's memorial stone, and his insult to her means that he will not be permitted to enter the Promised Land.

It is not only women who today reimagine the meaning of Miriam. The most radical update of the Miriam story I have encountered is by the storyteller Arthur Strimling. Composed in the witty voice of a gay man who has been a dancer in Pharaoh's court along with Miriam, "What ever happened to Miriam" recounts how, after the crossing of the Red Sea, while Miriam sings and dances with the people "at the hot center", the narrator comments, "So we were feeling free. But honey, feeling free is not the same as being free". At this moment a set of enforcers begins to separate the men from the women and to curse the narrator as an "abomination". A new repressive rule is in the offing. But as the narrator describes Miriam dancing, "I'm thinking . . . This is outrageous! This is like God moving!", and as she sings,

> It's not only about what just happened. It's about all the horses and drivers who hold us down, then and now and forever. And it's a prophecy, baby, and she's singing it right in the faces of the goons and the priests and the rabbis and the witch hunters and puritans and the KGB and the KKK and the FBI and the small town bigots and the big city bullies and the haredim and Evangelicals and all the haters for all time. And they all hear it . . . (Strimling, 1998, quoted by permission of the author)

In the end, Strimling's narrator brings us right up against our own historical moment: "So here we are, baby, out of Egypt. But free? Hah! Honey, for me and Miriam it's gonna be a long time!" To depict Miriam as the avatar of every form of freedom we have yet to win and to do so with Strimling's insistence on fusing art, politics, and myth, from the psychological perspective of the social outcast, is a stunning and timely move indeed.

Beyond the renewed celebrations of Miriam, feminism today has begun to explore the Shekhinah, who is the female aspect of God in

Kabbalah, the tradition of Jewish mysticism. The historian and anthropologist Raphael Patai in his groundbreaking 1978 study, *The Hebrew Goddess*, argued that worship of goddesses and the cult of the mother goddess under one name or another has always been present as an underground stream within Jewish culture. Patai was no feminist, but his work precipitated a flood of more woman-centered and detailed studies, among them the Assyriologist/biblical scholar Tikva Frymer-Kensky's *In the Wake of the Goddesses: Women, Culture, and the Biblical Transformation of Pagan Myth* (1992), the Syro-Palestinian archaeologist William Dever's 2005 book, *Did God Have a Wife? Archeology and Folk Religion in Ancient Israel*, and Rami Shapiro's *The Divine Feminine in Biblical Wisdom Literature* (2005), which identifies the female "Wisdom" figure of Proverbs and other biblical books with the Shekhinah. There has also been a cascade of writing on the image of the Shekhinah in the Zohar, in Lurianic Kabbalah, and in the women's spirituality movement of post-1960s America. All this has spilled over into newly created prayers and rituals. As a major instance relevant to therapists, Gottlieb (1995), in chapters devoted to the Shekhina as "The being who connects all life", as "The longing for wholeness", as "The call to justice", and, above all, as "She who dwells within", offers a range of prayers and rituals designed to engage women in acts of self-healing (pp. 109–113).

What has poetry to do with it?

Can poetry be therapeutic, as the work I have cited here implies? An immense literature exists on the subject, ranging from the saying Pagels quotes from the first century AD Gospel of Thomas, "Jesus said, 'If you bring forth what is within you, what you bring forth will save you. If you do not bring forth what is within you, what you do not bring forth will destroy you" (Pagels, 1979, p. xiv), to floods of current books on the subject by therapists such as Nicholas Mazza (2003) and Diana Hedges (2013), and by poets such as Greg Orr (2003), whose personal story stems from his accidental shooting of his brother, as a young boy. As a poet and as a teacher of prospective poets, I believe that one major role of poetry in our lives is to free ourselves and others by speaking the unspoken and the socially unspeakable. At the outset of every new workshop, I tell my students that the first task of the poet is to kill the censor, to write what they are afraid to write. I remember one young woman student who was silent in class and whose poetry was filled with highly charged but incoherent symbols, baffling to her classmates and to me. It took two hours of a conference for her finally to let me know that she was bulimic. At that time, the issue of eating disorders was not yet a major public one. I had never heard of bulimia, but I urged her to share with the class, which she did, offering an intensely moving poem that now made sense. By a stroke of luck, the best-looking girl in the class threw up her hands, laughing, and said *she* used to be bulimic, but had recovered and now, working as a waitress, she could walk into any dining room, look at the diners, and say to herself *that* one, *that* one, and *that* one. Opening up publicly was a breakthrough for the silent student, who proceeded to write clear, strong poems for the rest of the semester and a few years later was in law school. I remember a hulking football player reading a long poem about a brutal grandfather who had recently died; by the end of it he was in tears. He had not realised that beyond his conscious hatred of this grandfather was love. Writing and reading the poem enabled him to access what he had repressed.

As the poet Nick Flynn says in conversation with Beth Bachmann, we can see "poetry as an utterance from some inner realm that presses up against outer realities" (Flynn & Bachmann, 2014). Those outer realities may be social in origin; none the less, they function as inhibition and repression within the poet's psyche. To access the feeling, to express it, to bring it from darkness into light, to find language for what is inarticulate—that is the task. Here is where we find the overlap between poetry and therapy. To write what we are afraid to write, to say what we are afraid to say, is to ride a liberating wave of power we did not know we possessed.

Most of my students are women. Enabling women to access power they did not know they possessed is one of my chief goals as a teacher. For thirty years, I have used midrash writing assignments as one means toward that goal. I ask students to write in the voice of a biblical character, either one of their own choosing, or one from a text we are studying. I remind them that biblical narrative is essentially plot-driven, and does not give us the thoughts and feelings of its characters. I ask them to imagine their character telling something of importance to them that never made it into the text—an experience, a memory, a desire. I ask them to use words such as "I remember", "I

wish", "I hope", and to use physical images such as colour or clothing or food as part of what they write.

A key aspect of these assignments is that I give them very little
time to write, in order to short-circuit their inhibitions and rationali-
sations. It always works. Sometimes what they write takes the form of
prayer; sometimes it is angry, sometimes satiric, sometimes triumphant. Tears and laughter often accompany the readings as they go
around the room.

The "inner realm that presses up against outer realities" is, unsur-
prisingly, a major force in these writings. It does not take long for
students to recognise that the assumed voices in which they are writing are deeply personal, and that the device of the persona allows
them to say things that they would not have said directly in their own
voices. Writing with an urgency and intensity that may embarrass, yet
ultimately gratifies, them, my students experience in reality, and not
merely in theory, the liberating power of speech.

With a beginner's workshop, a simple and highly effective assign-
ment asks participants to imagine that they are Eve. We walk through
the text in Genesis involving the garden, the prohibition against eating
the fruit of the tree of knowledge of good and evil, and the dialogue
with the serpent who tells Eve that she will not die—that God knows
if she eats it her eyes will be opened and she will "be as gods, knowing good and evil" (Gen 3: 5). We follow Eve's process of decision
making up to the moment where she eats the fruit. This in itself is
revelatory, for "when the woman saw that the tree was good for food,
and that it was pleasant to the eyes, and a tree to be desired to make
one wise, she took of the fruit thereof and did eat" (Gen 3: 6). Rather
amazingly, we get an insight into Eve's mind, its physical appetite, its
feelings, and its intellect. We see what Plato thought were the components of the soul—bodily sensation, emotion, and intellect—in action
in a human being at this moment, for the first time, choosing (I point
out to them) to disobey, choosing to be free. I then give participants
one minute to speak in Eve's voice and express her first response to
what she has just done. What does she feel? As we circle the room,
when the daughters of Eve read aloud what they have written, there
is often an expression of sensuous pleasure. The fruit is sweet and
juicy. It can also be sweet with a bitter aftertaste. Other typical reactions include fear of punishment, anger towards, or mockery of, God
for the prohibition, an awareness of the body, an awareness of the

beauty of the environment, an awakening of sexuality. Once in a while, a participant will look around the room and shout, "Adam! Where are you?" When everyone has shared, I like to point out that transgression, the breaking of rules, is a basic human experience, a basic human need. The story of Adam and Eve is a parable about that need. Can transgression bring sorrow? Yes, but it can also bring freedom. I like to point out that Adam and Eve in the garden are like infants, and that disobedience is what enables them to become fully human.

Recently, I worked with a group of middle-aged women who were not poets or intending to be poets, but were ready to take the plunge of writing midrash. We read the story of Rebecca down to the moment when her son Jacob, on her instruction, flees home to avoid being killed by his brother. We spoke, on this occasion, of the recurrent depiction of dysfunctional families in the Hebrew Bible. We discussed the "ethical dilemma" of Rebecca tricking her husband to obtain a blessing for her own favoured son, the peaceful non-violent one. We remembered that when she asked God the meaning of the two sons in her belly making her life miserable, she was told that the elder would serve the younger. Did this mitigate the wrongdoing of her deception—and should it even be considered a wrongdoing? Finally, we wondered what was left to her, now that her favoured son was gone. At this point, I asked the group to imagine Rebecca at sunset of the day Jacob has disappeared over the horizon. Retired to her tent, she speaks to God—call it prayer, if you will. What does she say? I gave them five minutes. The first woman who read began with the guilty question, "What have I done?" The second went into a long set of anxious wishes for Jacob, while glancing meaningfully at her friend who was sitting next to her. Later, it became clear that she herself had a son who was in some kind of trouble, or perhaps was missing. Another woman challenged God, demanding to know why he created siblings who were doomed to conflict. Another wrote of her loneliness. And so on. The level of emotional intensity was high. You did not have to be a rocket scientist, or a psychoanalyst, to see that they were not only putting themselves into the matriarch Rebecca's sandals, but letting the exercise draw some otherwise inexpressible truths from them.

Are exercises such as these therapeutic? Obviously, they cannot in themselves turn anyone's life around, but they can contribute to self-awareness. In her breakthrough poem "Diving Into the Wreck" (1975), the feminist poet Adrienne Rich imagined a descent that seems equally personal and collective, a descent into the self that is at the same time a descent into history. "I go down . . . I go down", she wrote,

> I came to explore the wreck. . . .
> I came to see the damage that was done
> and the treasures that prevail.

For me, when I write and teach poetry, and especially when I write and teach midrash writing, it is essential to remember that discovering the deep truths of our lives means encountering obstacles both within and outside ourselves. "It's exhilarating to be alive in a time of awakening consciousness", writes Rich in her essay "When we dead awaken" (1975); "it can also be confusing, disorienting, and painful" (p. 167). There are rules, and we need to break them. How can we do this? How can we outwit the censors, slip past what one student of mine has called "the little policeman in our heads", to liberate what is enslaved in us, to help what is repressed return from the darkness of denial to the light of awareness? Is there a trick to it? For women, in the male dominated society we still all inhabit, it is commonly difficult to reconcile our femininity with our yearning for "might". We crave "might" in the sense of power—what is implied by the phrase "mighty woman". We crave "might" also in the sense of possibility—what is implied by phrases such as "I might do this" or "I might do that". I might study to be a lawyer. I might study astrophysics. I might take voice lessons. I might not want to marry. I might fall in love, if I let myself. It would be interesting to ask students or analysands to write, in their own voice, and then in the voice of a biblical character, a sentence beginning with the words "I might". I might try that.

The biblical women whose stories are sketched in the first part of this chapter are part of our heritage. They inhabit us, but, of course, we have repressed them. They can be fished from our unconscious to our conscious selves, so that we can watch them using their wits and breaking precedents and rules to accomplish their goals. We can let down the hooks of our minds for them. They can help us in the task of creating mighty women for ourselves.

Notes

1. The phrase *mi'lfanai* would literally be translated "from before my face", but its meaning, as indicated by other times it appears, implies personal rejection.

2. Originally an ancient rabbinic form based on a Hebrew verb meaning "seek or investigate, investigate". Midrash (pl. midrashim) has multiple meanings; for exegetical purposes, traditional midrash re-tells and elaborates on biblical stories, filling gaps and resolving contradictions in the narrative, and is often highly imaginative. Its primary object is to make texts spiritually and morally meaningful to the communities in which they are told. Contemporary midrash tends to be less interested in providing the stories with moral messages, and more interested in exploring the psychology of the biblical characters.

References

Dever, W. (2005). *Did God Have a Wife? Archeology and Folk Religion in Ancient Israel*. Grand Rapids, MI: Eerdmans.

Dinnerstein, D. (1976). *The Mermaid and the Minotaur: Sexual Arrangements and Human Malaise*. New York: Harper & Row.

Essick, R. N. (1991). William Blake's 'Female Will' and its biographical context. *Studies in English Literature, 1500–1900, 31*(4): 615–630.

Flynn, N., & Bachmann, B. (2014). In between words; a conversation on the extreme. *American Poetry Review, 43*(6): 7–12.

Freud, S. (1939a). *Moses and Monotheism. S. E.,* 23: 3–137. London: Hogarth.

Frymer-Kensky, F. (1992). *In the Wake of the Goddesses: Women, Culture, and the Biblical Transformation of Pagan Myth*. New York: Macmillan.

Gertler, P. J. (2007). Miriam: not an American success story. *Bridges, 12*(1): 72–73.

Gottlieb, L. (1995). *She Who Dwells Within: A Feminist Vision of a Renewed Judaism*. San Francisco, CA: Harper.

Hammer, J. (2001). Miriam under the mountain. In: *Sisters at Sinai: New Tales of Biblical Women* (pp. 129–133). Philadelphia, PA: Jewish Publication Society.

Hedges, D. (2013). *Poetry, Therapy, and Emotional Life*. Abingdon: Radcliffe Medical Press.

Lerner, G. (1986). *The Creation of Patriarchy*. Oxford: Oxford University Press.

Mazza, N. (2003). *Poetry Therapy: Theory and Practice*. New York: Brunner-Routledge.

Orr, G. (2002). *Poetry as Survival*. Athens, GA: University of Georgia Press.

Ostriker, A. (1993). *Feminist Revision and the Bible: The Bucknell Lectures on Literary Theory*. London: Blackwell.

Ostriker, A. (1994). *The Nakedness of the Fathers*. New Brunswick, NJ: Rutgers University Press.

Pagels, E. (1979). *The Gnostic Gospels*. New York: Vintage Books.

Patai, R. (1978). *The Hebrew Goddess*. New York: Avon Books.

Rich, A. (1975). *Diving Into the Wreck, Adrienne Rich's Poetry and Prose: A Norton Critical Edition*. New York: Norton.

Schwartz, R. (Ed.) (2001). *All the Women Followed Her: A Collection of Writings on Miriam the Prophet & the Women of the Exodus*. Mountain View, CA: Rikudei Miriam Press.

Shapiro, R. (2005). *The Divine Feminine in Biblical Wisdom Literature*. Woodstock, VT: Skylight Paths.

Strimling, A. (1998). What ever happened to Miriam (personal correspondence).

Walton, R. (2001). Lilith's daughters, Miriam's chorus: two decades of feminist midrash. *Religion and Literature*, 43(2): 115–127.

Warner, M. (1976). *Alone of All Her Sex: The Myth and the Cult of the Virgin Mary*. London: Weidenfeld & Nicolson.

Wilner, E. (1989). The Song of Miriam. In: *Sarah's Choice* (pp. 8–9). Chicago, IL: University of Chicago Press).

CHAPTER EIGHT

Contributions Part II: implications for psychoanalytic psychotherapy

Arlene Kramer Richards and Lucille Spira

The contributions of Matyszak, Spira, and Ostriker address the themes of victimhood, vengeance, and trickery. Aggression is a thread that runs through all of the contributions in this section. The challenges and conflicts of the dramatic, mythic, and biblical characters they discuss have their parallels today. The implication of these particular mythic stories to psychoanalytic psychotherapists is discussed below.

Hecate, Medea, and Psyche

The contrast between the goddess Hecate, the Titan Medea, and the human Psyche is a prototype of the choices available to a modern woman. By remaining a virgin, Hecate keeps her innate strength. She is beholden to no man; she is her own person. If she chooses not to become a mother, she is refusing to perpetuate her family, her clan, and her society. This choice is similar to the choice made by lesbians, single mothers, and career women who choose not to marry. Such a life is contrary to the mores of traditional middle-class families and, therefore, requires the strength of mind and heart to oppose what is expected.

Medea is also a woman who does the unacceptable. In choosing her lover Jason over her loyalty to her father, her clan, and her country, she is opposing all her supports: she is standing alone. But when she kills and dismembers her brother and dumps the pieces of his body into the water one by one to slow her father's ship because he needs to collect the pieces in order to bury his son according to ritual, she becomes an outlaw in any human society. Her later crime of killing her own children is an extension of the same rebellion. She deprives her faithless husband of his progeny and his family, clan, and society of members.

Psyche's rebellion is a more subtle one. She rebels by seeking knowledge. Her rebellion is looking at her lover. What is so terrible about looking? It is becoming the viewer, the originator of the gaze. By looking, she makes Cupid the object of the gaze. She has knowledge, and knowledge is power. That power enables her to choose rather than just be chosen. That is a threat in a social system that needs women to focus on reproduction rather than desire. To the extent that early analysts followed Freud's view that a girl's envy of her brother was compensated by the promise that she would have a baby when she grew up, they supported the refusal to honour a woman's right to acquire the power of knowledge. That this is still an issue in the modern world is shown in an article in the *Wall Street Journal* (Lagnado, 2015). Lucette Lagnado describes a situation that exists in parts of Africa and parts of the Arab world today. Many girls are denied education so that they will have no choice other than becoming mothers again and again in order to strengthen the society by producing more members.

All of these myths show mighty females choosing for themselves. Even today, women are facing the same choices. Waiting to reproduce until one has finished one's education and established a career has become more acceptable in affluent societies. For some women, this choice turns out to be a bar to ever reproducing. For some, it means having painful and difficult technology involved in the conception and delivery of babies. As therapists listen to young women struggling with these choices, it is difficult to keep our own understanding of the implications of these choices from clouding our ability to hear and empathise with those who make choices that are different from our own, or, worse yet, those who make choices that we made and regret.

Helen of Troy

The implications for treatment in the story of Helen's rape are clearly spelled out in Spira's account. Helen's story includes the possibilities for female power, female revenge for injustice, female loyalty and disloyalty to men, to ourselves, and to our children.

In some versions of her story, Helen is a transgressor. She deserts her husband and her young daughter, her family, her clan, and her country. If she leaves for love of Paris, she has chosen her own pleasure above her responsibilities. By abandoning her daughter, she has also devalued her own maternal creativity and power. This version of Helen is that of a person not to be emulated, but to be shunned. Yet, her husband takes her back as Queen. Does he do this for her wealth? Her beauty? Her willingness to leave when Troy is vanquished? Has he seen her as so shallow that she will be loyal to whoever wins a fight for her? Is she repentant? Does he forgive her because she stands for the prize the Greeks have won back? Is she a trophy wife?

In versions where she is raped and kidnapped, she is the victim and, therefore, innocent. In those versions she is powerless and, therefore, pitied rather than blamed. The charge of rape is the ticket to the restoration of her former life. This contrasts sharply with the story of Meng Jiangnü (this volume) who chose death rather than accept a second husband. In the Chinese myth, even if coerced, sex with anyone other than the first lover or husband is worse than death. Different cultures show their differing values in their myths.

These are complexities that the Greek myths do not explore, but are the stuff of psychoanalytic interest and investigation. In treatment, we look for feelings and meanings, not just for the actions that express those feelings. In myths, action tells the story; in treatment, words tell the story. It is this transition from action to words that is the essence of self-understanding. And self-understanding is empowerment (Warner, 2013). The rape victim can be empowered by understanding herself. She can become aware of her own motives and choices by explaining them to her therapist. This allows her to plan for a future in which she can protect herself. How can we expect this to happen?

For example, one woman who had been raped learnt in a rape victims' group that one should never yell "Help!" as this frightens onlookers. Instead, one can yell "Fire". This interests people and brings them to the scene. The response to victims is sometimes tainted with fear of becoming a victim oneself. By not arousing this fear, the person can attract helpers. Knowing her own fear, she was really able to see the fear in others and understand the importance of not arousing that in other people. Her understanding of herself enabled her to use the advice she had been given. Knowing that she now had a weapon against a potential rapist freed her to enter situations that she had been afraid to risk entering before this insight had been achieved.

And what if Helen had not been raped, but had entered the liaison with Paris of her own free will? Patients who choose to break up a marriage for an affair or another marriage have to face the reactions of their children, their spouses, their families, and the larger society. The woman who makes this choice can be helped to understand her own motivations, and her costs. She can feel empowered by this clarity of vision so that whichever choice she makes, she can preserve her self-respect and sense of self-worth. Contemplating the stories of Helen can normalise and detoxify the discussion of her own choice.

Heroines from the Hebrew Bible

Woman as transgressor, trickster, woman as mind is a wonderful reading of a great artefact of western culture—the Hebrew Bible. By showing the connection between the actions of mythic mighty women and their avatars and acolytes today, Ostriker shows the psychological uses of myths in the present. How can a woman become mighty? How can she shed the shell of fear that keeps her as secondary, accessory, possession, servant? For Ostriker, it is by using her wits.

She shows us a Bible we read, but did not see. Her Bible is full of unexplored meanings, each of which has implications for the particular issues of individual women. For example, the issue Eve faces is one many women face today. "Should I know more than my boyfriend? Will he hate me for knowing too much? Does he need to know more than his girl? Will he choose someone who doesn't compete with him?" Eve solves it by taking him on her journey to knowledge.

Rebecca faces every mother's problem when she has more than one child. Should she love them equally? What if one is the child she understands and sympathises with? What does she owe to a child she does not prefer? How can she feel equally towards two very unequal children? Can she force herself to feel what she does not feel? Will it help any of her children if she tries to fake her feelings?

Miriam faces the problem of many parentified children. If her primary responsibility is to her brother and her secondary responsibility is to her people, where is there room for her to have a husband, and/or children? This dilemma is not mentioned in the Bible, but any woman who reads her story must wonder how to fit her own life into that of her family.

Hannah is a mother who loses all of her sons to the glory of her tribe. Is this an ethical stance? In the Second World War, the last child of such a mother was exempted from dangerous duties because the sacrifice was deemed too great. Even though that was thought to be a war worth fighting, the right of a mother to protect her child was also thought to be worth a sacrifice on the part of the larger society.

Rachel stole the household gods from her father and cheated him through the power of her taboo menstruation. Since she knew he could not touch her if she was menstruating, she could protect herself from him. For modern women in societies that preserve this taboo, the menstrual taboo, it is a two-edged sword. On the one hand, it excludes women from many activities; on the other, it keeps unwanted approaches from men away.

All of these women and many others in the Bible stories are exceptions. They challenge the rules of the patriarchy. Since the work of Spitz (1957) shows how the infant at the breast already shakes her head back and forth until she reaches the nipple, it is clear that finding the nipple ends the state of frustration during which the infant is shaking her head from side to side. Shaking the head from side to side is easily transformed into a gesture of negation. It expresses a wish for a situation to end. It expresses a refusal. The infant starts with "no" and, thus, begins to establish a communication of feeling by gesture that will later become language. Refusal is the basis of selfhood. The rebellious heroines of the Bible are refusing; they are standing up for themselves or their children or siblings or family or tribe. In refusing, they are creating their own selves. The rebellious girl is the genesis of the proud woman.

In analytic treatment, a great deal of importance is attached to the development and expression of negative transference. The analyst welcomes anger, jealousy, envy, and competitive feelings because the negative feelings are the most difficult to express in normal life and because expressing them is the foundation of achieving a sense of self and an appreciation of one's own value as a person. By valorising the rebellious heroines of the Bible, by encouraging women to think of what they were feeling and thinking when they acted as they did, Ostriker achieves a similar empowerment for her students. The therapist who keeps in mind the power and importance of negative feelings can do no better than that.

References

Lagnado, L. (2015). Tunisian Jewish enclave weathers revolt, terror; can it survive girls' education? *Wall Street Journal*, February 14–15.

Spitz, R. A. (1957). *No and Yes: On the Genesis of Human Communication*. New York: International Universities Press.

Warner, A. (2013). *The Year After: A Memoir*. New York: CreateSpace.

PART III

THE POWER OF MOTHERS AND THE GODDESSES WITHIN

CHAPTER NINE

Boadicea, warrior queen: a baby's perspective and an analysand's perspective

Frances Thomson-Salo

I n this chapter, I summarise the history of the seventh century Celtic Queen, Boadicea, who was born about 30 AD and has been mythologised in British folklore as a formidable lady in history whose name will never be forgotten. (Fraser was the source for much of this material.) She has a special place, remembered for her courage, the warrior queen who fought the might of Rome, and brought them to ruin, causing them great shame. Then I turn the lens to suggest how a baby, while viewing the mother with awe and adoration, also sees her as a "mighty woman", all-powerful for good and bad, invested with desirable and awesome attributes, and I finish with a composited clinical vignette of how a male analysand might view his powerful mother.

Let me first turn to the commanding and fearsome Iron Age warrior queen, Boadicea, who was born into a royal family and married the king of the Iceni in Norfolk (Fraser, 1988). Boadicea led an uprising against the occupying forces of the Roman Empire, a powerful woman who paid the ultimate price of humiliation and death when, in the high stakes for which she played, she lost. She was the only woman to lead warriors into battle against the might of imperial Rome and win, at least initially. She had courage and pride, and in

leading the uprising she not only showed a capacity for strategic thinking, but went against the societal mores of the time—a woman leading
men—with gender implications for femininity and masculinity.

She had been queen of the Iceni, a Celtic tribe. When her husband
died in AD 60, he tried to protect his kingdom by leaving it jointly to
his daughters and the Roman Emperor, and the regency to his wife,
Boadicea. This was ignored by the Romans, and Boadicea was humiliated and viciously flogged in front of her family, and forced to watch
while her two teenage daughters were brutally raped by Roman
slaves. Much of the royal family was sold into slavery. The Iceni were
insulted and rose in revolt. Boadicea was chosen as their leader and
when she addressed her tribe about the difference between freedom
and slavery, she boasted of their hardiness. She said that it was not too
late to act if only for the sake of their children, lest they be raised in
slavery. Self-identifying as a quasi-goddess, she suddenly released
from her dress a hare, an animal that was sacred to the Britons, as a
form of divination; she had been astute enough to secrete the hare in
the folds of her dress and to ensure that it ran in the right direction.
She then prayed to Andraste, a war-goddess, for victory for the Iceni,
calling upon her "as woman speaking to woman".

Still about AD 60, while the Roman governor, Suetonius Paulinus,
was campaigning on an island off the coast of Wales, Boadicea led the
Iceni as well as the Trinovantes in revolt in the east of Britain. They
methodically demolished Colchester, burning it to the ground, and
overwhelmingly defeated those Romans who tried to relieve the city;
70,000 people are said to have been killed. The Britons had no interest
in taking or selling prisoners, only in killing by hanging, fire, or the
cross; the noblest of the women were impaled on spikes, and there
were sacrifices, banquets, and wanton behaviour in sacred places,
particularly in the groves of Andraste.

Immediately, Boadicea's army turned to the largest city in the
British Isles, London. Her army of Celts was victorious at first and
pushed the Romans back to London. Boadicea led an army of 100,000
tribespeople, sacking and burning London, and they massacred the
25,000 Roman citizens in it who had not fled. With the Romans not
having the numbers to defend London, Suetonius strategically abandoned the settlement.

Next, Boadicea and her army marched on St Albans, a city largely
populated by Britons who had co-operated with the Romans and who

were killed as the city was destroyed. Boadicea fought one more battle, though its precise location is not certain. Before this battle, Boadicea and her daughters drove round in her chariot to all her tribes, exhorting them to be brave. In a speech in which she presented herself not as an aristocrat avenging her lost wealth; she cried out that she was descended from mighty men but was fighting as an ordinary person, avenging her lost freedom, her bruised, battered body, and the abused chastity of her outraged daughters. She said that their cause was just, and the deities were on their side; the one legion that had dared to face them had been destroyed. She, a woman, was resolved to win or die. If the men wanted to live in slavery, that was their choice. Perhaps as a taunt to the men in her ranks, she asked them to consider: "Win the battle or perish: that is what I, a woman will do; you men can live on in slavery if that's what you want."

Boadicea's luck held until this battle, but at this point her strategic planning deserted her, and she chose the wrong way to fight the Romans. Her army, exhausted and hungry, attacked the Romans up-hill, and it was easy for the Romans to rout them. Suetonius, despite being heavily outnumbered, defeated them in the Battle of Watling Street: Roman troops of 1,200 defeated Boadicea's army of 100,000. Before that, an estimated 80,000 Roman and British had been killed by Boadicea's armies against their own losses of 400. Boadicea then probably killed herself to avoid Roman capture, by taking poison given to her by a faithful druid.

So successful was the Iceni uprising that the Romans were almost defeated and for nearly two years Boadicea had pillaged Roman settlements. Unfortunately for the Iceni and their allies, the military skill of the Roman army finally led to the crushing of the rebellion. Suetonius's eventual victory over Boadicea confirmed Roman control of the province.

By the Middle Ages, Boadicea had been forgotten. Her story became popular again during the reign of another English queen who headed an army against foreign invasion: in Queen Elizabeth I's speech before the fight with the Spanish Armada, there were resonances of Boadicea's speeches. But it was in Queen Victoria's reign that Boadicea became a heroic symbol of Britain and her fame took on legendary proportions as Queen Victoria came to be seen as Boadicea's "namesake", their names identical in meaning. Boadicea's name, Budica, derives from the Celtic feminine adjective for victorious.

Boadicea is seen as a great patriotic leader of the British, perhaps their first national heroine, but she was not an appealing character. She was described as a tall, terrifying-looking woman with fierce eyes and a piercing glare, a harsh voice, and reddish hair hanging below her waist. The Roman historian, Cassius Dio, wrote that she had "greater intelligence than often belongs to women". (Interestingly, all the history that comes down to us from those times is not from contemporary Britons, but from Roman historians. I am indebted to Philip Matyszak, personal communication, for this. Was there a secret admiration on the part of the Romans for this mighty woman?)

Boadicea exacted indiscriminate and ferocious vengeance on many of her fellow Celts who had the misfortune to live in the wrong place. Questions today are whether she was far subtler than usually portrayed, but nevertheless as fascinating as the myths associated with her name: in one woman's battle against an empire, and in terms of female power and colonial oppression, would she be seen today as a freedom fighter, terrorist, or martyr?

In recent years, the spelling of Budica (meaning, a bow) has come into vogue, a word that is more in line with the Celtic word for victory. Boadicea was a leader in every sense of the word. Her countrymen, both men and women alike, followed her. The Romans would regret inciting her wrath. Boadicea remains an important cultural symbol in the UK, although nowadays she might be less important than her statue at London Bridge suggests.

A baby's perspective

In thinking of the relevance of this story to the practice of psycho-analysis, I want to make a link primarily by thinking about the perspective of a baby. I want to consider first some positive aspects of the powerful mother (or carer), and what might be carried particularly in a mother's gaze: her adoration and awe, all carried in a luminous gaze to the infant and welcomed by the infant, the gratification of the sparkle in a mother's gaze sparking a baby's normal developmental pride. A cascade of infant research, particularly into intersubjectivity, suggests that what a mother feels looking at her baby, the baby feels, too, in his or her body in a kind of embodied communication (Bucci, 2009). Boadicea was courageous, and a mother helps impart courage.

The mother has, from the baby's point of view, all the power. The baby at birth tries to fasten on to the mother's gaze for security, for the social communicative system to click on (Porges, 2011), for safety in being held, for affirmation, for the beginnings of seeing themselves in the mother's mirroring gaze so that they know whom they are, and can then begin to develop their own identity. Current thinking is that a mother's capacity to help her baby develop reflective thinking and to mentalize is crucial for good self-esteem and sound mental health (Fonagy & Target, 2005).

A mother relates out of her sexuality to her baby, who encodes these sexual messages. Infant research suggests that a baby, from the beginning, turns outwards to include the third, the father (or mother's partner), and to identify with this Other. Whether infant sexuality is viewed from an infant mental health point of view as the rolling out of a developmental timetable, or from the more classical psycho-analytic viewpoint taken by Jean Laplanche (1995), who saw the enig-matic messages from the mother as having the power to be traumatic, a mother's role in helping her baby to cope with her withdrawal and to turn to the father is crucial for the baby's development, and gives massive power to a mother. The little girl identifies with aspects of both mother and father, each seen as having their own power valence, able to identify with the power inside the mother, if the little girl would allow herself to know it. We only have to remember the tie-in between these issues of power and the various maternal transferences that we see in psychoanalysis.

Yet, even from the first month, if a mother's gaze is angry, absent, anxious, or makes a baby feel ashamed—a quartet of "As"—this can attack a baby's fragile sense of connection with the world and their own identity, and the baby can feel devastated, powerless, and threat-ened, and may do everything possible to re-establish connection and please this powerful woman. A mother is felt to hold all the cards, and the power. Her lack of mentalizing can be felt as violent assault if there is sensed to be no place in her mind for a baby to find a psychic home. The power that mothers have over tiny enthralled babies can be almost total, particularly mothers who are very ambivalent, rejecting, and malevolent, and depressed withdrawal is currently viewed as having more traumatic consequences than other forms of maltreatment.

An infinite variety of roles have defined aspects of women, includ-ing warrior woman and evil temptress. In 1951, Marie Langer proposed the study of a modern myth for the "bad mother": that of a maid who, while the parents are dining out, roasts the baby who was entrusted to her (de Luca, 2014). There is also the myth of a monster mother indulging in a feast of naked power, of sadism run riot, with the power to forever cripple a young girl's sense of self and identity.

Perhaps we can think of the two names, Boadicea or Budica, the latter more explosive than the motherese implicit in the name of "Boadicea", that they could represent the powerful mother and the mother who whispers enigmatic signifiers in the baby's ear.

Clinical case

I turn finally to a clinical vignette to convey something of how for a baby, grown up to be an adult, the image of the powerful woman, the mother, transmutes but also remains so influential. This vignette of a male analysand is, for the sake of confidentiality, a composite, but nevertheless is accurate enough to the relational interchange between us. An educational executive in his thirties was seen in London in five times a week analysis on the couch. We can think about the babyhood he might have had and wonder what his relationship with a powerful woman, his mother, might have been. Although there are always many ways to think about clinical material, for the purposes of this chapter I have only focused on that of power.

Two months after starting analysis, he told me a dream in which I seemed to be vaguely seductive in the way I said goodbye, and he suddenly said, "You feel formidable, powerful, bloody hell!" If I was not completely attuned to how perceptive he was, he found me harsh and punitive. In contrast, when he approached his wife he felt like an adolescent and felt that being a powerful adult (sexual) man was terrifying.

> *Analysand*: If I hope, I'll be betrayed. I'm longing to be loved, acknowledged and understood, but I've been fooled, there's no warmth there, I've been betrayed. My mother would often see me as special but at other times didn't even know me, she was a million miles away. My mother can be very rejecting. The ways I tried to meet women were all non-verbal—like with sex, and starting therapy—like a terrified child. The end of the session is looming—I don't like putting it out there . . . (He trailed off.)

Analyst: (Drawing on earlier material as well.) As if you feel vulnerable not feeling clean or relieved.

Analysand: I feel unravelled. . . . I feel a bit on my own today. I shut down.

Analyst: That makes you powerful, against the despair.

Analysand: I'm polite about the end but sometimes I walk away with feelings (anger) about it. I don't understand all the stuff I've been saying today—talking about my relationship with women I guess, my mother.

He saw me as powerful like his mother; she could be completely attuned to him, followed by his feeling dumped, stranded, terrified, and unable to assume his own power. Some time later he felt down about not seeing me in a break, as though I would cease to exist.

Analysand: I'm worried about getting depressed in your break because I'm not sure if I'm in your mind about what happens to me in these separations. I'm not connected with you today and I don't give a fuck. . . . I've been saying to women all my life, "Who have I got to be for you?" and trying to figure it out? . . . To do something *with* you is the idea. I'm either helpless—or I have to do it all.

The following day, he felt that the analytic space was crowded with negative objects, and said that as a child,

Analysand: I heard my mother having sex loudly with my father and I rushed back to my room . . . every morning I wake with a feeling of dread, sensation of loss and I was terribly gripped by it . . . I worry I swear too much, am crass, over the top. . . . I have a feeling of helplessness and vulnerability and I just want someone to come and help me and it has plagued my life and set me up to be used or use others. You won't like this—I like the idea of castration and limits, being very clear—in case it offends you.

Analyst: I seem a bit more messy?

Analysand: Yes. You'll disapprove. My father—I'm not allowed to like him. It's true, you become a disapproving figure when it's a competing male—my mother had to be on a pedestal and adored. That's my mother in me, that's actually me, fuck! (He became sad.) A child on the receiving end of my parents hating me and it was devastating.

The following month, while thinking about his courage in the analysis, I suggested he had got something good from his mother in his first year before she became depressed. He brought a powerful dream, saying, "I had a dream that fucking shook me at the core—I didn't have a father who loved me. I've probably never grieved my whole life—my dream is to grasp my own power and be able to be expressive, and creative, and angry."

A few months later he returned to working on this, and, after feeling distanced from his mother, whom he said was scary, repulsive, and disgusting, he wondered about the kind of mother I had had, as though he had found within himself a good object and he could then remember and say reflectively, "My mother is deeply compassionate." We talked of something that came from her that was inside him and was passed on transgenerationally in the way that his young son felt loved by him. I was a strong mother with a strong father inside whom he might internalise to help him say no, in the transference, one who would be able to make a space for his feeling of not having a father who loved him.

Reflecting further, he said, "Women have such power over you, I give women power over me." He continued, "With my mother I felt so insecure I didn't have a sense of my own independence—I'm trying to appease all those perceived masters." This was one aspect of the transference when the firm setting was, at times, resented. Having been able to say that he feared I might attack him, he was then able to feel "really relaxed" on the couch and in the final session that week he had a dream that I was exhausted, perhaps my punishment, as he said, "You shouldn't be leaving me."

Three weeks later, he said, "Being listened to for ages, it's almost a beautiful feeling. I ache for the beauty of women, of goddesses." (Here the mother, as well as being mighty, is gradually transforming to have beauty.) But he then wanted to become excited with sex objects who were potent. "I'd love to be a powerful enough man to not have to crap on about this all the time ... My mother would throw some fucking shit if she didn't like something; she's so manipulative and I would pay. I guess I felt really owned by my mother. I want the heady sense of my own right to have independence." His wife had breast-fed their son, with the breasts seen as potent and he would look on with longing. In the way that Winnicott envisaged a good breast-feed as giving something to both baby and mother, he thought that his son had been helpful to him, and added, "I found some power."

I want to leave material there with his passionately expressed wish to grasp his own power. It was in the transference relationship, which swung between me being seen as both powerful and withholding my gaze and attacking, which gave the best chance of hope and meaning in integrating the pain of the early difficulties. Both female and male analysands find meaning in the myth of a mighty woman, and for an analyst, too, when they can deeply feel how a patient experiences them.

Conclusion

Here I allude only briefly to how myths about women permeate all cultures, with their power to have an impact on the development of girls and the psyches of women. Societal pronouncements about who women are, and who they might become, transmitted through the culture, affect the lives of all of us, necessitating women to adapt to them or to transcend stereotypes, although with more positive role models for today's young girls in the west than there have ever been: Margaret Thatcher in the UK, Indira Ghandi in India, Angela Merkel in Germany, Hillary Rodham Clinton in the USA. "The baby in his or her illusion of omnipotence, can imagine being one with the mother and particularly of her greatness and power" (Quagliata, 2013, Kindle locations, 953–965).

In 1902, a bronze statue of Boadicea riding high in her chariot, designed by Thomas Thorneycroft, was placed on the Thames embankment next to the Houses of Parliament in London. It has been described as Boadicea's revenge on the Romans. One wonders where Boadicea, whom I suggest indefinably colours the psyche of British women and girls, available as a mighty figure with whom to identify as a template at the base of identifications, rests. (Some say she lies buried only sixteen feet under a layer of clay in the city she defeated.) Where did she get her power, from a mighty woman-mother or from a father with whose aggressiveness she identified? And how in analysis, in taking in something of female mightiness does that allow greater access to the *power* in the self for all?

References

Bucci, W. (2009). The role of embodied communication in therapeutic change: a multiple code perspective. Available at: https://manhattan psychoanalysis.com/wp–content/uploads/TTC%202012–13%20 Readings%20uploads/ANDERSON_UPLOADS_2013/Bucci,W. Embodied_Comm.pdf, accessed 9. 1. 15.

De Luca, J. (2014). A particular kind of sterility. In: L. Tognoli Pasquali & F. Thomson-Salo, (Eds.). *Women and Creativity: A Psychoanalytic Glimpse Through Art, Literature, and Social Structure* (pp. 145–161). London: Karnac.

Fonagy, P., & Target, M. (2005). Bridging the transmission gap: an end to an important mystery of attachment research? *Attachment and Human Development, 7*: 333–343.

Fraser, A. (1988). *The Warrior Queens: Boadicea's Chariot.* London: Weidenfeld & Nicolson.

Laplanche, J. (1995). Seduction, persecution, revelation. *International Journal of Psychoanalysis, 76*: 663–682.

Langer, M. (1951). *Matenidad y sexo. Estudio psicoanalítico y psicosomático.* Barcelona: Paidos.

Porges, S. W. (2011). *The Polyvagal Theory. New Physiological Foundations of Emotions, Attachment, Communication, and Self-regulation.* New York: Norton.

Quagliata, E. (Ed.) (2013). *Becoming Parents and Overcoming Obstacles: Understanding the Experience of Miscarriage, Premature Births, Infertility, and Postnatal Depression.* London: Karnac.

CHAPTER TEN

Medea, almighty mother

Elina Reenkola

W omen have often been defined as mere objects and victims of oppression, deprived of power and subject to violence. Mother is often conceptualised as a subjugated victim or slave of the patriarchal society.

I want to challenge this view by arguing that a woman's potential for bearing new life inside her and giving birth to a baby represents formidable maternal power. This has several consequences. Female generativity may lead to intense envy of the female reproductive body by both males and females. The female body may excite horror and fear of monsters. The mother who gave birth to us may even take our life or be a terrifying castrator of men.

I use the myth of Medea to describe a woman who exerts maternal power, is aggressive, and acts as a subject. Medea uses her children as weapons of her violent revenge. Medea is not an idealised and good Madonna-like woman, but, rather, an abhorrent monster mother. The myth describes the dark side of motherhood. It also deals with the mother's unconscious phantasies of power and aggression. I describe the feelings aroused in both men and women by maternal power, and the psychic mechanisms they use for dealing with them, such as envy, fear, and devaluation of motherhood.

I have questioned (Reenkola, 2002, p. xi) why a woman's inner life continues to remain a closely guarded secret despite all the efforts female analysts have made since Freud to cast light on the prevailing darkness. Or is a woman's ability to give birth so powerful that men— and even women—must deny it? Or must women guard it as their secret in order to prevent its destruction?

A woman's ideals of "perfect motherhood" may be very demanding, blaming and shaming her if she does not fulfil them. They may be like a guiding compass and, simultaneously, a constricting corset that does not allow hate or aggressive thoughts (Reenkola, 2012).

The myth of Medea

The myth of Medea (Euripides, 2008) is a tragic story about the mother's tyrannical power over her children. Medea, with her magical skills as a sorceress, is a supremely powerful woman. She had the courage to leave Colchis, her fatherland, when she fell in love with Jason. She is an active, skilful woman who knows how to use her talents and magic powers to help Jason in his quest for the Golden Fleece. At the outset of the myth, Medea was an actor and a subject.

The myth begins with a rivalrous erotic triangle involving Medea, her husband Jason, and Glauce. Jason betrayed Medea by taking a new wife, Glauce, the youngest daughter of King Creon, in his quest for power. Jason left Medea, the mother of their sons, in favour of a younger woman who lacked the magical skills of a sorceress. Medea lost everything: her husband, her social status, and her honour. Her sons, too, lost their status. Did Jason do this because of feelings of both horror and envy as he encountered Medea's magic skills and maternal power?

Stripped of her position of power by Jason's creating this politically and erotically charged triangle, Medea felt depression and despair. She was humiliated and ridiculed as a scorned barbarian woman. She turned her aggression inwards at first and thought of death as an escape from shame and loss of power. Her combined shame and rage were fatally intensified when Creon told her that she and her children would be driven into exile. Exile was the last blow to, and humiliation of, Medea. As rage and vindictiveness took hold of her, her thoughts of death and suicide evaporated. Medea gathered her strength and what seemed like "womanly" timidity, accompanied by thoughts of suicide, gave way to the open fury of vengeance. Her motherly, feminine characteristics became irrelevant, and disappeared as she drew on her tremendous powers of sorcery to use as her weapons in vengeance. She transformed from a helpless victim into an active avenger. Medea prepared a poisoned gift for her rival, Glauce, to kill her, and used her own children as intermediaries in her murderous vengeance.

Jason had taken everything that was valuable to Medea; Medea did the same to Jason by destroying what was most valuable to him: their children. She made Jason go through what she had felt; humiliation, loss, and shame. She wanted her husband to suffer as she had suffered. Motherly love had given way to destructiveness.

Medea went through a harrowing struggle in the grip of thoughts and feelings of motherly love *vs.* filicide, life drive *vs.* death drive. Medea's burning rage and vindictiveness towards Jason ebbed and flowed, burdened by shame and guilt. Love and tender feelings towards her children made her hesitate time and again. Finally, she chose vengeance, hardening her heart to overcome her sorrow and shame. Medea also wanted to save her children from worse: the enemy's mockery. The only power and status left to Medea was her motherhood, which she used to hurt Jason by turning their children into weapons against him.

Euripides' play is searing and evokes conflicting feelings. Medea's destructiveness is horrifying, while her earlier pain and despair arouse sympathy in the reader.

Medea's myth reflects the universal unconscious phantasy of the mother's omnipotence and almightiness. In the unconscious, the mother has the power to give life and bring death. The myth poignantly delineates how closely the children's well-being and existence are linked with the mother's psychic balance and narcissism.

Maternal power and might

Despite the advances that several female psychoanalysts, beginning with Karen Horney, have contributed to psychoanalytic theory, the "law of the father" remains dominant while the law of the mother continues to exist as an undeveloped concept and the power and might of the mother are still devalued. The first dictator for the child is the mother. Although women do not have power in society and its leading positions in the same way men do, they do have it as mothers. The myth of Medea describes this. There are highly patriarchal societies, where men have the power and women are subjugated and denied social power. Even in these societies, women wield a type of unlimited power at home, by taking care of children. In the empire of the mother, the woman exercises invisible psychic power in contributing to the formation of the child's ego, ideals, and superego. Her power lies in the acceptance or denial of the child's feelings and desires, and the acknowledgement or suppression of the child's separateness. The law of the mother offers the threat of abandonment and loss of love. Mother also can threaten with castration.

Motherhood is seldom perceived by women today as being sufficient to what is necessary for a fulfilling life. Having children and taking care of them may be experienced as a pleasure and a treasure, but it might be experienced as the opposite: a disaster that imprisons the mother, or subjects her to the dictatorship of the child. Maternal ambivalence is inevitable.

A woman can use her invisible psychic power in motherhood without limit, tyrannically. A newborn child is completely helpless and dependent on the care of another person. Without the mother or a surrogate, the infant will die. Mothers can care for their children lovingly and attentively, or use mental violence. There is another side to the slavery of a full-time mother: the mother may keep her children as her slaves. There are no statutes to control mother's psychic power. The power may stem from the mother's unconscious motives or conflicts. The might of the unconscious can feel demonic and frightening.

In my chapter "Pregnancy, depression, and psychoanalysis" (Reenkola, 2002), I wrote that

> A woman's childhood disappointments are, indeed, profoundly reflected in her relationship to her own child. In a woman's psyche, growing to be a mother especially tests how, as a child, her own helplessness, desires, and dependency on the mother have been endured and received. The more feelings of unfulfillment and disappointment the woman has been left with when she was a baby, the more difficult it is for her to be concerned about the distress and demands of her own baby. (p. 40)

Even if the woman consciously wants only the best for her child, she often unconsciously repeats her own early, painful experiences, if she is not in touch with the agonising feelings they arouse. To alleviate this, it is essential that the mother reaches the painful emotions of her early traumatic experiences.

Mother wields concrete power over the fate of her child. She can even decide the death of the foetus. She may decide to interrupt the pregnancy. Abortion means the right of a woman to decide about her own body, but it also means the power to decide about the foetus and the rights of the child. The foetus is, after all, part of the woman's body and yet a separate being with its own genes. The decision to abort may arouse, besides relief, guilt-laden phantasies about being a killer mother, like Medea.

A woman might decide to give her baby away for adoption or fostering. The reasons for this may be manifold, and it is always a conflictual decision for the mother.

A woman might abandon an unwanted new-born baby. Some middle European countries, such as Poland, the Czech Republic, and Germany, provide so-called baby hatches, installed, for example, in a hospital wall. A mother can leave her baby in the hatch anonymously, if she does not want, or is unable, to keep it. The hatches help both mother and child. The baby survives and may be placed in a family that wants a child. On the other hand, giving away a baby unnamed deprives the child of the right to know her or his origin and the father of the right to know about his progeny. In many countries, the law prohibits the abandonment of a child. As an ultimate solution, mothers might kill their babies. I shall deal with this in the section titled "Monster mother".

The mother has the power to decide on the acknowledgement of fatherhood. The law in Finland today grants the mother the power to prohibit a paternity test. She can forbid DNA testing of the child, which would confirm fatherhood. According to contemporary concepts of justice, however, a child should have the right to know her or his origins, that is, both the mother and the father.

Apart from these sad aspects, the power of the mother appears as a positive support of the child's psychic development. The early relationship between mother and child has a deep influence on the mental well-being of the next generation. Society as a whole is founded on taking as good care of its children as possible and ensuring their mental well-being.

Fear of maternal power

The almighty mother who gives us life might be awesome and frightening, and this leads to various defence mechanisms. The powerful, pre-oedipal mother is reduced to a defective or devouring creature, or a horrifying monster, for several reasons. The repudiation of maternal power might be used as a mechanism to alleviate envy and fear of her might and the intolerable feeling of primal helplessness (*Hilflosigkeit*) that makes the infant completely dependent on the mother. In comparison with the ideal qualities attributed to the early mother-image, the castrated mother appears to be the result of a deep desire to free oneself from her domination and evil qualities, as Chasseguet-Smirgel (1993) sees it.

The Greek myth of Metis (Aeschylus, 1977) expresses these mechanisms. Metis, Athena's mother, was Zeus's wife. Zeus swallowed her when she was pregnant to prevent her from giving birth to children who would overthrow him. Instead, Zeus the father gave birth to a child, Athena, who sprang forth from his head fully armed and helmeted, thus escaping primal infantile helplessness. In this way, Zeus achieves the appropriation of the female procreative capacity. Athena magically nullified the significance of the mother by declaring: ". . . no mother gave me birth" (Aeschylus, 1977, p. 264).

The myth describes an actual matricide, the negation and destruction of the mother's importance and creative ability; this is what both father Zeus and daughter Athena do. In the myth, the mother's role as the one who bears life and gives birth to it is completely negated by a conversion to phallic defence and self-sufficiency. It is the man who gives birth, not the mother. The daughter is born from a man's brain, not the mother's womb! This alleviates envy and fear towards the birth-giving mother. The fear of mother's might is so powerful that the daughter is born in full armaments.

Has what happened to Metis also happened to motherhood in our culture? Has the mother's procreativity and power been denied and are mothers described as mainly suffering, subjugated, and victims of unequal treatment? Is only masculine power and spectacular creativity acknowledged?

Womb envy

We were all born of a woman. Only a woman can experience how it feels to have a baby grow and move inside her and sense its heartbeat as part of her and yet separate in full genetic makeup. Men do not have a similar experience. This is a point where men and women differ. This fact is apt to evoke intense envy. Men can, however, take upon themselves the maternal function (men-mothers) as Mariam Alizade (2006, pp. ix–xi) describes. Love and hate are influential powers in a human being and they do co-exist in motherhood, quite normally (Reenkola, 2008).

The Latin word for envy, *invidia*, refers to looking at someone with ill will. The evil eye, the malicious effect of a look, appears in Finnish folklore and in European folklore in general. The evil eye could turn on anything enviable, particularly fecundity, crop, children, and, specifically, the newborn. Everything desirable and admirable, including another person's contentment over what she or he possesses, is apt to cause envy. Envy is generally expressed in indirect ways. It often appears as belittlement and devaluation of the object envied as well as ill will towards those who are contented or well off. People may try to protect themselves from envy by idealising the object of the envy. What elicits envy is derogated and disparaged; people also may shield themselves from envy by causing envy in others.

"Envy is the angry feeling that another person possesses and enjoys something desirable . . . The envious impulse is to take it away or spoil it . . ." as Melanie Klein wrote (Klein, 1957, p. 181). She elaborated this by stating that the envious person wants to put badness, primarily bad excrement and bad parts of the self, into the mother, and that in the deepest, most frightening part of the phantasy, this means destroying the mother's creativity. Klein believed that envy might be unconsciously felt to be the greatest sin of all because it spoils and harms the good object who is the source of life (1957, p. 189). In her writings, envy originates in the earliest exclusive relationship with the mother, a view criticised by many.

Horney (1967) coined the terms womb envy and vagina envy to denote the unexpressed anxiety that men feel towards pregnancy, parturition, or breast-feeding. Several authors have described the envy of the female body and procreativity as womb envy. The concept applies to both genders, but has been undervalued and ignored in favour of penis envy.

Envy as a feeling can have various nuances. Benevolent envy entails admiration of another person and a wish to get the same for oneself, without wanting to destroy the object of the envy. Malignant envy wants to rob the object of the envy, to appropriate for oneself what is envied, and destroy or spoil it for the other. In Switzerland, people speak of "green envy" *vs.* "yellow envy", and, similarly, in Russia about "white envy" and "black envy": the first of each two terms entails the pain of felt lack (e.g., of youth and strength), and a wish and yearning to have or regain what the other enjoys without wanting to destroy either it or the person (Wurmser & Jarass, 2008). Envy may be conscious and vehement. Secret, unconscious envy causes despair, helplessness, rage, and desire for revenge. It wants the disempowerment and destruction of the object envied.

In the biblical creation myth prevalent in our culture, God, a man, created man in his own image. Eve he created out of Adam's rib. In this creation myth, the woman as giver of birth and giver of life has been annihilated and overlooked completely, and man has been placed as creator of the human being. The birth myth effectively alleviates man's envy of the mother and the womb. It operates in the nucleus of patriarchal culture and puts the woman in a secondary position.

The Paradise myth sums up one of man's core fantasies, his attempt to master in his psyche the fact that he was born of woman. The story assures us that the man is far from imperfect or deficient. It helps the man, and even the woman, to protect himself from the feelings of humiliation, shame, and envy in comparison with the woman who gives birth and breast-feeds.

It has been observed in analyses and psychotherapies of boys that they have wishes about giving birth to a baby and are disappointed at realising that they will never be able to do it, like mother does, not even as adults. A boy feels imperfect and shameful in comparison with the mother. Such observations are usually ignored, often as a result of womb envy (Lax, 2003).

The psychotherapist's pregnancy elicits a variety of feelings in patients. During my pregnancies, I was able to observe my female and male patients' envy towards me. Terminating treatment is a common male reaction to the analyst's pregnancy (Reenkola, 2002).

This aspect of womb envy has a profound psychological and cultural impact on the male quest for significance in the eyes of the cosmos (Shabad, 2008). Men want to undo their shame at being an inferior creature born out of woman and attain some sense of dignity by destroying the power of women.

For a girl, intense envy of the life-giving mother may have fateful consequences. Carolyn Ellman (2002, p. 644) writes about these:

> I believe that the fear of destroying the internal mother and the early identification with her heightens the girl's feelings of emptiness, because she fears that she is destroying not only a part of her feminine self, but also the life-giving, generative mother within her. The girl enters the oedipal period so frightened of her destructive feelings toward her mother that the oedipal stage is fraught with great anxiety. She believes that her wishes really can harm her mother. With this fear in place, the girl's inhibitions about her creativity can become heightened in adolescence, when envy and jealousy toward other women come out in full force ("*après-coup*").

Freud and maternal power

One of Freud's central insights was the profound impact of the body on the development of the psyche. He focused on observing how a boy's genitalia significantly affected his internal experience. Freud assumed that a girl was a castrated being, deficient by comparison to a boy.

Many psychoanalysts have challenged Freud's views. I have pointed out (Maenpaa-Reenkola, 1996, p. 47),

> A female's physical reality – which she does have – influences her mind more than what she does not have. Femininity and motherhood are based on experiences of a woman's own female body as source of physical pleasure and satisfaction and not as substitute or consolation for her defectiveness.

Chasseguet-Smirgel (1993, p. 115) writes how "the woman as she is depicted in Freudian theory is exactly the opposite of the primal maternal imago as it is revealed in the clinical material of both sexes".

The female pregnant body as precious and pleasurable is almost absent in Freud's writings. There are, altogether, thirty references to pregnancy in Freud's complete works, nine of which are in the *Interpretation of Dreams*. In this work, Freud describes three dreams of pregnancy (Freud, 1900a), presenting its negative aspects mainly.

In the first dream described by Freud (1900a), a friend's wife had dreamt about menstruation. Freud presumed that this was the fulfilment of a wish. The wife would have been happy if she could have enjoyed her freedom a little longer before "assuming the burden of motherhood". Another woman patient told Freud (1900a, p. 154) a dream.

> In the course of a longish dream, this lady imagined that she saw her only, fifteen-year-old daughter lying dead "in a case". In the course of analysis she found out that the dream-picture corresponded to a wish of hers. Like so many young married women, she had been far from pleased when she became pregnant, and more than once she had allowed herself to wish that the child in her womb might die. Indeed in a fit of rage after a violent scene with her husband, she had beaten with her fists on her body so as to hit the child inside it. Thus the dead child was in fact the fulfilment of a wish, but a wish that had been put aside fifteen years earlier.

Freud is describing pregnancy as insignificant and undesired. Freud (1900a, p. 357) also observes "Being plagued with vermin is often a sign of pregnancy". Freud, thus, recognises the mother's negative attitudes and even death wishes towards the baby, but only the negative side of the ambivalence of love and hate. Of course, women at that time could not use contraceptives, and this has an impact on women's attitudes.

Freud's third example (1900a, p. 374) is a flower dream that a young woman engaged to be married had told him. The dreamer was a girl who was not neurotic. Her dream: "I arrange the centre of a table with flowers for a birthday." The dream expressed her feeling of happiness. The floral symbolism in her dream reflected "sensual love and its organs". In this dream, Freud exceptionally connects pregnancy to pleasure.

The body of a pregnant mother is usually impressive and awesome to a child. Little Hans was three and a half years old when his little sister Hanna was born. Freud (1909b, p. 69) writes about his reactions to this, following the notes his father had jotted down in his notebook that day: "Later Hans talked about the big box (the mother's womb: "Really Daddy. Do believe me. We got a big box and it was full of babies; they sat in the bath."

> To my mind, this is the vagina . . . But what is striking is that Freud sees this too – the material leaves little room for any other interpretation – and yet, in spite of this, he continues to uphold the theory of

sexual phallic monism and the accompanying ignorance of vagina. (Chasseguet-Smirgel, 1993, p. 110)

Freud admitted the significance of the mother's womb and yet denied it.

Freud's concept of "uncanny" (*unheimlich*) denotes "something familiar that has been repressed" (1919h, p. 245). He refers to neurotic men who often feel that there is something uncanny about the female genital organs: "This *unheimlich* place, however, is the entrance to the former *Heim* (home) of all human beings, to the place where each one of us lived once upon a time and in the beginning". Here, Freud clearly writes about the womb as an uncanny, *unheimlich* place that is horrifying.

Freud's theories, thus, reveal a strong disavowal of the significance of female generativity and maternal power, and even horror of it.

Consequences of womb envy

I postulate that, in order to counterbalance the mother's crucial importance, dependency on the mother, and fear of the mother, and to alleviate the intolerable sense of helplessness (*Hilflosigkeit*), there is a universal tendency to see women as null and deficient in comparison to men. Another contributing factor is the envy a boy feels towards the mother, which often remains repressed in the unconscious.

Man's unconscious womb envy and the fear of the might of the mother may have serious consequences both at the social level and for the psyche: for example, the following (Reenkola, 2012):

- Unequal gender system.
- Institutions ruled by men.
- Exercising control over women's rights
- Disavowal of female generativity and maternal power.
- Belittling the significance of pregnancy and childbirth.
- Controlling the woman's body.
- Ignoring and disparaging women's ideas.
- At the other end, exaggerated idealisation of women; oppression by praise.

- Emphasising narcissistic–phallic pursuits as an ideal.
- Producing spectacular and respect-inducing creations in the field of technology and culture.

Various measures by which men can participate in so-called mothering can appease overwhelming womb envy and fear of the mother's power. In the Nordic countries, fathers no longer necessarily remain outside the mother–baby relationship, which alleviates the most destructive forms of the envy of motherhood. Ever since the 1970s, men have increasingly been able to take part in prenatal classes and childbirth. Men are allowed to participate actively in taking care of infants, for instance, by taking paternity leave. Men having the possibility of taking care of babies can diminish womb envy and alleviate fear of the power of the mother to a crucial degree.

Monster mothers

Love and hate are influential powers in a human being and they do co-exist in motherhood, quite normally. Aggressions are manifestations of the death drive when it is turned towards the outside world (Freud, 1920g, p. 44). The life drive, Eros, binds the destructive power of the death drive (Freud, 1940a, p. 148). Medea's love did not bind or tame her rage enough.

It is difficult to accept the idea that mother, the giver of life, could be destructive and aggressive. Mothers' aggression and violence aimed at their children fill us with outrage and horror. In women, aggression is often suppressed or directed against themselves, either against their bodies or against objects they see as parts of themselves, their children. Explicit violence is rare for women. Female aggression tends to be indirect and invisible because of the guilt and shame it evokes (Reenkola, 2013). Aggressive or violent mothers are considered abhorrent monsters.

It is difficult for a child to rebel against the mother or express hatred towards her, because the mother is vital to the child. Horrifying and bad aspects of the mother can be split off and projected into monsters, witches, evil stepmothers, goblins, or the Groke in the Moomin stories. In supernatural horror films such as *The Conjuring* (Wan, 2013) and *Annabelle* (Leonetti, 2014), the theme is a terrifying murderous mother who is projected into supernatural spirits. Mother's revenge and punishment are so frightening that we rather choose to idealise mothers. It feels safer to blame men for subjugating women in society than to blame the mother for subduing her child.

Medea's intensely disturbing ambivalence between her loving and hating feelings towards her children is inside every mother in some milder form, either unconsciously or consciously. That is why the tragedy of Medea still touches us. Maternal ambivalence is a normal and ubiquitous phenomenon.

To sum up

Fear and horror of the powerful pre-oedipal mother prevail in our unconscious. It is important to be aware of the secret fear and envy of the mother, because of the consequences that are harmful to both men and women. For the mothers, it is important to be aware of the power they may exert on their children, in both constructive and destructive ways. It is often invigorating to give words to the fear and envy of the powerful mother and this dark side of motherhood, or at least give them space in one's thoughts. Thought and talk are different from acts.

Acknowledgements

Translation is by Kaisa Sivenius.

References

Aeschylus (1977). *The Eumenides*, R. Fagles (Trans.). London: Penguin Classics.

Alizade, M. (2006). Foreword. In: M. Alizade (Ed.), *Motherhood in the Twenty-First Century* (pp. ix–xi). London: Karnac.

Chasseguet-Smirgel, J. (1993). Freud and female sexuality: the consideration of some blind spots in the exploration of the 'dark continent'. In: D. Breen (Ed.), *The Gender Conundrum* (pp. 105–129). London: Routledge.

Ellman, C. (2002). The empty mother: women's fear of their destructive envy. *Psychoanalytic Quarterly, 69*: 633–657.

Euripides (2008). *Medea*, R. Robertson (Trans.). New York: Free Press.

Freud, S. (1900a). *The Interpretation of Dreams*. S. E., 4–5. London: Hogarth.

Freud, S. (1909b). *Analysis of a Phobia in a Five-Year-Old Boy. S. E., 10*: 1–148. London: Hogarth.

Freud, S. (1919h). The "uncanny". *S. E., 17*: 217–273. London: Hogarth.

Freud, S. (1920g). *Beyond the Pleasure Principle. S. E., 18*: 7–64. London: Hogarth.

Freud, S. (1940a). *An Outline of Psychoanalysis. S. E., 23*: 139–208. London: Hogarth.

Horney, K. (1967). *Feminine Psychology*. New York: W. W. Norton.

Klein, M. (1957). *Envy and Gratitude*. New York: Basic Books.

Lax, R. (2003). Boys' envy of mother and the consequences of this narcissistic mortification. In: M. Alizade (Ed.), *Masculine Scenarios* (pp. 125–136). London: Karnac.

Leonetti, J. R. (2014). *Annabelle* (film).

Maenpaa-Reenkola, E. (1996). The fantasy of damage to the baby. *Scandinavian Psychoanalytic Review, 19*: 46–59.

Reenkola, E. (2002). *The Veiled Female Core*. New York: Other Press.

Reenkola, E. (2008). *Nainen ja viha* (Female Aggression). Helsinki: Minerva.

Reenkola, E. (2012). *Äidin valta ja voima* (Maternal Power and Might). Helsinki: Minerva.

Reenkola, E. (2013). Vicissitudes of female revenge. In: I. Moeslein-Teising & F. Thomson-Salo (Eds.), *The Female Body: Inside and Outside* (pp. 201–227). London: Karnac.

Shabad, P. (2008). Of woman born: womb envy and the male project of self-creation. In: L. Wurmser & H. Jarass (Eds.), *Jealousy and Envy* (pp. 75–90). New York: Analytic Press.

Wan, J. (2013). *The Conjuring* (film).

Wurmser, L., & Jarass, H. (2008). Introduction. In: L. Wurmser & H. Jarass (Eds.), *Jealousy and Envy* (pp. ix–xix). New York: Analytic Press.

CHAPTER ELEVEN

The mother of safety is the phantasied mother of power

Patsy Turrini

T he invincible image of the power and safety of the mother is determined by a multitude of experiences. Throughout this discussion, I use the word "mother"; however, any good-enough carer can provide the necessary safety and healing work that will then enable the baby to form a view of the invincible mother which organises the "good object", which, in turn, organises the capacity for basic trust in the good-enough-to-be-trusted people in this world. It is important also to recognise that babies at birth must have sufficient innate capacities to use the mother/carer as a "beacon of orientation". Some data demonstrate that babies without good-enough care are never able to trust others.

Although early biological evidence offers verifying data that there is an innate capacity for built-in trust in the mother, it is not well documented; there appears to be a connecting inner pre-wired biology that provides a turn toward the mother or carer. Erikson (1950) refers to the first year of life as the time for establishing basic trust and basic mistrust. The baby is primed (prewired) to connect and feel safe with a human being. Hartmann (1958) refers to innate "object seeking" as an apparatus of primary autonomy (innate capacities). Research has shown that the baby knows the mother's voice from others at birth;

when mothers have read to babies *in utero*, they then turn to the mother's voice right after birth, as opposed to another voice. The familiar is meaningful. There appears to be an intrinsic quest for safety and "the familiar", the sound of the familiar that, in turn, coincides with the wish for safety and relief from pain.

The mother cures and relieves pain; hunger pains, as described by Riviere,

> not only ... feel like biting, gnawing, wasting forces inside one, against which one is helpless, but the intense wishes to seize and devour (the breast) which accompany such hunger at its inception will be identified with these inner devouring agencies pains. (Riviere, 1991, p. 283, quoted in Turrini, 2003)

A baby's typical response, say to acute hunger, "is a reaction in which the whole body is involved: screaming, twisting, kicking". (Riviere, 1991, p. 279, quoted in Turrini, 2003). We should never underestimate the pain of hunger.

When pain is relieved, the remembrance of relief contributes to the wonderment about the mother and her invincibility. A "fix it" fantasy begins to form from this experience, and a belief in the mother's powers to control everything. Other magical cures have developed from early maternal relieving practices, and serve to underscore the images of cure, that is, the use of a talisman in many cultures (Turrini, 2003, pp. 156–157).

Gaddini (1987) also examines the pain, saying that the mother has to find ways to console the baby's experience of a lost union with her, "a union that preserves his(her) sense of being", a basic sensation connected with care aspects. The infant is unable to build defences. The pain is referred to as "primary agonies", a sensation observed externally in "hopeless crying", as the baby experiences sensations of being overwhelmed or annihilated. Then, too, the mother relieves pain with consolers and pacifiers to keep these pains away from the baby, which are critical to avoiding the build-up of the memory of pain. Lucky are the babies who have received pacifiers, for controversy in some eras and cultures prevents their use.

Surprisingly, one of the four causes of pains and crying observed from the second week of life is boredom. Brazelton and Cramer (1991) describe pain from boredom that is relieved by talking, playing, and offering new toys and friends. The human being can only tolerate a certain level of pain, after which all solutions are sought for; getting a fix and suicide are two terrible solutions. This might be an extraordinary way to examine the power of the mother to relieve pain, and the consequences when pain dominates, yet mothers and carers keep babies safe into adulthood and build in inner structures for the babies; they find cures, and take children to a paediatrician, who also may have solutions to relieve pain. She has the power to find and get help. Women—mothers and grandmothers—report a commitment to caring throughout their lifespan for their children and grandchildren, often unknown or unregistered by other family members. As Anne-Marie MacDonald (2003) says, in *The Way the Crow Flies*, "Between a mother's eyes and her son's face, there is not air. There is something invisible and invincible. Even though—or because—he will go out into the world, she will never lose her passion to protect him" (p. 117)

Other types of pain

Spitz (1959) describes the second organiser of the psyche that is universal and prewired as "eight-month stranger anxiety" (p. 37). Peto (1969) and Szekely (1954) also describe an anxiety-provoking response not to the perceived loss of the mother, but to fear of an unknown person. The stranger's eyes terrify, and the mother provides perfect protection. In our human memories, we carry the powerful conviction that mother cares, and we have experienced the feelings that she can keep us safe from all harm.

The nine-month-old turns to the mother, buries his head in the mother, and averts his eyes from the stranger, predator, and eyes that injure, and feels perfectly safe in her arms. The mother could be standing with a stranger pointing a gun at her head, but the baby only knows the safety of her arms. Anna Freud and Dann (1951) observed that children who stayed with their mothers in London during the Blitz felt safer than those who were sent out to the countryside for their protection, another observation on the belief in the mother's powers of safe-keeping.

Clinical vignette

I have a patient aged forty-five who suffers horrible panic attacks;

they have multiple causes, but one cause emanates from his experiences between the ages of three to ten. He slept at the far end of his house, and experienced predator fears, normal for a four-year-old at night, but he was not comforted by his parents. They would say, "Nothing's there, just go back to sleep," and he would lie there, hiding himself from the window where he knew, if he moved, the "monsters" and "murderer" would kill him. Hearing him describe the fear, and remembering my own predator fears, is a reminder of the importance of sitting with children during this phase, so they experience the safety and power of the adult, thus calming their fears and reducing the extent of the trauma. Predator fears can be mitigated, and need to be. Unfortunately, the patient was also banished to his room if he was rambunctious, which is expectable in children, and perhaps especially in a boy, and he felt constant fear over long stretches of time. He came to believe that there is no help in this world, and he does not as yet have an internalised good object (see object constancy, below).

Moro reflex

An infant fears falling, as witnessed by a response to a sudden loss of support, or a loud noise, or the banging of hands next to the infant on a table (a test given by paediatricians). The Moro reflex, as it is called, is present in new-borns up to about five months of age, when it disappears in normal infants. It is demonstrated as having three distinct components: spreading out of the arms, clenching the arms, and crying, and is believed to be the only unlearnt fear in human new-borns. It may have developed in the human infant in evolution to help the infant cling to its mother while being carried, or if balance is lost; the reflex causes the infant to embrace the mother (see Mahler et al., 1975, p. 42).

A personal vignette

Some time after my husband died, I dreamed I was descending into the Grand Canyon, down deep thin steps, and my husband was ahead of me. I yelled for him to wait. I woke, and realised again how safe I had felt with him, how much a bodyguard and partner representing safety he had been to me, and I also recalled my mother's praise for my ability to crawl down steps from the second floor when I was one (she used to tell others and brag about me), remembering the fear, but also my courage as I responded to her encouraging voice from below. A sense of falling, and awareness of height and the abyss, is an inborn trait, requiring appropriate caring to mitigate the fear. The mother who represents safety provides calm holding. The fantasy and belief in the mother being able to create safety is easily transferred to a selected partner, and is a common attribute in the selection of the good enough partner (Turrini, 2013).

Mother as the early object of power

Maternal caring provides the baby with profound equipment. Spock and Parker (1998) say,

> For decades, scientists believed that the human brain was shaped solely in accordance with the child's genetic blueprint. Biology is destiny. The real picture is far more interesting and complex. It turns out that . . . a young child's environment actually helps to determine the structure of the brain, and the richness of the brain is pretty much set in the first two to three years.

Talbot (2015, pp. 19–20), in her paper, "The talking cure", reviews some reports about words spoken to the early infant and child that raise IQ and increase language capacity.

Songs that mothers sing to babies are soothing, offer a sense of being loved and safety, and are remembered. Words are conveyed through songs, and can contribute to neuronal development. In a paper entitled, "A dream while drowning", Greenson (1971) describes a patient who suffered a traumatic gas attack during the Second World War, which he associated with drowning. The patient reported that during the attack and in his rehabilitation period, strange words came into his mind that seemed to have a soothing effect. With the help of his analyst (Greenson), he discovered that the the words were from Flemish songs that his mother had sung to him during his infancy (his mother had died when he was two years old). Greenson postulates that this demonstrates the powerful effect of the pre-oedipal mother's soothing, since her words returned to her son when he was faced with trauma as an adult.

Freud relates the attachment of the mother to her narcissism. He postulates that

> a person may love: (a) what he himself is (i.e. himself); (b) what he himself was; (c) what he himself would like to be, and (d) someone who was once part of himself. Parental love, which is so moving and at bottom so childish, is nothing but the parents' narcissism born again, which transformed into object-love. (Mahler & McDevitt, 1980, p. 135)

Each parent views their loved newborn as invincible and confers power to them because their archaic self retains the parental love they received, which gave them power. Maternal love and the provision of safety thus pass from one generation to the next.

One can say that we are programmed to believe in an omnipotent being, and our wishes make it so, and the experiences with the good-enough mother set the stage for that perception and belief and strengthens it.

Wish fulfilment includes the longing for a pain-free life, and the power to attain all wishes. My twenty-two-month-old son ran across the room and announced, "I am the fastest runner in the world", a thought he had long before he had seen television heroes or runners winning races.

In a somewhat different vein, the mother seeks parenthood to reclaim the joy, wonderment, union with another, her mother–father of her past, the earliest warmth and safety of her remembrances, complete love, and connection to the perfect painless life. In good enough circumstances, she will please her parents, providing them with more family connections and a continuity of being for them; another form of safety and power to which mothers contribute. According to popular belief, mothers continue the opportunity for the planet to be populated and survive.

Bernardez (2003) discusses the inherent contradictions in these views, saying that "we hold an unconscious fantasy of the mother as an omnipotent being with magical powers and no needs of her own who is also potentially capable of ferocious destructiveness" (pp. 300–301). This view elicits fear in women who express anger and aggression. The fact that a woman believes that she should have no needs of her own when she becomes a mother is a major cause of depression in women. (See the section below on the imaginary mother of safety.)

Mahler's view

Mahler and colleagues (1975) refer to the "safe haven" of the symbiotic oneness experience organised in the first six months of life. In this "sense" experience, we are never alone, never in danger, with someone who can undo all pain, and will always be with us; the perfect ideal mother, a caring, giving other, who is omnipresent. If we had a good-enough mother, and were a good-enough baby (who could be soothed, and benefit from the caring), then we know perfection and the ideal safe mother. The two hearts are said to beat as one. Through this lens, the mother who provides the warmth and opportunity for oneness is the mother of power who creates (wires into the infant's brain) the ability to know and seek deep partnerships and ongoing love. The baby internalises the vitalisation of self, and can deny the "painful awareness of separateness" (Mahler et al., 1975, p. 96).

Emotional libidinal object constancy, defined by Mahler and cited in Edward and colleagues (1992, p. 250) as "a mental representation of a positive libidinally cathected (lastingly formed internal in the mind) inner image of the mother", implies maintenance of that mental representation regardless of the presence or absence of the love object (mother) and despite internal stress or need. It also implies the unification of the good and bad object into one whole representation, fosters fusion of the drives, and tempers hatred for the "object" (caring) person. The child with object constancy can go off to nursery school quite confident that the mother will come to fetch her or him at the end of the day, and optimistic that the teacher is a good caring person, who will take care of him/her. The father's, or other carer's, contributions to safety and the provision of food and pain relief, not just mother's, are important to include in assessing what helps the infant to organise an inner awareness of a trusted good other, but is not the subject of this discussion.

Self-constancy is an enduring individuality, including the awareness of being a separate and individual entity and a gender-defined self (Edward et al., 1992, p. 345; Mahler et al., 1975). For Eisnitz (1981), the self comprises an infinite number of self-images and units that construct our complete sense of our self that is consistent and endures. The parent contributes to the pre-oedipal child's sense of who he/she is through many inputs, including speaking well of them, encouraging their competency, and admiring and loving their personalities and ways of being. The mother's or carer's input powers the child's self-love, self-competency, self-regard, and positive self-esteem, as well as the positive units of the self.

A perspective on the loss of mother

Anna Quindlen (1994) says, in *One True Thing*,

> After my mother died, I had a feeling that was not unlike the home-sickness that always filled me for the first few days when I went to stay at my grandparents' house and even, I was stunned to discover, during the first few months of my freshman year at college. It was not really the home my mother had made that I yearned for. But I was sick in my soul for that greater meaning of home that we understand most purely when we are children, when it is a metaphor for all possible feelings of security, of safety, or what is predictable, gentle and good in life. (p. 213)

The power of myth

One dictionary definition for myth is: "Natural objects of pleasure; fictitious people. A belief or set of beliefs often unproven or false; without foundation or fact". The invincible mother concept is both a myth and an expectable, normal, structural fixture of a well-developed psychic life.

Film-makers and comic-book writers carry forward the idea of the invincibility of mankind: superman and superwoman. During the practising period, around fourteen months of age, toddlers are observed to experience a sense of invincibility, which soon changes to painful fear when they cannot reach the mother. Seeking for myths and heroes helps to mitigate feelings of helplessness. Mendell (2003) describes three typical maternal fantasies, components of the feminine self that accompany a woman and inform her feelings during her mothering. She says of the cornucopia fantasy,

> In Greek mythology, the cornucopia, the horn of plenty, is born of the goat that suckled Zeus. In common images it is associated with an overflowing fullness, abundance, the magic container of fairy tales which is never empty and renews itself. Demeter, the goddess of agriculture and fruitfulness and the protector of marriage, and the Earth Mother are celebrated for their maternal aspects, frequently pictured carrying a cornucopia bursting with the fruits of the earth. (p. 193)

In the parthenogenesis fantasy, noted in the myth of the virgin birth, only one parent, the mother, is registered. Mendell notes Finzi's archaic fantasy of spontaneous procreation of an imaginary child. Observations of doll play affirm the child's belief in the alive baby, and, as Kestenberg (1956) has described, the four-year-old experiences the "death of the doll baby" that affirms the significance of the fantasy of being like the great mother, caring perfectly for a baby (doll). Mendell's third fantasy is the one-body fantasy, which refers to the mother's fantasy in the unconscious that her child is a physical part of herself (p. 201).

Women as icons of power and safety

Eleanor Roosevelt held many in her thrall from the 1930s through the early 1960s. She comforted, chided, and spoke to the public during the Second World War. A quote from her is in keeping with the aspiration and conviction in the concept of her power, and her attribution of that power to the people of the USA. As she responded to the attack on the USA at Pearl Harbor, when war was declared, she said,

> We must go about our daily business more determined than ever to do the ordinary things as well as we can and when we find a way to do anything more in our communities to help others, to build morale, to give a feeling of security we must do it. Whatever is asked of us I am sure we can accomplish it. We are the free and unconquerable people of the United States of America. (Given on 7 December 1941, at the Pan American Coffee Bureau in ER's regular weekly talk)

Both she and her husband, Franklin Roosevelt, continuously (as parental substitutes and cultural–governmental social mentors) gave constant credit to the people, through lectures, fireside chats, and news statements.

The Statue of Liberty

The Statue of Liberty is a symbolic presence, a woman who stands at the entrance to the harbour of New York. Her history traces back to the figure of Libertas, in 228 BC, before the Second Punic War. Having formerly been a Roman diety, Libertas assumed goddess status. Libertas, along with other Roman goddesses, has inspired many modern-day symbols, including the Statue of Liberty.

Ken Burns' (1985) documentary about the statue records many immigrants' expressions of joy as they entered the harbour, feeling welcomed and safe. The symbol for many is a woman of power, holding up hope and offering the world safety from oppression and the protection of freedom, care, light, and love.

The Madonna (religious tradition)

The Virgin Mary (Madonna) embodied power rather than maternal tenderness in the Byzantine world. As the Mother of God, she was seen as a guarantor of military victory and, therefore, of imperial authority. In Pencheva's book, *Icons and Power: The Mother of God in Byzantium* (2014), he connects the fusion of the Marian cult and imperial rule with the power assigned to images of this All Holy Woman. As mentioned before, she is presented as giving birth as a virgin—a one-person power. She is depicted as caring, soothing, and always available.

The imaginary mother of safety and perfection is a myth

Unfortunately, this wonderful sense of power and safety that forms in a woman's ego ideal archaic self, her libidinal self, and object constancy and belief system is not real, yet it is a normal developmental acquisition, and governs an internal, and mostly unconscious maternal state. It causes great agony, and contributes to depression in women when they become mothers. A person raised with a good-enough parent tends to form an unconscious expectation that they will know everything about being a mother and do it right.

Then, to the shock and surprise of the majority of mothers, and fathers too, there is (a) a long recovery from delivery that can last up to six months, most often painful and physically exhausting; (b) a total inability to know why the baby is crying after the nappy is changed and breast or bottled feed has been given; (c) a fear that the baby is dying; (d) a feeling of failure to comfort that causes self-recrimination; (e) a serious feeling of failure that develops; (f) a belief that all other mothers are perfect—only they are the bad, inferior ones; (g) a feeling of shame takes over; and (h) a tendency for mothers to feel they are crazy.

When women attend groups with other mothers, for example, at a mothers' centre, and feel confident they can share their inner fears and inadequacies without censure, they report that they love to meet and talk; they learn the universality of anguish and shame, and that they are not crazy. Each has failed their inner expectations of themselves, and then they learn that others, too, carry these feelings of shame and failure. The reality of the colossal work required in caring for a baby becomes known.

"Babies do not come with instructions" is a comment I once heard and thought so on-target. Millions of things can go wrong, and paediatricians' offices are bombarded with phone calls at the beginning of each day. Now mothers search the Internet for answers, but continue to hide their inferiority feelings. Such feelings last a lifetime, and are frequent elements of therapy in adult women who are mothers, involving reworking the guilt and shame connected with their caring. There is a predictable depression that will occur for almost all mothers. Fathers, too, become depressed.

Bernardez (2003) voices concern for mothers as she explains that the mythical standards women hold and that are internalised prevent them from making accurate assessments of their tasks. She says,

> until this portrayal of the all-powerful mother is brought to consciousness and rectified, and until the social forces that continue to devalue women and mothering are understood and altered, the split of the omnipotent mother in the unconscious and the devaluation of the mother in real life will continue to exist. (p. 301)

Sandberg and Scovell (2014) refer to the "myth of doing it all" and "having it all" as the greatest trap ever set for women (p. 153). "Having it all" is best regarded as a myth, and, like many myths, it can deliver a helpful cautionary message. Think of Icarus, who soared to great heights with his man-made wings. His father warned him not too fly too near the sun, but Icarus ignored his father's advice, and crashed to earth. According to Sandberg, superwoman is the "adversary of the women's movement" (p. 156). Women's and mothers' moods crash when they face the actual baby—even the most placid baby has bouts of terror and pain that cannot be soothed. Then mothers need great support, kindness, and help to understand that they are not failures as mothers and women.

Robert Furman, a paediatrician and analyst (1924–2002), was an active member of the Cleveland psychoanalytic community, and, in a speech to a Cleveland business community, said,

> It is important to me to make certain your group of community leaders knows of the crucial significance of mothers, of the mother–child relationship, and the importance of all doing all we can as a society to strengthen and preserve that relationship.

Furman (personal communication) emphasised the crucial significance, citing Winnicott's ideas to conclude that individuals and society have a debt to women as mothers. He thought masculine pride prevented individuals from accepting the idea that it is only the mother who can carry the baby *in utero*, deliver the baby, and provide essential sustenance for life and growth.

Men come from their mothers' wombs, but cannot themselves carry babies, give birth to babies, or sustain them in their early months. This fact may motivate American male politicians who vote against adequate wages and time off for family care to compensate for their own inadequacy in this regard by denigrating mothers. This envy and denial prevents adequate maternity leave compensation and other needed services for women and mothers.

References

Bernardez, T. (2003). The good enough environment for good enough mothering. In: D. Mendell & P. Turrini (Eds.), *The Inner World of the Mother* (pp. 299–317). Madison, CT: Psychosocial Press.

Brazelton, T. B., & Cramer, B. (1991). *The Emotional Relationship: Parents, Infants and the Drama of Early Attachments*. London: Karnac.

Burns, K. (1985). *Statue of Liberty* (documentary film). PBS.

Edward, J., Ruskin, N., & Turrini, P. (1992). *Separation, Individuation, Theory and Application*. New York: Brunner/Mazel.

Eisnitz, A. (1981). The perspective of the self-representation, some clinical implications. *Journal of the American Psychoanalytic Association*, 29: 309–316.

Erikson, E. (1950). *Childhood and Society*. New York: Norton.

Freud, A., & Dann, S. (1951). An experiment in group upbringing. *Psychoanalytic Study of the Child*, 6: 127–169.

Freud, S. (1912–1913). *Totem and Taboo. S. E.*, 13: 1–161. London: Hogarth.

Gaddini, R. (1987). Early care and the roots of internalization. *International Journal of Psychoanalysis*, 14: 321–333.

Greenson, R. (1971). A dream while drowning. In: *Separation Individuation: Essays in Honor of Margaret Mahler* (pp. 374–384). New York: International Universities Press.

Hartmann, H. (1958). *Ego Psychology and the Proble of Adaptation*. New York: International Universities Press.

Kestenberg, J. S. (1956). On the development of maternal feelings in early childhood—observations and reflections. *Psychoanalytic Study of the Child*, 11: 257–291.

MacDonald, A.-M. (2003). *The Way the Crow Flies*. Toronto: Knopf Canada.

Mahler, M., & McDevitt, J. B. (1980). The separation–individuation process and identity formation. In: I. S. Greenspan & G. H. Pollock (Eds.), *The Course of Life (Volume 1): Infancy and Early Childhood* (pp. 395–406). Madison, CT: International Universities Press.

Mahler, M., Bergman, A., & Pine, F. (1975). *The Psychological Birth of the Human Infant*. New York: Basic Books.

Mendell, D. (2003). On the exploratio of three typical maternal fnatasies: the cornucopia fantasy, the fantasy of parthenogenesis, and the one-body fantasy. In: D. Mendell & P. Turrini (Eds.), *The Inner World of the Mother* (pp. 187–208). Madison, CT: Psychosocial Press.

Peto, A. (1969). Terrifying eyes—a visual superego forerunner. *Psychoanalytic Study of the Child*, 24: 197–212.

Quindlen, A. (1994). *One True Thing*. New York: Random House.

Riviere, J. (1991). *The Inner World and Joan Riviere: Collected Papers 1920–1958*. London: Karnac.

Sandberg, S., with Scovell, N. (2014). *Lean In*. New York: Alfred Knopf.

Spock, B., & Parker, S. (1998). *Dr. Spock's Baby and Child Care* (7th edn). New York: Pocket Books.

Szekely, L. (1954). Biological remarks on fears originating in early childhood. *International Journal of Psychoanalysis*, 35: 57–67.

Talbot, M. (2015). The talking cure. *New Yorker Magazine*, January 12.

Turrini, P. (2003). The capacity to cure: inevitable failure, guilt, and symptoms. In: D. Mendell & P. Turrini (Eds.), *The Inner World of the Mother* (pp. 149–168). Madison, CT: Psychosocial Press.

Turrini, P. (2013). The death of the loved spouse, the inner world of grief: a psychoanalytic developmental perspective. In: A. K. Richards, L. Spira, & A. A. Lynch (Eds.), *Encounters with Loneliness: Only the Lonely* (pp. 253–270). New York: International Psychoanalytic Books.

CHAPTER TWELVE

Contributions Part III: implications for psychoanalytic psychotherapy

Arlene Kramer Richards and Lucille Spira

P art III, with contributions from Thomson-Salo, Reenkola, and Turrini, brings us into the world of mothers, children, and mother–infant pairs. Ambivalence, envy, power, and agency are prominent themes in the myths discussed by these authors. The implications for clinical work of the chapters in this section are discussed below.

Boadicea

Thomson-Salo focuses on the story of Boadicea, a Celtic queen with mythic qualities. This character is a mature woman, a mother, who stood up against the powerful Romans. She did this to protect her daughters, her countrymen, and her self. The daughters were raped by slaves at the instigation of the Roman overseers, while Boadicea was degraded.

In treatment, we see women who, as children, were raped or sexually abused. The rapist or abuser belonged to a band of invading warriors in Boadicea's time. In our own time we hear of rape and/or abuse by fathers, uncles, grandfathers, mother's lovers, brothers, sisters, even mothers. In many instances, the mother helps or tries to help and protect her daughter. In other cases, the mother denies the abuse or just does not take action to protect her daughter. This can be the result of her own sense of powerlessness or actual powerlessness. Where she does not protect her daughter, she is complicit in the abuse.

Later on, women who were abused as children hold an image of their mothers as weak, or as silent partners to the abuse, not having been powerful, or loving, enough to protect them. Daughters wish for an active and powerful mother like Boadicea, although the history of the actual Boadicea may be unknown to them. This wish is built on the fantasy of the omnipotent mother, a theme that is taken up in this volume by Turrini. Such a wish or fantasy might not be expressed in words, but is, rather, enacted.

This has implications for the transference. One way in which it manifests is in how the daughter sees and reacts to her lovers or husband. Having been abused, some women choose abusive lovers. Some see any activity or initiative on the part of their lovers as domineering.

If they report the men in their lives as abusive, coercive, and insensitive, they induce the therapist to protect them from perceived or actual aggressive acts, much as they wanted and needed protection from their mother. However, as adults they need to examine their own wishes to be dominated. They need to see the conflict between the wish to be in thrall to a powerful partner and the wish to be a separate, independent, self-protective person. The phantasy of being powerful competes with the phantasy of being in the shadow of a powerful person.

The analyst can conceptualise this as the "mirror transference" competing with the "idealising transference". Understanding the wish for the other to be a powerful idealised person enables the patient to distance herself from the need to enact the conflict.

The Boadicea story, as Thomson-Salo details it and the case of her composite male analysand, is a reminder that we still long for the mother's "gaze" and fear that powerful mother. Some of us enact this longing in our daily life, bypassing the possibility that we can identify with a mother's power, as after all, all mothers were initially powerful to us when we were babies.

The infant observation studies that are of interest to Thomson-Salo remind us how much babies and mothers teach us about development and its role in later life. They illuminate how powerful mothers are and also ask us to consider how powerful a therapist is in the eyes of the patient, as was the case for Thomson-Salo's patient. Unlike the mother and child, the analyst–therapist contains and interprets aggression, rather than throwing a fit when things do not go her way, as the mother of the patient whom she describes reportedly did. The power of interpretation and understanding is highlighted in Thomson-Salo's work.

Medea

Reenkola's discussion of "Medea, almighty mother" presents Medea as a powerful, aggressive woman who acts as a subject. We are familiar with Euripides' Medea as the mother who vengefully kills her children after being humiliated by Jason, her husband and the children's father. In this action, she is exerting what Reenkola sees as women's mightiest and most enviable power: to adopt or negate the role of mother. By her actions, a mother has the power to deny life to her offspring just as she does to nurture them. We know that most of the aggressive behaviours by mothers toward their children are more subtle and less frightening than that enacted by Medea. Some of the less sensitive and sometimes sadistic behaviours that a mother enacts can contribute to severe physical or psychic damage. Fortunately, abusive actions on the part of mothers toward children are not the norm.

A therapist's support of a mother's ego strength in her relations with her children and in general helps both mother and child. The mother does not have to think of herself as a "monster" mother just because she sometimes feels as if she wants to kill her child. By pointing out the mother's self control in not acting on these feelings and thoughts, the therapist can help the mother to respect her own restraint. This restraint is what we call ego strength.

The Medea drama displays the truth that aggressive actions by mothers toward their children can be fuelled by factors beyond the child's behaviour or the mother's resentment of motherhood. Father has a role. By being abusive, absent, or rejecting, father can enrage a woman to the point where she destroys his and her children. Children and mothers may be at risk where the child's father is perceived as the persecutory other. We, as therapists, must keep in mind that for the mother, the children who share aspects of the father, and also, where concrete thinking replaces symbolic thought, there can arise the idea that the child is the same as the father. One message here for psychoanalytic psychotherapists is that feeling desperate, a sense of being humiliated and powerless, can lead to desperate actions on the part of any of us, including mothers.

With mothers, we must be sensitive and empathic about their sometimes ambivalent feelings and help them to differentiate feelings from planned actions; often, desperation results in anger that subsumes love. The therapist creates potential space for all feelings, even those of the mother who seems to us an avatar of Medea.

Reenkola's work suggests that women who have had abortions or are considering an abortion might be at risk of suffering a severe blow to their self-esteem as they feel unable to meet the idealised image for women—unambivalent motherhood. As such, they can experience themselves as Medea figures. In such circumstances, they might be at risk of doing harm to themselves through self-punitive behaviours and depressed feelings.

That male therapists as well as female therapists might envy their pregnant patients for the power inherent in motherhood is an issue to consider as we examine our countertransference. Also, we may identify with the child as we connect with what we see as the Medea aspect in our patients, or even in ourselves. Our negativity towards mothers comes from what we feel towards ourselves as less than perfect nurturers and towards our own mothers, where we still have poorly resolved issues *vis-à-vis* self and mother.

The myth of "the mother of safety and protection"

Turrini's focus is on baby and her/his mother. Using psychoanalytic developmental theory, she suggests that the infant needs to phantasise an image of an invincible mother for a sense of safety and protection. The familiar becomes meaningful and the voice of the mother has magical power to soothe. In the eyes and skin of the baby, the mother as she soothes or rescues the baby from pain is the "fix it" mother.

The wish for the "fix it" therapist might very well stem from this early need/perception fostered in the infant–mother pair. However, analytic therapists do not "fix it", but, rather, help patients to find their unique solution to their problems and conflicts that give rise to painful affect. Turrini's description of the early infantile wish and experience suggests that the phantasy of returning to the time when omnipotence predominated—baby screams, mother comes—provides pleasure. When the therapist becomes the phantasy vehicle for this return to paradise, these wishes can elicit corresponding feelings in therapists. Therefore, therapists need to attend to the discomfort engendered by our own limitations. Optimally, therapists make serious efforts to accept the patient's perception of the degree of their suffering, thus providing symbolic holding in Winnicott's sense, and awareness of the wishes, fears, moral judgements, and compromises inherent in the phantasy.

Disillusionment sets in bit by bit rather than in one fell swoop, and the pain is tempered by the sense that the therapist and patient are both adults who can master the conflicts they experience. But, as Turrini makes clear, even the "good enough" mother does not always succeed; illness and other vicissitudes of life cause ruptures and threaten the development of basic trust; a therapist's vacation, pregnancy, or perceived withholding of voice can trigger ruptures.

The importance of the mother's voice to baby for soothing and supporting is paralleled by the importance of the therapist's voice. Our failure to provide enough of this has a negative impact on a therapist's self-esteem, just as the mother with an uncomforted baby described by Turrini feels. In that case, we have bought into the phantasy that we can provide perfect safety and protection.

Often, we see women in treatment whose children are now grown but are not faring well. We hear the pain and self-blame on the part of the mother for the perceived failures and problems in their offspring. We can recognise that such women believe their children's failures result from their own failure to be the mothers of safety and protection. Such descriptions of their role in their children's failings need to be explored as phantasies that express the wishes, fears, and moral judgements that all phantasies are built of. Mourning the loss of such beliefs is helpful to these mothers. Similar mourning of the belief that one should be the all-powerful therapist is helpful as well.

Giving up the idea of omnipotent mother or omnipotent therapist allows the therapist to accept her need for support in the form of supervision and the mother to accept her need for help from the spouse, partner and/or family, as well as the wider community.

PART IV

THE POWER OF WOMEN'S SEXUALITY

CHAPTER THIRTEEN

The last word: Molly Bloom*

Paul Schwaber

J oyce told his friend Frank Budgen that he would give Molly
Bloom the last word (Ellman, 1982, p. 501). Famously, it was
"yes", three times repeated, reaffirming her love for her husband
and her delight in remembering how she got him to propose.

Joyce took big risks in *Ulysses*, his extraordinary novel that transformed Homeric precedence, democratising the epic with a very
funny, deeply discerning tale of a middle-aged Dublin advertising
canvasser, a tormented young man he protects, and the canvasser's
intriguing wife. The Greek hero Odysseus's adventurous struggles to
return after the Trojan War to his wife Penelope and son Telemachus
is reconceived in distinct persons and interactions of a single Dublin
day, 16 June 1904 (and a bit of 17 June), as Leopold Bloom (Jewish on
his paternal side) wends his alert, troubled, often lonely way home,
eventually accompanied by young Stephen Dedalus, to his wife Molly,
who that afternoon has committed adultery for the first time.

So, let us contemplate her in *Ulysses'* last and her only chapter, as
she lies awake in their old brass bed at No. 7 Eccles Street. Poldy, as

---

* A previous version of this chapter appeared in *The Cast of Characters: A Reading of
Ulysses*, 1999. Reprinted by permission of Yale University Press.

she sometimes calls him, sleeps soundly beside her. He kissed her on the buttocks getting into bed and woke her, but that, like his wily account of his day and surprising request for eggs and tea for breakfast, is over for him. Having wandered, the exhausted Jewish Odysseus of Dublin sleeps, his "cold feet" (18.906)[1] as usual where his head should be.

That afternoon Molly has been to bed with a man other than him for the first time—Hugh "Blazes" Boylan, her musical agent and a known womaniser. At nearly 2.45 a.m. she is well on in her thoughts, taking note at the moment of her teenage daughter Milly's angering behaviour, the inadequacies of her cleaning lady, and an assignable cause: Leopold's deficiencies as a provider. She begins to pity herself, when suddenly she realises she is menstrual:

> every day I get up theres some new thing on sweet God sweet God well when Im stretched out dead in my grave I suppose Ill have some peace I want to get up a minute if Im let wait O Jesus wait yes that thing has come on me now wouldn't that afflict you of course all the poking and rooting and ploughing he had up in me.

Boylan's forcefulness brought it on, she supposes, discomfited by their intention to do it again four days hence: "wouldn't that pester the soul out of a body," she sighs, "unless he likes it some men do." Sorely disappointed, she airs a general complaint: "God knows theres always something wrong with us 5 days every 3 or 4 weeks usual monthly auction isn't it simply sickening" (1102–1110). Soon we learn of her relief not to be pregnant by him. But her period surprises her. Hers may not be predictable—"5 days every 3 or 4 weeks", she thinks, and before long she calculates three weeks since her last. Perhaps she's inattentive. Later, wondering whether something might be wrong with her "insides", she thinks fleetingly of seeing a doctor.

At once she recalls a similarly unexpected onset one night at the theatre. It was their "one and only time" in a box. A fashionable fellow stared through glasses at her, Bloom talked on impercipiently about "Spinoza and his soul that's dead I suppose millions of years ago", while she smiled, leaned forward, and, trying to look interested, felt "all in a swamp". They had gone expecting "a fast play about adultery", but some "idiot" in the gallery hissed and shouted at the adulteress all the same. Molly fancies the fellow finding a woman in the next lane after the show "to make up for it", adds "I wish he had what

I had then hed boo", and whisks back to the present: "I bet the cat itself is better off than us have we too much blood in us or what O patience above its pouring out of me like the sea anyhow he didn't make me pregnant as big as he is". She goes on:

> I don't want to ruin the clean sheets the clean linen I wore brought it on too damn it damn it and they always want to know youre a virgin for them theyre such fools too you could be a widow or divorced 40 times over a daub of red ink would or blackberry juice no that's too purply O Jamesy let me up out of this pooh. (1111–1128)

This glimpse into the midst of things may help us to fathom Joyce's gamble on her, her husband's abidingly detailed fascination with her, and her lasting fame. Through the windings of the book she has been a source of entertainment and pride to Leopold, the powerful magnet of his regrets, guilts, pleasurable self-punishments, and attempts at recovery. Not with total consistency, she has seemed from afar a scold and layabout, a disloyal if much tried wife, a singer possessed of a strong but untrained voice and heaving *embonpoint*, a goad for masculine jokes, timidities, and stories, and once even earth mother Gea-Tellus. She did not leave the house and much of the time was in bed. We saw her toss a coin from her window to a crippled beggar—an uncommon act of charity in the book—and we know of the singing tour to Belfast to be managed by Boylan and their appointment that afternoon. But, for the most part, except as we might have gauged her more complexly through Leopold's thoughts, she has been the stuff of gossip and wish. She attracts attention in Dublin while remaining subject to its expectations, like the other women we have met: the milkwoman and midwives, Josie Breen, Stephen's sister Dilly, the barmaids Misses Kennedy and Douce, Mrs Purefoy at last delivered of her ninth child, and others. Molly's private ruminations, furthermore, proceed from male stereotype: a woman in bed and on her back, emotional and garrulous, with little to do but conjure sex, endure biological vulnerability, and *be*.

Yet, as we follow her thoughts, Molly proves alert, witty, and playful, though in pain, complaining and engaging in distress. Her perceptions tumble into one another, suggesting acuity and mental richness, if also muddle. Her spontaneity allies with sharply etched images to produce exaggerations that resonate: "its pouring out of me like the sea"; "a widow or divorced 40 times over". Divorce or Bloom's death:

the thought has occurred formulaically but more than once. She has an eye for fakery, whether her own or others': "a daub of red ink would do". She lacks education, has a knowing, cunning intelligence and ready opinions. Dismayed here, she shows willingness to find fault and distribute it. Her mind moves swiftly, liltingly. "Flow" or "stream" are the usual metaphors for it, as in "stream of consciousness". Molly's reflects both stereotype and her variety: her zest, fun, and shrewdness, her acerbity, outrage, wonder, and pain—and more.

Because, although earthy and direct, she is evasive, too. Her surprise about her period jibes with her diction: "that thing" has come upon her: something in her "insides" has produced "pooh". There are specifics she ducks, even with herself. "I was coming for about 5 minutes with my legs round him," she has exulted; "I had to hug him after O Lord I wanted to shout out all sorts of things fuck shit or anything at all". But she didn't. She said nothing: "who knows the way hed take it . . . I gave my eyes that look with my hair a bit loose from the tumbling and my tongue between my lips up to him the savage brute"—only to go on: "Thursday Friday one Saturday two Sunday three O Lord I cant wait til Monday" (587–595).

Molly functions within constraints, her inner ones flexible enough to displace her aggression ("fuck", "shit") to Boylan (who has enough of his own, "the savage brute") through time and, retrospectively, to increase her pleasure. She wanted to shout but did not; as she remembers it, she came for five minutes, and through the length of her reverie the number of times they had intercourse increases from at least two to "5 or 6". It might be by way of compromise with her contradictory impulses, therefore, that she slips into comical but contained metaphors like "all in a swamp" and the "usual monthly auction".

She seems comfortable with half-knowledge ("he didn't make me pregnant as big as he is") and with superstitious explanations ("the clean linen brought it on too damn it"). Perhaps she is straining here for distancing humour, but, typically, Molly fuzzes or distorts a bodily focus of knowledge. She also imposes precipitous finality on what she knows ("unless he likes it some men do"), with the dependable focus of switching her objects of attention rather than pursuing any one. Of course, she is tired, still excited, and thinking associatively. She does run her diverting idiom to absurdity, however. That Boylan hoped to find her—Bloom's wife and Milly's mother—a virgin is much to be doubted, though the drift may alert us to a wish. Neither Gea-Tellus nor Penelope, Molly Bloom evokes both and more, because she is realised, contradictory, idiosyncratic, wilful and winning—a specific woman who combines lively curiosity with puzzling limitations on it. From that bind she indulges in philistinism, like her dismissal of Spinoza, as elsewhere she notices, only to disdain, politics, religious disputes, nationalism, and wars—matters of import to others in *Ulysses*. She continues untroubled about countering frankness with avoidance because apparently unaware of it.

Given her many mentions of God, her chiselled memory of the hissed stage adulteress suggests guilt, and earlier she remembered awakening terrified to the thunderstorm: "as if the world was coming to an end God be merciful to us I thought the heavens were coming down about us to punish" (134–135). Overridingly in this passage, however, Molly is angry: bitter about her marriage and the demandingness of men ("theyre such fools"), distressed by the monthly exigencies of her body, thus encompassingly disgusted when she calls out for help—"O Jamesy let me up out of this pooh"—to Joyce! A vaudevillian flash relaxes the tension, breaking up our suspension of disbelief that we have been following an actual woman's thoughts. She calls to him familiarly, moreover, reminding him and us that she is only a creature of words, a character in his book. What are we to make of it?

It is a joke, of course, a test of our wakefulness, but also, paradoxically, an assertion of her reality; she's no less real than Poldy or Stephen, indeed, equal in claim here to her creator, Joyce, and implicitly, thereby, as real as any of us. So we had best attend. The liveliness and disparate movement of her mind impress, and before long one adjusts to its persistence. She is in no hurry to sleep; her thoughts pulsate on and on. Her reverie, its logic and focus elusive, its contiguities insistent, admits little inner silence. For thirty-six unpunctuated pages the only cessations occur when she cries out to Jamesy—a moment instantly closed round by more thought—and at eight paragraph endings, the last of which ends the book. We know her closely only this way: keyed up, mulling present and future, and remembering her past, hours after frolicking with Boylan and soon after her husband requested breakfast in bed.

Not since the City Arms Hotel has he asked that, and then he did it under guise of being ill. They lived at the City Arms more than a decade ago when he worked for Mr Cuffe at the Cattle Market, at the time their son, Rudy, was born and after eleven days died. Leopold now gets breakfast for her—did so, in fact, that very morning. Yet, in big and little as *Ulysses* ends, Molly ponders change. Too fed up to continue as she has—witness the first adultery, the cry to be let up out of pooh—she explores other of her feelings as well: guilt, as above, but, far more recurrently, indulgence and appreciation, nostalgia, sadness, anger, competitiveness, joy, and desire. Several of these converge to anxiety when she comes close to fantasising murder, contemplating a Mrs Maybrick, who poisoned her husband—Molly imagines for love of another man. She remarks disliking being alone in the big "barracks of a place" (978) at night. But usually anxiety is not something Molly feels. It is what she avoids—what translates into the press of her thoughts. Her mind here has a runaway tone, suggests an implicit panic attributable only in part to the specialness of the day. Her thoughts push on, I believe, to fill the unknown and to suppress or otherwise contain what frightens her, because, given who she is, who she reveals herself to be, the changes already begun endanger her.

Diverting anxiety to pulsating consciousness, she reveals a good deal about herself. She was born on Gibraltar. Her father, Brian Tweedy, an Irish Sergeant Major in the British Army, raised her with the aid of several elderly women, most notably pious and stern Mrs Rubio, whom Molly remembers with annoyance, an attitude she transfers easily to her cleaning lady and to Mrs Riordan, Stephen's aunt, whom the Blooms knew in the City Arms Hotel. Old women do not please her. Contrastingly, her father figures kindly in her thoughts. As a soldier's daughter, she has glowing memories of parades, ceremonies, and colours, of officers' talk and bandnight strolls on an officer's arm. She remembers Gibraltar's hot sun, the flowers and the sea, the multiplicity of peoples on the island and her discoveries of early adolescence there. Although she mentions no presently close women friends, she longingly invokes Hester Stanhope, a Gibraltar friend nearly her own age and married to a much older man. Molly and Hester's husband had begun to be somewhat aware of one another when the Stanhopes left. That was awful: "it got as dull as the devil after they went I was almost planning to run away mad out of it . . . so bored sometimes I could fight with my nails". She goes on, sadly, "people were always going away and we never" (668–678).

Eventually, she and her father settled in Dublin, she met Bloom, and at eighteen married him, already pregnant with their first child, Milly. By now they have been married for sixteen years. Milly, herself an adolescent, lately has left home to work as a photographer's assistant in Mullingar. Her mother supposes Bloom behind the move, suspecting his prescience and possible implied permission about herself and Boylan, but she recognises that she and Milly no longer could abide under the same roof. None the less, Milly leaves an empty nest: only Molly and Leopold at 7 Eccles Street. Molly has to remind herself not to shop for three. And since their infant son Rudy died, sexual contact between them has been exceedingly strange, involving attentiveness and often tenderness, varieties of fore- and alternative play, his selecting pornographic books for her to read, and, as the parodically objective previous chapter report it, "a period of 10 years, 5 months and 18 days during which carnal intercourse has been incomplete, without ejaculation of semen within the natural female organ" (17.2282–2285).

So, Molly turned to Boylan after an epic wait—one as long as the Trojan War. The aftermath we can observe in her rushing stream of consciousness, which halts only when specific contents cause paragraphs to end. The first occurs when she reflects about Mrs Maybrick, who put arsenic in her husband's tea. "Theyre not brutes enough to go and hang a woman surely are they" (244–245), she wonders—and halts, presumably not liking the retort she could adumbrate. Then she darts in a different direction, towards men who have desired her. This drift ends when she recalls trying to persuade Mr Cuffe, whom Bloom had insulted, not to fire him. Cuffe refused—Molly notes with pride—regretfully: "I just half smiled I know my chest was out that way at the door when he said Im extremely sorry and Im sure you were" (533–534). Puffed with her attractiveness, she holds for a moment, delighted. The third paragraph ends passionately: "Thursday Friday one Saturday two Sunday three O Lord I cant wait til Monday" (594–595), and the fourth desperately: "my goodness theres nothing else its all very fine for them but as for being a woman as soon as youre old they might as well throw you out into the bottom of the ash pit" (745–747).

Equally charged thoughts mark the ends of the other paragraphs. She passes wind with the accompanying mental rebuke of her husband while a distant train whistle provides cover. She urinates

gleefully, attending to her period on the chamberpot. After articulat-
ing a prolonged imaginative scenario about Stephen, who would be
her young, clean, intelligent poet lover, curiously linked to Rudy, who
would now have been the age Stephen was when first she saw him,
she startlingly remembers Boylan: "O but then what am I going to do
about him though" (1366–1367). So many men to keep track of! It
brings her up short. At the last, her lyrical "yes" ends the book as she
merges Bloom with her first beau, Mulvey, who kissed her under the
Moorish wall, and Gibraltar and father with Howth Hill, where she
got Bloom to propose, affirming felt continuities between her happiest memories, her present and her future—at least for the moment.

These intensities arrest her inner flow of language. For moments
they cannot be contained. Our focusing example, which has its own
breakthrough (Molly's associations of menses and pooh), provides
more clues about the range of what has stirred in her, and the urgency.
After calling out to Jamesy, she follows with grumbles about women's
lot, thoughts about sex being better in the afternoon, and this fantasy,
combining retaliatory hostility and exhibitionism with a wishful flight
to pre-puberty: "I think Ill cut all this hair off me there scalding me I
might look like a young girl wouldn't he get the great suckin the next
time he turned up my clothes on me Id give anything to see his face".

In turn, this issues to concern that the chamberpot might break
beneath her weight, self-conscious snippets of herself and Boylan
("he was so busy where he oughtn't to be") and a tendentious thought
about urinating: "God I remember one time I could scout it out
straight whistling like a man almost", before ending a paragraph with
overt fantasising about being a man like Boylan admiring her soft
white thighs: "God I wouldn't mind being a man and get up on a
lovely woman O Lord what a row youre making" (1133–1147).

This material bespeaks wayward desires awash, psychic fluidity
that approaches boundarylessness and diffusion, that sweeps forward
to renewed genitality and back to the earliest stages of development.
It includes bisexuality, murderousness, dire vulnerability, and a resur-
gent, flamboyant assertiveness so pleasurable, so intense, that she
backs off. It dovetails, too, with aggressive and libidinous preoccupa-
tions throughout by being presented, diverged from, and recurred to.
Her thoughts press on: "Goodbye to my sleep for this night" (925).
Molly's act of adultery and these early morning ruminations show
oedipal triangulations. She has made one by adding Boylan, perhaps

to replace the one with Milly. She considers one in which Stephen would replace Boylan, connects Stephen and Rudy, remembers her father and Mrs Rubio, and her own incipient awareness of Captain Stanhope. She is fascinated by male arousal: "can you ever be up to men the way it takes them"; for example, quiet, mild Mr Mastiansky taking his wife from behind, Bloom's fondness for stockings and drawers, smutty pictures and rumps, his "mad crazy letters" during their courtship ("Precious one everything connected with your glorious body everything underlined that comes from it is a thing of beauty and a joy forever") (1176–1178) that had her masturbating four or five times a day—though that is not a word she uses, Boylan attracted by her foot, Boylan sucking at her breasts, making them firm and her thirsty. sailors flashing, all men "mad to get in there where whey came out of youd think they could never get far enough up" (806–807). Her arousal is palpable and polymorphous, stretching to all areas of the body and to pre-oedipal rebelliousness, rage, and orality. She would like to suck a young boy's penis, she'd like to give Boylan a "great suckin", and she can feel her soul in a kiss: "theres nothing like a kiss long and hot down to your soul almost paralyzes you" (105–106).

So, as Molly Bloom, a somewhat exotic but discreet Dublin housewife, who until that day, even by strict Victorian or Edwardian standards, was a respectable one, who, committing adultery, wanted to shout obscenities but did not, thinks through what to do now about Boylan and what about Bloom, including the possibility of having another child with him ("yes thatd be awfully jolly," she thought early and rushed on) (168), she simultaneously gives expression to a press of id impulses and struggles to control it. She is not always like this. She is in crisis—when potentials always present clamour to the fore. For example, she remembers herself at ten years of age "standing at the fire with the little bit of a short shift I had up to heat myself I loved dancing about in it then make a race back into bed Im sure that fellow opposite used to be there the whole time watching" (919–921).

I have emphasised that the persistent process of her thoughts counts for much. She is also markedly ambivalent, which provides a kind of ballast. She gives and takes back, asserts and lightens, expresses distaste only to find something admirable. She intends to take her ring off going to Belfast with Boylan, "or they might bell it round the town in their papers or tell the police on me but theyd think we were married" (408–409). Critical of her cleaning lady, she notes, "arent they a nuisance that old Mrs Fleming you have to be walking round after her putting things into her hands sneezing and farting into the pots well of course shes old she cant help it" (1082–1084). When concerned about her "insides", she brings Dr Collins to mind, whom, before her marriage, she consulted about emissions she now thinks were caused by her masturbating:

> asking me had I frequent omissions where do those old fellows get all the words they have omissions with his shortsighted eyes on me cocked sideways I wouldnt trust him too far to give me chloroform or God know what else still I liked him when he sat down to write the thing out frowning so severe his nose intelligent like that. (1169–1174)

Later, feeling possessive and ruefully proud of Poldy, she thinks of his coming in late, of Paddy Dignam's funeral and the men who attended it:

> well theyre not going to get my husband into their clutches if I can help it making fun of him when behind his back I know well when he goes on with his idiotics because he has sense enough not to squander every penny piece he earns down their gullets and looks after his wife and family goodfornothings.

She goes on:

> poor Paddy Dignam all the same Im sorry in a way for him what are his wife and 5 children going to do unless he was insured comical little teetotum always stuck up on some pub corner and her or her son waiting Billy Bailey wont you please come home. (1275–1283)

Or consider her asseverations on women: "either he wants what he wont get or its some woman ready to stick her knife in you I hate that in women no wonder they treat us the way they do we are a dreadful lot of bitches I suppose its all the troubles we have make us so snappy" (1457–1460). Molly cannot be nasty without making amends, or flatly changing the subject.

Writ large, her pattern of doing and undoing becomes her path for deciding about Boylan and Bloom. Clearly, Boylan thrilled her: "O thanks be to the great God I got somebody to give me what I badly wanted to put some heart up into me" (732–733). But early on she resents him slapping her behind, just as if she were one of his father's horses. She plays with running off with him and provoking a scandal. In time, however, his crassness and stupidity compare terribly with her hopes for Stephen:

> the ignoramus that doesn't know poetry from a cabbage . . . of course hes right enough in his way to pass the time as a joke sure you might as well be in bed what with a lion God Im sure hed have something better to say for himself an old Lion would. (1370–1378)

By the end, via the fantasy about Stephen linked to Rudy and leading to Bloom, Blazes Boylan seems dismissed from her thoughts. A similar route going the opposite way affects Leopold, answering in kind his odyssean return to her. Molly's inner oscillations contain and ventilate, can serve stasis or adaptation.

For, no matter how far she travels mentally, she always returns to him, and whether puzzled, annoyed, dismayed, fascinated, amused, or pleased, her attention plays on him. Thus, she complements him, answers his consistent preoccupation with her during the day. They each note quietly the other's secretiveness about correspondence. She thinks he has been having sex elsewhere: "so very probably that was it to somebody who thinks she has a softy in him . . . and then the usual kissing my bottom was to hide" (50–53). She has other traits like his. She gave charity, as did he, more than he could afford, to Dignam's family, and he acted charitably towards Stephen. When Molly hears the train whistle's "weeping tone", she pities the "poor trainmen" (597–598) far from their families and, remembering bull-fights on Gibraltar, she registers dislike for the violence done to the horses. There is kindness to her. She fits the lonesome man who threw Banbury cake to the gulls.

Several times she affirms his preferability to other women's husbands. She likes his manners and cleanliness, his caring and his learning, such as it is—though she mocks it: "still he knows a lot of mixed up things especially about the body and the insides"—that she respects. And he is polite to old women. Her anger and complaints are manifest:

> any man thatd kiss a womans bottom Id throw my hat at him after that hed kiss anything unnatural where we haven't 1 atom of expression is

us the same 2 lumps of lard before ever I do that to a man pfooh the
dirty brutes. (1401–1410)

Still, "something always happens" with Leopold. He is always interesting. She enjoys the oddity in him. Fondly and laughably she
remembers her swollen breasts hurting her after weaning Milly,

> till he got doctor Brady to give me the Belladona prescription I had to
> get him to suck them they were so hard he said it was sweet and
> thicker than cows then he wanted to milk me into the tea well hes
> beyond everything I declare someone ought to put him in the budget
> if only I could remember the one half of the things and write a book
> out of it the works of Master Poldy yes. (575–580).

Poldy is her problem, but psychologically, in her crisis ruminations,
she may be said to organise around him.

There is one more pattern of containment co-operating with the
ongoing process of her thoughts, her balancing ambivalence, and her
recurrence to Bloom: her narcissism. Molly refers everything to
herself—assesses herself validated by it or not, triumphant or failed.
That is why she is so competitive. It accounts for the edge of battle in
her pride of beauty, as with Mr Cuffe, her temper about men who dis-
tract Poldy from attending to her; her shortness with causes and learning. Her self-reference bears on her generalised dislike of men or
women at different moments, her fascination with who has what, with
who gets more: "nice invention they made for women for him to get
all the pleasure"; "they have friends they can talk to weve none"
(1456–1457). She thinks of Boylan at her breasts:

> he couldnt resist they excite myself sometimes its well for men all the
> amount of pleasure they get off a womans body were so round and
> white for them always I wished I was one myself for a change just to
> try with that thing they have swelling up on you so hard and at the
> same time so soft when you touch it. (1379–1383)

Compliments gratify her deeply, and ordinariness appals. She has tart
things to say of other Irish women singers. It is a nice touch that Molly
remembers whistling "there is a charming girl I love" (347–348) when
tossing the coin to the crippled sailor. For self-regard preserves her,
just as crucially as what she knows about Bloom does: "I saw he

understood or felt what a woman is and I knew I could always get round him" (1578–1579). Without both, but especially that sense of her power over him, she could be nothing.

Why, then, did Molly commit adultery, and why the tremulous aftermath? After long holding to a pattern of complicitly limited genital interaction with Leopold, one they both trace to the death of their infant son Rudy and obviously different from their preceding pattern, which produced two children, the first conceived prior to their marriage, Molly has pushed forward again to completed intercourse. Her adultery with Boylan broke a regressed tie to Bloom, and that inner change contributes to her tremulousness. What apparently provided the impetus, however, was Milly's puberty—her attendant acerbity to Molly and flirtatiousness with Leopold—and the path she has now taken towards a separate life. Molly reflects on the family name she acquired in marriage, prefers it to Breen, Briggs, Mulvey, Boylan "or those awful names with bottom in them", then suddenly links three generations of women:

> my mother whoever she was might have given me a nicer name the Lord knows after the lovely one she had Lunita Laredo the fun we had [Mulvey and she] running along Willis road to Europa point . . . they were shaking and dancing in my blouse like Millys little ones now when she runs up the stairs I loved looking down at them. (844–851).

Milly's development has revived Molly's wishfulness about her mother and vibrant memories of her own young sexuality. Annoyed with, but proud of, Milly, Molly registers delight in herself and fears of getting old:

> [Leopold] helping her into her coat but if there was anything wrong with her its me shed tell not him . . . I suppose he thinks Im finished out and laid on the shelf well Im not no nor anything like it;

> her tongue is a bit too long for my taste your blouse is open too low she says the pan calling the kettle blackbottom and I had to tell her not to cock her legs up like that on show on the windowsill before all the people passing they all look at her like me when I was her age. (1023–1036)

Before confronting the empty nest, Molly knew the enlivening challenge of an all-too full one and began to reclaim her desire.

Her thrust forward includes her thought, briefly aired early on, of trying for another child with Leopold, and near the end, during the prolonged fantasy about Stephen through which she arrives at her decisive acceptance of her husband, she has a poignant series of associations about "goodfornothing" men: "where would they all of them be if they hadnt all a mother to look after them what I never had that's why I suppose hes running wild now". It is Stephen she refers to, whose mother died and whose father she's called "a criticizer": "well its a poor case that those that have a fine son like that theyre not satisfied and I none". The imagined lover to replace Boylan thus leads to her dead infant:

> that disheartened me altogether I suppose I oughtn't to have buried him in that little woolly jacket I knitted crying as I was but give it to some poor child but I knew well Id never have another our 1st death too it was we were never the same since O Im not going to think myself in the glooms about that any more. (1441–1451)

This sequence unlocks a good deal, I think. Their little son's death long ago touched Molly's ache of absence, and she retreated from genitality—Poldy did too, but that is another complicated story—to avoid another such loss. Rudy's was *their* first death, but not Molly's. It evoked hers: the core inner one of the mother "to look after" her that she never had, though everyone else did. Hence the halt to full intercourse, though she knew she could bring Poldy round if she wanted to. Hence the importance to her of Hester, who taught her and held her:

> we used to compare our hair mine was thicker than hers she showed me how to settle it at the back when I put it up what this else how to make a knot on a thread with one hand we were like cousins what age was I then the night of the storm I slept in her bed she had her arms round me then we were fighting in the morning with the pillow what fun. (638–643)

Hence the idealisation of Gibraltar—an inclusive, warm, colourful, nurturing place, a maternal substitute or screen—compared to which her life in Dublin seems grey. Other strands connect with her missing mother, too: Molly's aggrandising narcissism—a compensation; her vulnerability, which she counters with competitive thoughts; her store of anger and ambivalence; her fear of ageing; her nostalgia. Her imprecision about bodily knowledge may well derive from this. She had no mother whose dependable touching, washing, hugging, and overseeing could help her to define her boundaries. So she thinks about Milly, "of course she cant feel anything deep yet I never came properly til I was 22 or so" (1050–1051), as if the two statements relate simply and logically. Even her belief in God has maternal echoes: "for them saying theres no God I wouldnt give a snap of my two fingers for all their learning why don't they go and create something I often asked him atheists or whatever they call themselves" (1563–1566). Create something—the way mothers, she knows, even when not there, can.

"[P]eople were always going away and we never" (668); "I suppose theyre dead long ago . . . its like all through a mist makes you feel so old" (636–637); "were never easy where we are" (677–678). Loss is what she is heir to, what she guards against most, in living memorial to an old injury of soul. However much she accepts or wants the present changes in her life, they reverberate deeply and frighteningly. She has lost Milly now, and Poldy too, not actually or completely, but as she has depended on them being for quite a while. Of the mother for whom she still longs, she knows only a name and that her eyes and figure were like her own. Careful and perhaps ashamed about the mystery of her mother, she did not tell Leopold about it until they were engaged. That fact alone invites speculation. But one thing Molly has believed: that Lunita Laredo either was Jewish or looked Jewish. Thus, Lunita's daughter was ready for Leopold Bloom. She remembers their first meeting vividly:

> he excited me I don't know how the first night ever we met when I was living in Rehoboth terrace we stood staring at one another for about 10 minutes as if we met somewhere I suppose on account of my being jewess looking after my mother. (1181–1185)

Their mutual recognition was mutual transference; "we stood staring . . . as if we met somewhere". From that instant, Poldy fulfilled her abiding wish for a *maternal* person, whatever else she saw and liked in him. And since the blow to them both of Rudy's death, he has "looked after" her: caring, making breakfast, being the butt of her assertiveness, and making no demands for coital completeness. For more than a decade they have maintained a holding environment involving mother and child. Consequently, Molly's desire to leave it now and her new experience of adultery bestir her from core to periphery.

With Molly Bloom, Joyce extended the democracy of his epic interest from Stephen and Leopold to her, and potentially to everyone. Presenting a woman, he made her specific, real, and free—capable of talking to him. So thoroughly did he render her that one can perceive and ponder her and offer a psychoanalytically informed interpretation of her. Molly has an actual situation, inner dynamics, and an internalised past. She exists, a superbly engaging, believable, and sustained illusion of verbal art. About her silence I trust we all agree. She is no more silent than Stephen, Leopold, or anyone in *Ulysses*, because, like them, she is a creature printed in words in a book. A creature of words: she restores the weight of *creature* in that phrase.

Notes

1. Unless otherwise noted, all quotes are from Chapter Eighteen of *Ulysses: The Corrected Text*, H. W. Gabler (Ed.), with W. Steppe & C. Melchior (Random House, 1986), pp. 606–644, and cited by line numbers.

Reference

Ellmann, R. (1982). *James Joyce: New and Revised Edition*. Oxford University Press.

CHAPTER FOURTEEN

The old crone

Elizabeth Haase

An archetype of myth and media, the crone performs characteristic structuring functions across the generational structures of a family that are underexplored in the psychoanalytic literature. For good or ill, confrontation with the ravaged flesh, critical wisdom, and controlling power of the matriarchal figure of the crone forces the hand of those under her influence. Queen, grandmother, dowager, she sets the standards, holds the rules and the traditions of the family, and allows or blocks the emerging sexuality and self-assertion of those beneath her. Either they are buried under her need for admiration and dominion, or she provides the skeletal structure of historical stability, family nurturance, and rituals upon which obligations are organised and roles remain clear. Either the crone deadens and suppresses the vitality of the emerging generation, or she enables them to grow.

The crone is also a description of a woman at a phase of female development, as she embraces the changes in her body and social role engendered by menopause and the emergence of the next generation into their fertile years. If she can accept her losses and imperfect flesh as proof that she is old, she functions as a tool for others' awareness of time, by which they may come to relinquish magical childlike delusions and get on with coping in a real adult world. She can, in her role in family, myth, and society, allow others to separate from excessively depressive states of dependency, self-preoccupation, and stagnation in transitions between life stages. Thus, she becomes the moral structure that cajoles and encourages others: grow up!

Confronted with Erikson's (1984) eighth stage of development, integrity *vs.* despair, the crone must decide, have I been and done enough? Perhaps the answer is no: she must preserve her status as alpha female, maintaining her beauty and maternal role. If so, she will be greedy of attention and deference, dissatisfied, and so undermine the autonomous development of the young women in the familial order. However, if she is satisfied with herself and her accomplishments, she will answer yes, and be content to pass her wisdom on, guiding and pushing them. She will turn instead to holding and reflecting the female ideals of the family in her bickering, critical, and injunctive way, beloved despite it all.

In so doing, the crone becomes a repository for the individual and collective superego function of her community, supporting its ego adaptation over time and providing it with an ongoing approving reflection. Where this wise old superego is not too rigid, its ideals for continued liveliness and achievement not too idealised, its punishments not to harsh, the crone superego becomes the familial structure for drive and reward, maintaining order without oppression when crisis strikes, motivating familial and community accomplishment. When this superego does not deprive by binding too much libido to its ideals and demands, it becomes, like her, the matriarchal inspiration for the female legacy, the spark that ignites their imagining of their own lives.

The crone typology

Who is the crone? Witch, hag, gorgon, sorceress: she is most often identified by physical characteristics that repulse and wound. Her yellowed shark teeth bite and ravenously consume; her sagging teats, colder than winter, provide no nourishment; her matted hair is a tangle of poisonous snakes; her nose a hook; her eyes turn us to stone; her sharp-nailed fingers emit a dangerous curse. Yet, as terrible is her beauty, as difficult and envious is she, she is clearly in charge, respected, capable of managing large kingdoms and executing complex schemes, all the while cackling at her own secret wisdom. She is a crank and a pain, but a lovable one, to whom all are loyal.

The crone is the representation of the post-menopausal female in the eyes of younger women and men. Two myths are presented as example of how this archetype has been conceived in narratives of their development.

In the Hellenistic tradition, the paradigmatic story of the crone and her mid- to late-life relationship with the younger woman is the myth of Demeter and Persephone. The virgin Persephone is abducted by Hades after becoming seduced by a beautiful flower that opens a portal to his underworld of sexuality. Demeter, her middle-aged mother, goddess of the harvest, is grief-stricken at the separation from her daughter. She becomes immobilised in her role, leading to droughts and famines that symbolise the loss of fertility, sexuality, and maternal nurturing capacity associated with the departure, and emerging sexuality, of her child. She becomes falsely excessively old, disguising herself as an old woman, to play the falsely young role of carer, or still-fertile substitute "mother", to a male infant, yet still grieving and refusing food and drink. It is the servant woman and even older crone, Baubo, or Iambe, who saves Demeter from starvation by lifting her skirt and displaying her genitals, this playful sexual act leading Demeter to laugh and take sustenance again. She is able to negotiate successfully with Hades to get Persephone, both daughter and representation of her own ongoing femininity and sexuality, partially back. While Persephone becomes sexually bound to Hades through the ingesting of pomegranate seeds that represent her passage into the adult woman's world of menstruation and egg production, she returns to her mother every spring, a return linked to the Eleusinian mysteries that celebrate the female developmental quest and mother–daughter bond.

The Persephone myth has been considered the central myth of adult female experience, a metaphoric representation of the Triple Goddess of maid, mother, and crone in some interpretations, in others, of the two perhaps most important transitions of a woman's life: leaving home to enter a dangerous world of sexuality and childbearing ability, and confronting the loss of these roles with the empty nest and onset of menopause. Bereft, Demeter's first solution is to assume the roles of both an older and newer mothering figure than she is, a perversion of the ageing process. Her error and grief are righted only by the ongoing sexual reach of Baubo, an even older crone, who restores Demeter's proper and still vital role as intermittent model and support to her young adult daughter.

In the *Kalevala*, the national epic poem of the Finnish peoples, the crone plays her more punitive role as castrating mother of a middle-aged man striving to remain a youthful lover and leader. Similar to other Nordic myths of journeys across the oceans to recover desired treasures, this is the story of numerous warrior suitors who attempt to advance into adulthood by sailing north to take a maiden bride. They are thwarted by Louhi, the shaman matriarch of Pohjola, dark land of the North. Even the shaman leader of the group, a middle-aged king named Väinämöinen, is unsuccessful, the flagging of his phallic power reflected through an episode of the story in which his horse is struck from under him by a younger warrior. After drifting for six days at sea, during which he recreates the world, the king washes ashore, and must promise the crone a fertility object, a Sampo, in exchange for passage home. Instead of making his own Sampo, Väinämöinen sends Ilmarinen, a young and virile smith, to do so. Ilmarinen builds one while simultaneously making love to the crone's maiden daughter, "one foot in a German boot" working, the other "between her thighs". This impressive male display, as in the Persephone myth, restores the harvest, here through the awakening of sexuality in a younger woman rather than the revitalisation of the older woman in the Persephone myth. Still, Ilmarinen returns home without a bride, controlled and defeated by the crone. The story then continues with a long series of unsuccessful suitors, all prevented by the witch mother from establishing their own families. Finally, the king and his warriors wage a vicious battle against her in which the Sampo, its power too deeply embedded in the earth to pull free, is destroyed, even as the Sun and the Moon are pulled down by the wrathful crone rather than allowing the king a legacy. Here, the crone represents the mother who holds too tightly to her phallic power, literally embedded like Arthur's sword, a phallus stuck in the earthy vagina of the maternal homeland. Unable to let go, she destroys the ability of both her offspring and their male suitors to achieve full and separate potency by making their own families. Väinämöinen's journey is described by psychoanalyst Thomas Hägglund (1985) as an adolescent regression to replace his lost childhood after losing the phallic power he had inherited from his parents in which ultimately he leaves no heirs, but only his songs as legacy, an apt representation of the unsuccessful midlife male in Erikson's stage of generativity *vs.* stagnation.

Together, these two myths, variations on which occur across cultures, encompass the good and the ill of the crone, both she who restores vibrancy to the midlife mother and sexual freedom to the daughter, and she who denies fulfilment to the midlife male and new marital couple.

To the grieving mother and virile suitor, the crone is the provider of sexual experience and sexual power, manifest in her children, which will restore and continue life across generations. She is also the provider of wisdom and healing. It is she who has survived the affairs, the uncertainties, the rejections of love. It is she who knows lay remedies and sits by the bedside of the sick child, who has weathered the deaths of children and soul-mates, who has multi-tasked, protected and avenged, negotiated transition, and has gained spiritual and political wisdom from her experience. This is the version of female ageing that is celebrated in croning rituals, in which women shed the mantles of Maiden and Mother and adopt the new role of Elder or Crone at a ceremonial women's coven (Le Guin, 1990).

To the frustrated man and suppressed younger woman, however, the crone is experienced as the maternal need that deadens through her possessiveness and demands, cruelly enslaving them in the Hansel and Gretel roles of subservient little boy and girl. To the man, she is the frightening and taboo aspects of the maternal body that kill sexual liberty: the hungry *vagina dentalis* that will suck in his energy, the proof and oedipal threat that a young sexual wife will become his mother and must be denied to avoid the incest taboo, imperilling the marital bond. To the woman, she is the proof that the influence of her own beauty will fade, the competitor who makes the full love of fathers, suitors, and husband impossible, the critic who denigrates her attempts to establish her own role as a mother and homemaker. It is no wonder the crone is a figure both unwanted and unloved.

The crone as the split mother

These dual functions of the crone are often split into two figures, most easily observable in the fairy tale. Cinderella is abused by her wicked stepmother, but rescued by a fairy godmother; Sleeping Beauty is sentenced to death by Maleficent, but rehabilitated to merely a long sleep by fairy Merryweather. Little Red Riding Hood must feed her beloved grandmother to avoid being consumed by the split-off rage of the same invisible grandmother, literally inside the greedy wolf, who has not been so attended. In some versions of the Persephone myth, too, the good witch, Hecate, goddess of the healing power of medicinal plants, must lead Persephone back from entrapment.

While, traditionally, authors such as Bruno Bettelheim have viewed this duality of crone roles as a split of good and bad representations of the mother protecting the magically good pre-oedipal mother from the punishing mother of oedipal rivalry, most often these split figures are, in some way, invisible, ethereal, or far away, disembodied, one step removed, or far too old to be a mother. The crone is not mother, but stepmother, or "the witch next door"; she is not the age of a mother, but of grandmother or dowager: Madame Armfeldt from Sondheim's *A Little Night Music* (1986) substitutes for her granddaughter Fredrika while actress daughter Desiree is away on tour, and is often found in some odd wrong rooms or secluded garden, cut off from the action. These mothers are family, but not too close for comfort.

Suggestive of a superego function in these split images of the crone is their disembodiment: Old Grandmother Willow advises Walt Disney's Pocahontas by appearing magically inside a local tree; the good witches of the *Wizard of Oz* and *Cinderella* emerge from shimmering balls. Often, the mother is literally dead, and what remains of her to assist her daughter's sexual flourishing is an abstracted bit of nature: a flock of birds frees Cinderella, corn silk liberates Rapunzel, the harvest in the *Kalevala* is restored by a Sampo talisman made of milk, grain, and wool.

The crone as structuring superego

This transformation of maternal function into grandmother and stepmother and then of this crone into the abstracted, mysterious, and advisory role of the older sorceress or magical talisman is part and parcel of how the family crone comes to function as its superego as well. Where she does not meddle but lends her earthy, been-there-done-that wisdom, the crone functions as a healthy superego ideal, the hoped-for self projected into the motivation force of conscience, but realistic enough to accept mistakes. Where she is too removed from them by narcissistic self-involvement or righteous intrusion of her own views, the crone becomes anachronistic and demotivating. Her irrelevant rules and constant dissatisfaction come to function as a superego whose excessive "shoulds" do not lead to effective behaviour, introjected from parents who did not relate empathically to their child's actual needs or generated excess guilt and shame. In this second case, the crone functions intrafamiliarly and intrapsychically like the constant but ineffectual monitor of the poorly structured superego, correcting and admonishing, but failing to provide real guidance for day-to-day challenges. A contrast between two crones who embody such superego types is seen in the television show *Downton Abbey* in the lower status Mrs Crawley, mother-in-law to the heiress, and dowager Countess Violet. The dowager is stubborn, certain, highbrow, and well bred, like a too uptight superego. Her attempts to influence her family to follow traditional social etiquette are only effective when she is present and her tyranny impossible to ignore, or when she softens her precepts to hold the family together in times of crisis. Standing in contrast is Mrs Crawley, who, through attending to the wishes and moral strivings of the young heiresses, inspires one to become a nurse and the other to find an unusual but appropriate love after years of spinsterhood. Hers is a morality that transforms rather than controls.

The crone in crisis

For the crone, however, the central conflict is her relationship with herself, not others, as she loses romantic and sexual attention and the often coincident waning of need-based attention from her children.

The responses of the crone to her crisis can be segregated into two major types. In one category are those older women who have fallen into a depression over losses and are frozen in time, looking back, or spending their energies trying to retrieve what is already gone. The biblical character of Lot's wife is fixed as a pillar of salt because she looks back at her old town. While no reason is given for her disobedience to the biblical command for which she is punished, theologians have speculated that she is looking back for her lost married daughters, who did not leave with the family, or that she is unable to lose the material comforts associated with the iniquities of Sodom. Demeter falls into a depression from the loss of her daughter, immobilised as well.

In the second category is the crone who rages, equally unable to lose the roles of maiden, lover, wife, mother, and queen imposed by the ascendance of the new generation. Snow White's evil queen will kill her rather than give up her role as fairest maiden in the land. In Walt Disney's *Little Mermaid*, sea witch Ursula uses Ariel's voice against her to retain her own seductiveness and keep Ariel from winning her prince. Rapunzel's witch holds her in a tower to avoid relinquishing her role as protective mother. Maleficent of Sleeping Beauty transforms into an enormous dragon rather than let Aurora out of a position of sleeping little girl subservience and have her role as powerful queen replaced.

Just as the physical risks of childbirth can enhance her early awareness of mortality, the crone faces again the experience that perhaps she is done: irrelevant and unnecessary. At the heart of every angry old hag is a Medusa, so angry at her lost beauty that her despair literally turns its witnesses to stone until, through some alleviation of her psychic pain, represented in the Medusa story by a literal decapitation from which a sword-bearing giant and winged horse emerge, she finds new power and takes flight again.

Many of the characters who challenge the crone must leave hearth and home and enter a space of profound danger. Similarly, the crone herself is in a place of great darkness. Stephen Sondheim's characters in *Into the Woods*, like Snow White and other fairy tale heroines, go deep into a psychic forest, where size is distorted by dwarfs and giants, round fruit poisons, cow's teats dry up, stomachs are ripped open, toes cut off, eyes plucked out, phallic wands made half their length. It is as if they share with the crone the loss of her plump protuberances and height, a despairing reversal of the changes of size and shape she endured with pubescence and impregnation. If they do not die, fairy tale heroes and heroines who encounter the crone come dangerously close, poisoned, pricked, and zapped by her curses, often teetering on a literal precipice. The crone teeters there, too, on the brink of death and despair.

The crone as guide through transition

The crone is, thus, both co-traveller and villain of the voyager's most difficult passageway. She provides the magic potion that saves, but she seeks the total control of a curse or the literal destruction of those attempting their own transition. As conceived by Nancy Ann Parker (2011), she is "a regeneratrix who initiates change through death-like experiences. She is a mode of consciousness that values endings and completions" (pp. iii–iv). The crone destroys to create again, an embodiment of natural and creative cycles. Unlike the male, whose power comes from triumph over nature and weakness, the crone's death-inducing curses move us through death to something new. Persephone is kidnapped to the Underworld; Väinämöinen drifts on a dark sea, both near death.

Both in myth and in psychoanalytic understanding, transitional phases are conceived as places of absence, confusion, and resultant magic. For Donald Winnicott (1953), creative illusion was used to gain knowledge of the unknown in the child's play. For Jacques Lacan, the missing other causes desire, and the incompleteness of linguistic and psychic structure facilitates creativity (Rowland, 2014). Carl Jung, based on his own mid-life experience, called the crises of the croning years a metanoia, a word combining meta, "great change" and nous, "higher consciousness". Jung derived this word from the Gnostic myth of Nous. In it, Nous is a spark of the divine that breaks free from the heavens. He sees his own reflection in the dark chaos of real matter below in the form of Physis, the essence of matter, and they join, bringing about new creation (Prétat, 1994, pp. 13–14).

Jungian analyst Murray Stein (2014) has also explored the dangerously mad, exaggerated world of the midlife passage:

> The midlife crisis typically brings about the astonishing recognition of our own hidden-away madness. Midlife crisis turns persons inside out and tears up their crafted worlds (p.1)

> . . . [In a] dark night of psychological crisis, when the light of day is eclipsed, the figures of the psyche stand out and assume another magnitude. Dreams can strike like thunderbolts and leave you shaken to the core. The prevailing feeling is one of alienation, marginality, drift. (p. 8)

> ... To do this thoroughly and decisively, the person needs to "find the
> corpse" and then to bury it: to identify the source of pain and then to
> put the past to rest by grieving, mourning . . . (p. 27)

The crone in crisis puffs herself up with magical solutions and self-delusion, and her psychosis draws the others around her into its curse. Her particular matriarchal myth comes to dominate the family's behaviour. Then what is not magically hers but already a corpse, taken by time, becomes recognised as such. The crisis in the crone story is resolved when she is shaken from her delusion; the magical object loses its power, becoming again part of nature: the wand becomes a stick, the witch melts in water, the coach turns back to a pumpkin, the Sampo breaks, the flash of Baubo's genitals reminds us what is still alive and what is not. Stein (2014) continues, "Persona is mere persona, only a hollow mask full of lies and preposterous posturing, to be ridiculed and mocked, as the soul looks out from its position of submersion in the depths of liminal experience" (p. 55).

With the breaking of her powers, the witch of *Into the Woods* (Sondheim, 1986) articulates this accepting disgruntled regret that there will be no magical solution and one's ideals will always be slightly unfulfilled, saying to the other characters with great disappointment: "You're so nice. / You're not good, / You're not bad, / You're just nice . . . / Give me claws and a hunch, / Just away from this bunch".

Of course, the crone also exists in the minds of the younger generation. As such, their telling of her story reflects their own fantasies about her, and the stories of her control and their resistance fantasies about themselves. A separation–individuation paradigm and developmental fantasies are often implicit in the transitional battle with the crone, one in which the repeated theme is of losing power to her temporarily in order to wrest it back and become truly independent. Why? Through fusion or submission to the crone, the younger hero or heroine gains narcissistic supplies; for some, this is a parturition fantasy: gaining what grows in the mother's body. For others, it is a fantasy of independence, through the battle becoming as powerful as she. For others, the submersion into her identity is a defence against smallness, a narcissistic identification with the magical gleam in the adoring mother's ideas (Hägglund, 1985). Writes Swan (1975), following Holland, the hero has a kind of death-and-rebirth through magic: a submerging of his self (from a "bridge") into an underworld of matriarchal magic, then a disillusioning re-emergence into rationality and the real world at the end. He acts out again [an early, infantile stage of] oral fusion followed by an infant's discovery of his own [separate] identity. (p. 7)

For the clinician, the patient's use of a crone, besides its implications for transference, can be mined for these underlying fantasies about independence, achievement, and creative power and for the impact of the maternal relationship on her superego. Second, the crone can be seen as a projection for the hopes and fears of both male and female patients about female bodies—their mother's, their own, their partners. Finally, the difficulties posed by the crone can be seen as the patient's representation of deficits in herself, what she is up against in herself and her current developmental struggles as exaggerated by the transitional phase of the treatment.

This passage back from the creative world of the transition and the superego ideal to the ordinary is part of a fuller humanity for both the crone and her younger co-travellers. It represents the resolution of narcissistic preoccupation into every day self love, the overcoming of the shameful indignities of both dependency and the ageing body with self-acceptance. In it, the magical reunites with the real, the divine with the mundane, the awake vitality of life with the death of sleep, and time is transcended.

Dedication

To my mother-in-law, Helen Meyers, my favourite old crone in the best sense, who sometimes worked magic and always held tight.

References

Erikson, E. H. (1984). Reflections on the last stage—and the first. *Psychoanalytic Study of the Child, 39*: 155–165.

Hägglund, T. (1985). The forging of the Sampo and its capture: the Oedipus complex of adolescence in Finnish folklore. *Scandiavian Psychoanalytic Review, 8*: 159–180.

Le Guin, U. (1990). The space crone. In: R. Formanek (Ed.), *The Meanings of Menopause: Historical Medical and Clinical Perspectives* (pp. xxi–xxv). Hillsdale, NJ: Analytic Press.

Parker, N. (2011). The mythical and mortal crone, recollecting and reclaiming the sacred generatrix. *Dissertation Abstracts International, Humanities and Social Sciences, 72*(5-A).

Prétat, J. R. (1994). *Coming to Age: The Croning Years and Late-Life Transformation*. Toronto: Inner City Books.

Rowland, S. (2014). Crumpled or purloined? The sublime and feminine creativity in destruction in Jung and Lacan. Unpublished paper presented to "The Notion of the Sublime", New York, 13 September.

Sondheim, S. (1986). *Into the Woods*. New York: Theater Communications Group/Crown.

Stein, M. (2014). *In Midlife: A Jungian Perspective*. Woodstock, CT: Chiron.

Swan, J. (1975). Giving new depth to the surface: psychoanalysis, literature, and society. *Psychoanalytic Review, 62*: 5–28.

Winnicott, D. W. (1953). Transitional objects and transitional phenomena: a study of the first not-me possession. *International Journal of Psychoanalysis, 34*: 89–97.

CHAPTER FIFTEEN

Contributions Part IV: implications for psychoanalytic psychotherapy

Arlene Kramer Richards and Lucille Spira

T his section moves the discussion of myths and psychoanalytic psychotherapy as it focuses on a woman character as she embraces her sexuality and a folk tale with mythic-like characters. Issues about marital relationships, self-relations, love, ageing, and the power of a woman's body are prominent themes.

Molly Bloom

What has the character of mighty Molly Bloom to tell us about psychoanalytic therapy? She thinks as a mature woman, a woman of thirty-five who has a teenage daughter and has lost a baby son. She is a mourner who has spent ten years avoiding mourning. Her never completed mourning prevented her from allowing herself sexual intercourse for all of those years. Her fear of mourning prevents her, as Dr Schwaber so persuasively shows us, from allowing herself to conceive another child who might die as her son did. Dr Schwaber shows us that she hates menstruating. The thought that the menses is "pooh" connects it with death. Faeces is "pooh" and faeces is death. Her hatred of "bottoms" is hatred of connection to faeces and death.

A woman who cannot bear the thought of death destroys the possibility of creating life. She cannot tolerate those atheists who cannot create. She refuses to create. She hates that in herself.

This hatred of the non-creative is something we struggle with especially in women patients who refuse to bear children, whether they are already mothers of as many children as they think they can take care of, or whether they are women who have no children and do not want to undertake taking care of them. For many women, this is a sensible choice. For some, it provokes guilt and/or shame. Ambivalence might lead to conception and abortion; sometimes, repeatedly, the woman tries to work out her competing impulses to create and to protect herself from the loss of what she creates. Working with such women, the therapist needs to be careful not to be on the side of maternity or the side of refusal of maternity, but the therapy involves considering the aetiology of each choice, the possibility that it might be connected to unmourned loss, and the consequent fear of repetition of the loss.

This line of thinking contrasts with the Freudian idea that femininity depends on motherhood as a substitute for the penis. It devolves from the idea that to be female is to have the pride and pleasure in her own genital that Molly Bloom recalls having before her loss of her baby. For women who have had abortions, like women who have lost babies, part of the work of analytic therapy is the mourning of the loss of their creation.

The old crone

The old crone is a concept that can calm: the no longer sexually enticing or demanding woman can be seen as a grandmother figure, soothing, nurturing, and undemanding. The therapist who is herself an old crone can be that soothing figure. However, the reverse is that the old crone also can be the envious one who wants what she no longer has and destroys anyone who has the beauty and fertility of youth. The therapist can, through her awareness of this double nature of the patient's vision of her, enable the patient to talk about the less socially acceptable side of the patient's view of her and her own vision of herself. Seeing herself as an old crone can be painful for the clinician who, as a human being, wants to see herself as benign, and as a professional wants to help the patient rather than destroy her with envy.

The clinical implications of the old crone are three:

1.   When treating a woman of middle age or older, the idea of age as ugly needs to be addressed.
2.   The older woman needs to know that age is seen as power and is therefore frightening.
3.   The diminishment of physical and mental powers needs to be talked about.

All of these are matters for discussion. Will the patient bring them up directly? Not usually, but the prepared mind of the clinician will see the possibility of bringing each of these aspects of the ageing woman into focus as a corollary of feelings of envy, fear of being envied, guilt, and shame, as well as disappointment, rage, and other negative affects.

PART V

THE FATHER'S CONTRIBUTION
TO WOMEN'S POWER

CHAPTER SIXTEEN

Athena, Antigone, and their modern avatars

John Munder Ross

Introduction

Karen Horney was perhaps the first mighty woman to challenge the Sphinx—in her case, the Egyptian half-male prototype of Greece's half-woman in the person of Freud—and was herself a "[wo]man most mighty". Horney turned Freud's phallocentric theory of gender differences in sexual identity development on its head (see Freud, 1923e, 1924c,d, 1925j). Woody Allen was not alone, Horney implied: all little boys have "penis envy"—indeed more so than their sisters. Confronted by the engulfing vagina and womb of The Great Mother, they feel inadequate to the job, daunted and narcissistically wounded (Horney, 1924, 1926, 1932, 1933).

The misogyny of the male gender—the notorious misogyny in Freud's theory—is a defensive strategy in which boys and the men they become try to diminish and contain women in order to feel better about themselves. Furthermore, an adult woman's penis envy as opposed to a pre-oedipal girl's is, as Jones suggested (1948), largely a cultural artefact of the male chauvinism and patriarchy that prevailed at the turn of the century, when women were deprived of an education, and what today's feminists call a "voice" and "the phallus".

In fact, it is the girl who typically lingers in the positive oedipal position, from which the boy flees for a host of developmental reasons. Yes, to an extent these have to do with a fear of castration at the father's hands, in which Hans Loewald (1952) long ago saw an ingenious strategic retreat from the threat posed to an ever fragile masculinity and individuation by the omnipotent and enveloping mother of his earliest years. In contrast to their male counterparts, girls have nothing to lose in the way of femininity and self-identity in loving their fathers (Ross, 1990).

Freud, who believed the clitoris to be an "inferior organ" and a "poor substitute for the penis", might himself have told a woman guest in the film *Manhattan* that though she had "finally had an orgasm . . . it was the wrong kind". But what did he know? Unlike Horney—who also defied gender stereotypes in her personal conduct—Freud was a sexual *naïf*. Four decades after he laid out his speculations about male and female sexuality, Masters and Johnson (1966) would use first-hand observational data to prove Freud wrong and Tereisias right: a woman's libidinal capacity is far greater than any mere man could begin to fathom.

The ancient seer Tereisias learnt this the hard way, as a transitorily transgendered woman who was then blinded by the gods for this dangerous insight. Nabokov (1966) to the contrary, I guess that "old Greek myths" applied to one's "private parts" do have something to say about desire. But I shall stop there. I shall not be talking about sexuality any more—not in the concrete sense at least—but, rather, about imagination, power, and creativity.

In point of fact, Oedipus's story, an interlude that has more to do with intergenerational power struggles and aggression than libidinal desire, is a relatively minor story in Greek mythology compared to the depictions of Olympian fathers and sons—notably the story of Zeus's emasculation of Kronos, in which his mother Rhea plays a critical role. And what about array of other mortal family dramas in which mothers also have a crucial part to play? In this vein, consider Agave's decapitation of her son Pentheus in the city of Thebes, which was founded by her father, Cadmus, long before his descendents— Oedipus, Laius, and Jocasta—came into being.

With this panorama in mind, in considering the many mighty women that people this mythology as well as other polytheistic religions, we are calling into question not only the one-person, but also the one-myth and one-complex psychoanalysis of the past century. The Oedipus complex was, as Freud put it, the "Shibboleth" that defined psychoanalysis itself (Freud, 1905d) and in so doing contributed to the undeniable decline of our discipline and practice in this millennium. A consideration of the goddesses and mortal women in this collection has a great deal to tell us about both the inner life of women and the ways in which men perceive them, and, thus, pays tribute to the "infinite variety" of individuals who seek our counsel. Thus, a foray of this kind into applied psychoanalysis proves more than applicable to the contemporary clinical situation.

In a similar vein, an interdisciplinary caveat: whether or not unconscious fantasies about omnipotent women and the mythologies that reflect these translate into real power in social relations is moot. Jim Sidanius, Professor of Social Psychology and African American Studies at Harvard, regrettably thinks not. I shall return in closing to his cogent if pessimistic social dominance theory (Sidanius & Pratto, 1999). Melding cognitive psychological and sociological perspectives, and after exhaustive empirical research, the authors emphasise the tenacity of a hierarchy in gender relations as in racism and other forms of discrimination and oppression. For starters though, with the caveat that this is not the whole elephant, let us do what we analysts do best—home in on individual women as well as their archetypes.

Her father's daughter

Some time ago, my twelve-year-old daughter and I were having lunch with my friend from college, Honor Moore, who has been, among other things, a pioneer feminist. My daughter attends an all-girls private school here in New York, whose avowed mission it is to "empower" young women to have those "voices" of their own. However, that day, preparing to go to a co-ed summer camp, she said that she was tired of hearing about "Women, women, women."

To this lament Honor replied with the grace of a Boston Brahmin by birth, "Well dear, you weren't there with us and so you don't understand what we had to do to get you where you are today."

However, having been "there" with her, I could. When we arrived in Cambridge in 1963, Matina Horner, celebrated for her research on how girls defer to boys in co-educational academic settings (e.g., Horner, 1972), had just assumed the Presidency of Radcliffe College, which was then a separate entity. The 1600 students in her college were a more select group than the 4,800 Harvard undergraduates, and their braininess showed. None the less, they were still called "Cliffies" in the 1960s and catered Geisha-like to their male counterparts, sometimes even sorting our laundry and typing our term papers.

Radcliffe women were further subjected to all sorts of ignominious insults by the institution itself, ranging from exclusion from Lamont Library to downright sexual harassment by teachers. Thus, in our twenty-fifth reunion book in 1992, the renowned psychoanalyst and sexologist Jenny Downey, who was then my rather shy fellow student in a Freshman writing class, wrote about how our seemingly prissy instructor, who was Lamont's Chief Librarian, came on to her. When she shot him down, he lowered her grade from an A to a C—something none us knew about at the time.

Vindicating themselves, the women in the Class of 1967 took over that reunion programme, marginalising most of their male classmates while reminding us of what they had endured. In the era before Marjorie Garber became Harvard University's pre-eminent Shakespeare scholar, Elena Kagan its Law School Dean, and the scholarly Drew Gilpin Faust its first woman President (perhaps with exceptions that I myself cannot recall), the senior faculty, who were well-served by brilliant but often doting female section leaders, were overwhelmingly male.

As its President, Honor would assume the leadership of the Harvard Dramatic Club at a time when undergraduates actually ran the Loeb Theater. Even so, rather than as an artist in her own right, Honor defined her place at the Loeb mostly in her capacity as a producer, serving the vision of male directors and applauding their actors. Indeed, while I can remember some riveting actresses who later rose to fame, not a single woman director comes to mind. Only years later, concurrent with the merger of Harvard and Radcliffe as one college with absolute gender parity, would Honor herself also come fully into her own as a brilliant memoirist, poet, playwright, and sought-after instructor in these arts.

In her controversial memoir, *The Bishop's Daughter* (Moore, 2008), she described a lifelong struggle to free herself from her longing to please her distant father, Paul Moore—Episcopal Archbishop of New York, hero of Guadalcanal, inspirational Civil Rights activist, father of

nine (Honor was the first), and closeted gay man. The book is a courageous confessional in which the author relates not only the intricacies
of this publicly great man's double life—reminiscent of so many other
mighty men—but also the vicissitudes of her unconscious identification with her father's disavowed homosexuality. Freed in her artistic
life to find and proclaim her own aesthetic vision, none the less Honor
retreated from relations with men and, while she truly and dearly
loved her lovers, assumed what in the end was a pseudo-homosexual
identity.

Like a self-analysis, writing the memoir brought her back to her
true self. In this she does not decry having been a lesbian, but simply
demonstrates that this orientation was not her own. Needless to say,
the book sent shock waves through the Episcopal dioceses at a time
when this and other churches found themselves sorely challenged—
as does psychoanalysis today for not dissimilar reasons.

Merger and over-identification with, and surrender of the self to,
the powerful and potentially empowering father—these shared male
and female fantasies have represented the primary routes to influence
and ascendance for women since Apollo stole the oracle and the realm
from Gaia.

Athena, Antigone, and Elektra

I am by no means a classicist. However, when asked to contribute to
this volume, the epic journeys of two such mythic personae—the one
an Olympian, the other the daughter of psychoanalysis's favourite
hero—came immediately to mind as allegories for a woman's empowerment in a man's world. Consider two icons devoted to ensuring
their fathers' legacy: wise Athena, born from the head of Zeus, and the
heroic Antigone, Oedipus's self-sacrificing and noble daughter
(Graves, 1955; Matyszak, 2010; Sophocles, 1977)

I shall explore the reciprocal male and female fantasies embedded
in the narratives about them—including the "myth of the birth of the
heroine", to paraphrase Otto Rank (2010)—as well as their modern
day and real life avatar in psychoanalysis's very own Miss Anna
Freud. Next, I shall consider the apparent revival in the twenty-first
century of the dominion of Mother Earth—that is, of courageous
women who appear to be powerful, dominant, and creative in their

own right. And I shall briefly illustrate the impact on women patients of these emerging "paradigm shifts" in the clinical situation.

I should add at the outset that I am guided by the sweeping world-view of Erik Erikson, with whom I began my journey back into psychoanalysis. That is, by his emphasis on what he called "historical actuality" (Erikson, 1964) in both the "growth and crises of the healthy personality" (Erikson, 1950) of the individual and the evolution of culture and society.

Wise Athena, born from the head of Zeus—fully formed, fully armed, and very wise! And a "divergent" versed in so many divine arts. What a gratifying ambisexual, parthogenetic conception in the creation of the most sagacious and honourable of the Olympians.

"But not to worry, gentlemen, she owes it all to Daddy!"

Of course, it is not really that simple, as a classical scholar would be quick to point out. As with real life individuals, the transmission of unique life historical and intergenerational patterns of relatedness, as well as traumas, endows a baby in the womb and cradle with what Spitz reminded us is the parents' conflict-laden past.

For example, in one variant of Athena's conception, Zeus had a Laius-like fear of the progeny of his paramour, Metis. No wonder he was nervous, given what his mother Rhea had incited him to do to his father Kronos, who earlier on had himself castrated his father, Uranus. Fearful of a similar demise, Zeus swallowed Metis, suffering labour pains in the form of a horrible migraine before his daughter burst from his brow. Inherent in this, of course, is a boy and man's envy of a mother's childbearing powers, which I myself happened to research and write about four decades ago (Ross, 1975, 1977, 1994). I shall let that pass for the moment and focus here on the phallocentric illusion that a powerful woman owes her very existence to a man, specifically her father.

Thus endowed with a masculine basic core, Athena was able in turn to either best or mentor a whole lot of males: beating her uncle Poseidon in their competition for what became her City State of Athens; outsmarting her impetuous and pugnacious half-brother Ares in, of all things, warfare; wisely guiding an already wily Odysseus in his circuitous journey back from Troy to Ithaca; and many more. No god or goddess—except perhaps for her father—was a match for Athena, much less any mere mortal, to which the miserable fate of Arachne attests.

Within the mortal sphere, we have Antigone as the exemplar of
nobility by virtue of self-abnegation and devotion to her father and his
legacy. In Sophocles' trilogy, she tends to the old and blind Oedipus
in a sequence of images that reverses the course of the universal
human life cycle as depicted in the Riddle of the Sphinx. We analysts
all remember it, of course: Yes, most men walk on four legs in the
morning (as crawling infants), two in the afternoon (adults in their
prime), and three in the evening (old men with walking sticks). But
not Oedipus, it seems, whose feet were pierced with a spike when he
was abandoned as a baby so that, effectively, he crawled on three
limbs, who stood tall as the Theban king in his prime, and who
required the eyes and, therefore, the two legs of his devoted Antigone
when he ended his life as a sightless wanderer in his old age, peram-
bulating on four feet. In this instance, unlike Zeus and Athena, father
and daughter do not begin, but, rather, conclude, their life's journey
in a state of union or merger.

Mortal that she is, Antigone does not succeed in defying and surviving the rule of men after Oedipus's death. Attempting to bury her
brother against her uncle Creon's decree, she is jailed by her maternal
uncle, whereupon she hangs herself. Creon's son, Haemon, also kills
himself when he discovers his dead fiancée. I suppose that this terrible *dénouement* attests to a certain power over men in Antigone's
martyrdom. But all that is another story.

I might have discussed Elektra, especially given Freud's well-
known repudiation of the notion of an "Elektra complex". However,
famous and poignant as this persona may be, I still do not see her as
all that mighty, counting as she does on her brother Orestes to do the
deed.

Miss Freud

What better example can one find of the Athena/Antigone complex
or—if you prefer—*motif* than our very own Anna Freud? When I
trained in the late 1970s at the downstate NYU Institute, Miss Freud
was venerated as a sort of latter day Sybil, or, better, a Delphic priestess of the Freudian oracle. I remember her holding forth seamlessly in
her signature interminable skirts and sensible shoes, after which a
coterie of overawed male child analysts, ascending the stage, would

virtually genuflect before her. The "Miss" in Miss Freud is important here, suggesting that she was an avatar of Parthenos Athena— "Parthenos" meaning virgin. And this, I would venture, as a possible counterpoint to the divorced Mrs Klein, her co-pioneer and rival in child analysis.

A bit of biography: Anna seems to have been an afterthought as a child. According to some, the Irma dream expresses Freud's frustration that his wife Martha refused to open her mouth and perform fellatio on him as a form of birth control after his sixth child's birth. Growing up, Anna felt spurned by her father in favour of her more beautiful sister, the ill-fated Sophie. Further troubled in her adolescence by disturbing daydreams and sadomasochistic masturbation fantasies, she was depressed, possibly anorexic, and isolated as a teenager. Indeed, so severe was her mental state that it required sanitorium stays and other remedies reminiscent of her father's pre-psychoanalytic interventions with his caseload of hysterical women (Menaker, 1989, Young-Bruehl, 1994).

From an early age, Anna sought Freud's attention as the "brains" among the six siblings, ultimately sacrificing her sexual being in her devotion to him. (Much as Honor had.) She said that Sigmund Freud's library and person provided a version of a "university" for his youngest daughter. Like most young women of her ilk and era, Anna attended not a gymnasium but a lyceum, never progressing to a formal higher education, whereas most of the women in Freud's inner circle were both highly educated and worldly. And as Freud himself put it, with her ministering to him in his losing battle with the oral cancer that plagued him for the last sixteen years of his life, Anna was anointed as "the Antigone of [his] old age".

As a young adult, Anna continued to recoil from sexual yearnings that were fraught with perversity and conflict. Thus, according to her gay biographer, Young-Bruehl, she might not even have consummated her lifelong relationship with Dorothy Burlingham. Frustrated, she seems to have been "dyspeptic" and moody. Her nephew, Lucian Freud, who loved his grandfather, could abide neither his aunt's "unpleasantness" nor the lack of mirth in Maresfield Gardens, which he abjured once Sigmund Freud had died (also Blos, personal communication).

Living the life of an old-fashioned spinster, none the less Anna progressed professionally. With her father's belated blessing, at the age of thirty and having presented her own analysis in disguise to qualify for admission to the Vienna Psychoanalytic Society, his daughter assumed the helm of the organisation. Soon enough Anna became psychoanalysis's expert on her father's "ego" and on her very own "mechanisms of defence". After Freud died, the childless Miss Freud became a veritable authority on "normality and pathology in childhood".

The stark clarity of her contributions—whether or not on a creative par with those of Margaret Mahler, Horney, or Klein—is undeniable. And yet, one can only imagine her fate in the world had she not been Sigmund Freud's legacy.

So, Anna fits the bill. Born from the head of Zeus and sacrificing herself in the mode of an Antigone, imbued with Freud's aura in the eyes of his, and subsequently her, acolytes, she proceeded to set herself up as the counsellor for future generations of psychoanalysts.

Well, this was true as long as they did not betray her or her father. She never did forgive Erik Erikson for leaving her couch to marry Joan and emigrating to the USA or, later on, for his adulteration of Freud's "pure gold" in his appreciation of the impact of society, culture, and history in the construction of "identity" (Friedman, 1999). Without her imprimatur, Erikson would find his ground-breaking contributions during the 1950s and 1960s—which I believe to have been equalled only by those of Margaret Mahler at roughly the same time—woefully absent in the curriculum of our institutes, even to this day, when these centres have begun to wither on the vine. As some who knew her have remarked, the more parochial Miss Freud was in no way as cultivated as her erudite and passionate father or her truly cosmopolitan analysand (Blum, personal communication).

Although only a few have run its institutions, other innovative women did become intellectual and organisational forces in psychoanalysis: Horney, Klein, Mahler, as I have already noted, along with Phyllis Greenacre, Hannah Segal, Betty Joseph, Ethel Person, Helen Meyers, and many more. Indeed, as a profession, for many years we were ahead of the game when it came to both *de facto* gender parity in our ranks and the freedom of particularly brilliant women to declare themselves.

What distinguished Anna Freud was her insemination by the originator of psychoanalysis and her steadfastness as the keeper of the Freudian flame. Her status as a "brainchild" in the flesh and as a latter-day Vestal Virgin suffused her with an almost mystical aura—

even for those fundamentalist atheist analysts who had long ago consciously repudiated religiosity and cultism.

Another anecdote from another distinguished woman classmate of mine, this one from Nancy Wexler, who later discovered the gene for Huntington's disease. The daughter of child analyst Milton Wexler and in appearance very much "a California girl", Nancy spent a post-graduate fellowship year from 1967 to 1968 at what was then the Hampstead Clinic. Impressed though she might have been by the clinical gifts of Milton's daughter—Wexler senior had studied with her—none the less Miss Freud often chastised Nancy regarding the length of her miniskirts, which were then very much in fashion, especially in London. At the close of their final meeting that year, with Nancy about to embark for the USA and ultimately a whole new career outside her precincts, Miss Freud made a tell-tale Freudian slip. Anna smiled warmly and nostalgically as she said goodbye to Nancy with these words, "Remember me to . . . *my* father."

Women and men in the secular world: transition and conflict

At just about the same time, I embarked on my own travelling fellowship and tried my hand at reading anthropology at the London School of Economics. That peripatetic year brought me face to face with the roiling emotions and contrasting conditions of women around the world.

I spent three months in India staying with my friend, and perhaps Erik's most prized *protégé* and future Goethe medallist, Sudhir Kakar, in the Corbusier-designed compound in Ahmedabad of his aunt Kamla, a Ford Foundation Director and future cabinet minister. Kamla Chowdri had been widowed early on when an embittered ex-convict murdered her magistrate husband, after which she became the most independent of women, professionally and romantically.

When Sudhir and I were not taking on Malinowski in his strident challenge to Freud and searching through the autobiographies of his students for evidence the universality of the Oedipus complex, even among the matrilineal Nayars of Kerala, we would spend our evenings discussing, over contraband cocktails, world events with Kamla, who was herself a force of nature, and her politically prominent guests. Indira Gandhi, Jawahartal Nehru's only child and, thus, his

anointed heir, had just become Prime Minister and soon enough—
during the Emergency—would be wielding absolute power greater
than that of Nehru himself

"The times—they [were] a-a-changing" in this, the Third World.
Talk about mighty women! None the less, Indira Gandhi, who would
leave her own legacy and dynasty, had been propelled to power
initially by virtue of her parentage. She was both a pioneer and a transitional figure.

Fighting off four parasites that had devoured forty of my pounds, I
returned from this developing nation to London and the already developed western world in the autumn *en route* back to the USA. Two
nights after my flight back, I found myself erupting in sweat and
nearly febrile at the surreal dinner to which my father and stepmother
invited me with the now notorious *fakir*, Masud Khan, and his wife,
Svetlana Beriosova, *prima ballerina* and second only to Dame Margot
Fonteyn at the Royal Ballet. As Khan held forth while heating his
brandy snifter with a Zippo lighter, this great *danseuse*, whom I had
seen partner with Nureyev the previous spring, seemed to become
almost concave. Hunched over, Svetlana, who was far more famous
than her infamous husband, disappeared into herself. Just like the brilliant girls in Horner's studies, I reflected, who twirled and munched
on their hair and batted their eyelashes when the boys spoke up.

Such was Khan perhaps: character is character. But, then again, so
was the stature of most other women in what was still a man's world.
The 1960s had only begun to see the emergence of the second feminist
wave, Simone de Beauvoir, her name linked inextricably to Jean Paul
Sartre, having spearheaded it. Betty Friedan's *The Feminine Mystique*
served as its new manifesto, followed by the works of Germaine
Greer, Gloria Steinem, and others. Ordinary women were just beginning to enter the workforce for real, though their status and remuner-
ation would only approach a par with those of men when economic
exigencies were such that dual income families became the norm.

Women on the couch

Coexisting and contrasting with this new consciousness was the
womanhood embodied by Beriosova that night in Mayfair. Despite
the women in their midst, psychoanalysts were perhaps the slowest to

move forward in their thinking. With the stamp of approval of a woman, Helene Deutsch, and fearful of Medusas and "the phallic woman", analysts still clung to their unsubstantiated notions of penis envy and to their misunderstanding of Freud's "feminine masochism". In his initial formulation, Freud had meant by this construction a male fantasy of what it meant to be a woman, and not an actual female characteristic (Freud, 1924c,d). Analysts discouraged women in their professional ambitions, interpreting these as futile efforts to be what women were not—men with penises. In effect, they discouraged their patients from entering the work force, enjoining them to remain "stay-at-home mums".

At that time, our patients complied. I do not know about others, but well into the 1980s my caseload consisted mostly of women. In those days, female patients of mine said that they had sought out my services because, as one of them put it, "Dr Ross, I don't know what it is, but as a man you have a certain 'something' a woman does not."

As this woman's analysis progressed, we analysed what Jones called her "deutoro" or secondary penis envy (Jones, 1948), or, better, the sense that in the political sphere men possessed the "phallus", embodied in something similar to what the Hindus deify as Vishnu's "lingam", an image that, in fact, often alternates with bisexual renderings of this deity. The socio-cultural oppression of women from Freud's era into much of the next century fixated or perpetuated the inevitable wish to "be both sexes", as Kubie put it (1974), with the attributes thereof—especially among the subjugated second sex. Ms X went on to elaborate her fantasy of merging with me—my "mind" in particular—and being reborn. Hence, her "Athena complex".

Not so today. Coinciding with the feminisation of so many fields—notably, medicine—and, thus, starting in the 1990s, women have tended to seek out women when it comes to health care providers, especially obstetricians and gynaecologists and psychotherapists. Thus, at present, yours truly—a purported man *maven*—now has far more men than women in his practice.

And most of these men have a tale to tell.

Female aggression towards males: an epidemic?

It might be that the women who inundated my practice towards the end of the previous millennium failed to report it adequately because of their shame and guilt and need to please me, a male practitioner. However, in the past ten or fifteen years, the men who have occupied my couch and chairs have described—almost to a man—what appears to be a veritable epidemic of female aggression coming at them from their wives and life partners. This seems true no matter what the couple's particular demographics—whether the woman works on a par with the husband or is a frustrated "housewife". Neither does the husband's professional success seem to me to be a significant variable in this regard.

As we now know, denied a chance to succeed in her own right as a gifted violist, "Little Hans's" mother, Olga Hoenig Graf, had assaulted and tortured her husband along with her children 100 years earlier (Ross, 2007). Yet, impressionistically, I cannot help feeling that what I have been witnessing, beginning with this latest *fin de siècle*, is a phenomenon specific to our epoch and *Zeitgeist*.

The big thaw following the big chill, I speculate, might have to do with women's waking up and feeling pain and attendant rage after aeons of oppression. With what amounts to a consensual "license to kill", they are no longer taking it out only on the children, but directly on what they perceive as males who are, by definition, slave masters. No matter that the husband might actually be a "nice chap" or even a "new man", he serves as a stand-in—a collective transference figure—for all the Torvals and far worse who ever were. Women want that phallus at last and so now see men's paltry penises as signifiers of weakness, selfishness, or sheer stupidity.

The future: social dominance and gender

Erikson once remarked to his devoted head section leader, Pamela Daniels (who, once he retired, would become Dean of Students at Wellesley), that if women ran the world, there would be fewer wars. From the aggression that I have just remarked on, this might seem unlikely. Yet, who knows? Indeed, I wonder whether once women's frustration has dissipated and their individuation completed in such a way that they need not employ anger to declare their boundaries and selves, if they will then feel free to tap into their natural nurturance and generativity in leading us.

None the less, the question remains as to whether Gaia will ever be able to reclaim her oracle from Apollo and rule the world of real-life people. According to Sidanius, like it or not, male dominance hierarchies in human as in other mammalian species—notably primate troops and wolf packs—might be inevitable because of their adaptive value from a purely evolutionary point of view. Evolutionary psychologists have further explained the psychological processes that reinforce and perpetuate hierarchical systems. The bottom line is: males are bigger and stronger and, thus, more capable not only as predators and territorial protectors, but also as peacekeepers within social units, while females are freed to concentrate on bearing and rearing the young. There are notable variations and exceptions with regard to these functions: the now celebrated emperor penguin, an ice house-husband; the lioness huntress; the female grey wolf who rules the roost, or den, even of the alpha male. None the less, Athena *vs.* Ares to the contrary, when it comes to the social organisation itself, the warrior gender prevails.

Until now at least: in our ever more cyber focused and metrosexual universe—Lawrence Summers to the contrary—women's prowess today in science and finance is undeniable. With technology mushrooming as never before in history and women working on a par with men, with brainpower supplanting physical strength, and with third party childcare and other outsourcings of maternal functions, again for better or worse, physical strength matters less and less in structuring gender relations and politics. It may take some time for human nature to catch up with human civilisation, but the adaptive advantage of male dominance is probably becoming obsolete. To which world leaders such as Angela Merkel and the proliferation of female CEOs of Dow companies attest.

We may think of Hillary Clinton has having ridden on Bill's coattails. Not so, I think, when it comes to this power couple. Even as the twentieth century came to a close, it was political exigencies that forced her to take a back seat to her husband for the time being. So, let us see what happens in 2016.

And by the way, consider the New Deal sixty years before the ascent of this iconic couple. Well, that was originally Eleanor's idea, was it not?

With these times-a-changing, the myth of mighty women might very well be on track to become a reality.

References

Blos, P. Personal communication.

Blum, H. Personal communication.

Erikson, E. (1950). *Childhood and Society.* New York: Norton.

Erikson, E. (1964). *Insight and Responsibility.* New York: Norton.

Freud, S. (1905d). *Three Essays on the Theory of Sexuality. S. E., 7*: 226–. London: Hogarth.

Freud, S. (1923e). The infantile genital organization *S. E., 19*: 411–148. London: Hogarth.

Freud, S. (1924c). The economic problem of masochism. *S. E., 19*: 159–172. London: Hogarth.

Freud, S. (1924d). The dissolution of the Oedipus complex. *S. E., 19*: 173–179. London: Hogarth.

Freud, S. (1925j). Some psychical consequences of the anatomical differences between the sexes. *S. E., 19*: 243–258. London: Hogarth.

Friedman, L. (1999). *Identity's Architect: A Biography of Erik H. Erikson.* London: Free Association Books.

Graves, R. (1955). *The Greek Myths.* Harmondsworth: Penguin.

Horner, M. (1972). Toward an understanding of achievement-related conflicts in woman. *Journal of Social Issues, 28*: 157–175.

Horney, K. (1924). On the genesis of the castration complex in women. *International Journal of Psychoanalysis, 5*: 50–65.

Horney, K. (1926). The flight from womanhood. *International Journal of Psychoanalysis, 7*: 324–339.

Horney, K. (1932). The dread of woman. *International Journal of Psychoanalysis, 13*: 348–366.

Horney, K. (1933). Denial of the vagina. *International Journal of Psychoanalysis, 12*: 57–70.

Jones, E. (1948). *Papers on Psycho-Analysis.* London: Baillere, Tindal and Cox.

Kubie, L. (1974). The drive to become both sexes. *Psychoanalytic Quarterly, 43*: 349–426.

Loewald, H. (1952). Ego and reality. *International Journal of Psychoanalysis, 32*: 10–18.

Masters, W., & Johnson, V. (1966). *Human Sexual Response.* Boston, MA: Little Brown.

Matyszak, P. (2010). *The Greek and Roman Myths: A Guide To Classical Stories.* London: Thames and Hudson.

Menaker, E. (1989). *Appointment in Vienna.* New York: St Martin's Press.

Moore, H. (2008). *The Bishop's Daughter: A Memoir*. New York: W. W. Norton.

Nabokov, V. (1966). *Speak, Memory*. New York: G. Putnam.

Rank, O. (2010). *The Myth of the Birth of the Hero*. Baltimore, MD: Johns Hopkins University Press.

Ross, J. (1975). The development of paternal identity: a critical review of the literature on nurturance and generativity in boys and men. *Journal of the American Psychoanalytic Association, 23*: 783–817.

Ross, J. (1977). Towards fatherhood: the epigenesis of paternal identity during a boy's first decade. *International Review of Psycho-analysis, 4*: 327–347.

Ross, J. (1990). The eye of the beholder. In: C. Colarusso & R. Nemiroff (Eds.), *New Dimensions in Adult Development* (pp. 47–72). New York: Basic Books.

Ross, J. (1994). *What Men Want: Mothers, Fathers and Manhood*. Cambridge, MA: Harvard University Press.

Ross, J. (2007). Trauma and abuse in the case of Little Hans. *Journal of the American Psychoanalytic Association, 55*: 779–797.

Sidanius, J., & Pratto, F. (1999). *Social Dominance: An Intergroup Theory of Social Hierarchy and Oppression*. Cambridge: Cambridge University Press.

Sophocles (1977). *The Oedipus Cycle*, D. Fitts & R. Fitzgerald (Trans.). New York: Harcourt.

Young-Bruehl, E. (1994). *Anna Freud: A Biography*. New York: Norton.

CHAPTER SEVENTEEN

Heroines and mythology of contemporary girls

Ellen Sinkman

Introduction

Mythological heroines have inspired girls throughout history. This chapter proposes that features of long-ago heroines resonate with contemporary girls' concerns.

History's heroines have had attachment, narcissistic, and gender identity issues, just as contemporary girls do. A psychoanalytic look at current mythological heroines can be quite revealing about girls now. I explore a number of heroines of girls under seventeen years old, through three recent film and television chronicles: *Beasts of the Southern Wild, Buffy the Vampire Slayer*, and *Juno*.

Girls' unconscious fantasies are reflected in these media, and their fantasies become part of the mythology shared by others. In addition, society accepts the girls' internal worlds. The media help in locating their inner selves in the outer world. At the same time, society—via films and television—shapes the forms that intrapsychic fantasies may take, by portraying young screen heroines.

A look at early mythological goddesses and heroines can be informative. Myths were the media then. However, goddesses tended to be less complex than current mythological women.

In Greek mythology, Mother Earth gave birth to Heaven/Sky, and then married him. Goddesses could often conceive and give birth to children without a male's participation.

Despite her having done all of this, Heaven/Sky banished their first children back into her womb. Grief-stricken and furious, she conspired with subsequent children to emasculate their father. She was forced to wield her power "behind the throne". She accomplished this through her sons' loyalty to her.

As constrained as goddesses were, they were still vastly powerful. Hesiod, the primary source on Greek mythology, described why goddesses were worshipped by mortals. Goddesses listened and had the power to help, as well as the prerogative not to help (Hesiod, 1988, p. 15). Male gods did not intervene in people's daily lives.

The classics scholar Lefkowitz noted that goddesses were "closer to humankind" (Lefkowitz, 2007, p. 22) than male gods. Also, without the intervention of the female deities, world events might have turned out quite differently. Plus, the goddesses were concerned with childbirth. Thus, the future of humankind was very much their province. For all of these reasons, goddesses were worshipped.

The Roman goddess Juno was tremendously powerful, although less so than her brother/consort Jupiter. Juno was envious of other women—very often with good reason, as Jupiter indulged in countless sexual affairs. She directed her murderous fury at the women rather than at her husband.

Juno turned women into objects, or part-objects, mere whispers of their personae, or she banished them into the cosmos. This queen of the gods brooked no competitors in her surge for power. Mere mortals undoubtedly wanted to invoke Juno's superpowers.

Persephone was the daughter of Demeter, goddess of agriculture. Hades, lord of the underworld, kidnapped Persephone. Demeter, depressed and enraged, stopped crops from growing while Persephone was underground. Hades was forced to allow Persephone to return to Earth and her mother for part of the year. Otherwise, life for mortals was threatened. Her annual but temporary return to her mother facilitated renewal and growth on earth. Many humans hoped for Demeter's powers when they lost loved ones.

Shifting to the recent past, 1950s girls looked for heroines in the adventures of the ever-inquisitive Nancy Drew, the brushed-by-fame

Marjorie Morningstar, the tragic but talented Sylvia Plath, and others for their mythologies.

An important consideration about heroines is that readers and viewers, our patients, look for heroic powers as they are developing themselves. Of course, genetics, attachment dynamics, and vicissitudes of object relationships should never be given short shrift. But accessing and reworking themselves out of powerful raw materials reverberates in the heroines our patients embrace. Centuries-old mythologies are the prototypes of contemporary mythologies. Below are key points of several film mythologies.

Beasts of the Southern Wild

The mantras of Hushpuppy, the five-year-old waif of the film, are "When you're small, you gotta fix what you can", and "There's no time to sit around cryin' like a bunch of pussies" (Alibar, 2013; Alibar & Zeitlin, 2012).

Hushpuppy has almost nothing. She wears threadbare boys' underwear and is small, but she declares to her father "You think I don't know? I got eyes." Hushpuppy's tiny face, though often looking stoic, also reflects her confusion, terror, and fury. She seems unlikely to be a heroine.

Hushpuppy imagines having loving conversations with her mother, who left when she was born. Hushpuppy's father, a destitute alcoholic, cares deeply for her, but has only the vaguest notion of how to be a parent. Prone to violence, he is often absent. Plus, he is dying.

They reside in decrepit shacks in an almost isolated, watery Louisiana bayou called The Bathtub,[1] "a sinking island on the wrong side of the levees" (Alibar & Zeitlin, 2012). They live with partially feral animals around them. "School" is a shaman woman who tells tall tales about cavemen battling ancient animals called aurochs. Her terrifying "lessons" are full of violence and obscene language. Like Hushpuppy, young patients from deprived backgrounds often do not have solid role models or resources in their lives.

An early image in the film is of Hushpuppy walking a wooden "tightrope" wearing her trademark hip boots, a scene embodying the tightrope Hushpuppy walks in life, threatened with annihilation while trying to navigate to safety.

Soon, Hushpuppy "accidentally" sets her shack on fire, after carefully donning a helmet to heat water with a blowtorch. She climbs into a cardboard box—presumably thinking that if she cannot see the blaze, then it will not get her.[2]

Hushpuppy feels that the destructive fire (i.e., her anger) has hastened the end of the world, certainly the end of her world. She says to her mother (who exists for her somewhere between outside and inside), "Mama, I've broken everything."

She also feels that she has killed her father. He tells her that she is killing him. Additionally, Hushpuppy knows that just being born led to her mother's running away from her. Hushpuppy's world is very much like the emotional world in which some patients feel they live.

Her mother has vanished from the face of the earth. Her father is only an intermittent presence. She tells him that she fears that if he dies, she, too, dies. When she cannot find him, she draws his image and lies down next to it. She tries to keep the relationship alive, using materials around her. This is part of her being a heroine.

Hushpuppy has a few of her mother's possessions, which function as transitional objects. Perhaps they will also function as the base for certain sublimation activities.

Trying to find her mother, she swims to swaying women. Her desperate search (possibly a merging fantasy) for a mother turns up only a mirage, a comforting but fleeting fantasy. Nevertheless, it is also part of Hushpuppy's active search to attach herself to a safe object.

A hurricane floods and destroys their community. Hushpuppy says, "The fabric of the universe is coming unravelled . . . Everybody lose the thing what made them. They stay to watch it happen. They don't run." Heroically, Hushpuppy does not run. She stays to wrestle with her fears.

Aurochs, dinosaur-sized hogs, are unleashed from primordial glaciers. These ferocious creatures, enormous versions of hogs around Hushpuppy,[3] go on a stampeding rampage. She says, "Strong animals got no mercy. They eat their own mamas and daddies." This belief reflects her own projected self image, verbalised by her stating that if her Daddy does not reappear soon, she will have to start eating her pets.

Hushpuppy's inner world is projected on to the external world, and the outer world supplies ample material with which to do so. Beastly aurochs and Hushpuppy's father represent derivatives of her aggression. As with patients, external events often unleash psychodynamic forces. Film-goers and clinicians are witnesses with Hushpuppy to the mutual influence of inside–outside turmoil. The lush cinematic display shows a pint-sized Hushpuppy as heroine.

Part of the film's mythology reflects a baby's primitive primary process fantasies. The infant's fears of her annihilating rage, and of being abandoned, are rampant. The boundaries of Hushpuppy's world explode and collapse, sometimes by ice, other times by fire. Her attachment to people is the "insecure" type (Ainsworth and colleagues' 1978 research).

Projective identification animating Hushpuppy's world means distinctions between internal and external are tenuous. Dwarfed by events and beastly aurochs that swallow their own families, even her name is a type of food.

The precariousness of existence shows in her reflecting that "The whole universe depends on everything fitting together just right. If one piece busts, even the smallest piece, the entire universe gets busted." Many young patients identify with Hushpuppy's intense vulnerability. Many can also identify with her magical feelings of defensive omnipotence (e.g., being "the one whose fault it is", or "the one who has to take care of everybody else").

Hushpuppy heroically tries to keep her world intact. Part of her attempts to deal with her world involves a counter-phobic front. She, her father, and community promote their lives as profoundly superior, although these efforts often require splitting off affects and reality. Self-reflective mourning and depressive feelings are kept out.

It is unclear how Hushpuppy's gender identity will evolve. Periodically teaming with a group of girls, she is their leader. Her father, the only parent present, gives her survival lessons. But his efforts are confusing about gender identity. For example, he tells her she "will be the last man in the bayou". He shows her how to punch, and how to be nonchalant when her hand gets cut in the process.

When they mindlessly fight, the father shouts for Hushpuppy to show him her "guns" (i.e., biceps). Hushpuppy enthusiastically flexes her tiny biceps. When she wins in arm-wrestling, her father congratulates her with "You the man!" She is proud to find this gleam of herself in her father's eyes and she chants, "I'm the man!" Hushpuppy also drinks moonshine, learning to "burp like a man".

Hushpuppy's psychosexual identification will be complicated. She has acquired lore about her mother, whose sexuality was so "hot" that she caused spontaneous combustion on the stove. Saying "Hushpuppy popped into the universe four minutes after that", her father perpetuated a myth of an elusive but sensual super-mother who, dressed only in her underwear, shot an approaching alligator with a shotgun and then cooked it and fed it to her family.

Hushpuppy is consciously proud of this goddess of a mother, but how to bring her down to accessible, nurturing earth-size? Hushpuppy needed to idealise a maternal image whose powers she could acquire. But idealising worship comes with the price of shutting off components of an evil, abandoning mother. Her father is Hushpuppy's primary role model, but eventual gender identity might have less to do with any basic identification as a male, and more to do with staying alive and staying lovingly attached to her father.

Despite sparse resources, Hushpuppy's desires (whether maternal or paternal) to repair and nurture are evident. Hushpuppy makes a nest from mud and plops an almost dead chick on to it. The chick twitches to life. Hushpuppy listens to hear what the chick's heartbeat has to say. She listens to other animals, trying to decode their communications. Later, she rushes with magic herbs to where her sick father had collapsed. He is no longer anywhere to be found, so she puts the herbs into her "storage unit", the hollow of a tree. This is the equivalent of her womb, and she is trying to keep him alive.

There are swings in Hushpuppy's narcissistic structure: she can feel like an insect-sized morsel about to be squashed into the mud; she can also feel omnipotently, defensively empowered to save the world. Like the goddess Mother Earth, Hushpuppy feels entrusted with keeping life in her world. Also like Mother Earth, she observes that life sometimes being swallowed up.

There are aspects of a creation myth in *Beasts of the Southern Wild*. Hushpuppy has gleaned pieces from her difficult childhood to forge her own identity.

Basic themes in *Beasts of the Southern Wild* involve destruction and loss. There are also themes of creativity and hope. Like Mother Earth, Hushpuppy perseveres. She uses the most of what little life has given her thus far.

She works to craft a life for herself. Hushpuppy and the goddesses are fiercely indomitable yet also tender. They try to listen to the beings around them. Ultimately, Hushpuppy emerges victorious, facing down a stronger civilisation and aurochs and confronting the death of her father. She heroically faces her own future.

Buffy the Vampire Slayer

Buffy the Vampire Slayer (Whedon,1997) is the second film the chapter addresses. This extremely popular television series ran for seven years and inspired academic studies and a cult-like following. The chapter looks primarily at the first several episodes.

Unlike Hushpuppy, Buffy is a beautiful fifteen-year-old in an affluent suburb. Like Hushpuppy, Buffy has only one biological parent. She lives with her divorced mother, who is kindly, but impossibly unattuned to her daughter.

The plots (i.e., the mythology) involve Sunnydale High School's adolescent population. The name Sunnydale belies the truth: it actually sits on a "Hellmouth", which is a portal to the underground catacombs of Hell where vampires and other monsters are trapped. They periodically escape, bringing violent torture and death to the earth's surface. This situation recalls Hades' abduction of Persephone.

As in ancient mythology, these creatures have supernatural powers and superhuman strength. They can live forever. Vampires suck the blood of ordinary people, thereby changing them into vampires, too. Some demons turn humans into werewolves. They can cast magic spells and curses.

Reminiscent of the goddess Juno's powers, there is "shape shifting" and inhabiting other people's bodies. Monsters can take on the look of animals or acquire lethal objects for body parts. The monsters mask horrendously repulsive bodies beneath the appearance of everyday people.

Appearing to be ordinary, Buffy is attractive, bright, and steeped in popular culture. She has familiar teenage interests: her hair, boys, social life, and the latest fashions. However, she is not ordinary. She can do everything a girl might wish—and without worrying about how she is seen by other people. She is the heroic "Vampire Slayer". The mythology states that in every generation, fate chooses one girl (always a girl) to combat evil. The Slayer role means that her powers must be used to save humankind from annihilation. She must prevent

Hell from spilling on to Earth. Like Superman's family, hers are mere mortals. She is special and very different from them.

Buffy's superhuman strength and perceptive powers enable her to accomplish this goal. In addition, she is extraordinarily brave. Buffy can wreak superhuman havoc, too. She is helped by two social outcasts whom she has befriended. They form a close bond, although the "popular" crowd ostracises her because of her friendship with a geek and a nerd. In addition, she must keep her identity as a heroic Slayer a secret, to protect people from danger. When she seems to be behaving strangely in her "chosen" role, she is further isolated socially.

Buffy has an older mentor, the Watcher, who specialises in focusing her on honing the skills for destroying monsters. Functioning as Buffy's superego, he can be forbidding or approving. She finds his regimen constricting and is defiant about being given orders. Nevertheless, Buffy is dedicated to her chosen work, and she courageously throws herself into the path of danger to save others. There are still many moments when she feels torn between id derivatives (that is, sexual desires) and superego imperatives to attend to her responsibilities.

The show's creator said the series is about "high school as hell, as a horror movie". It is, in fact, a study of one version of experiencing adolescence, which can feel hellish. Understanding one's changing body, solidifying gender identity, and moving towards sexual inti-macy are critical tasks of adolescence. Another adolescent task is to continue differentiating and separating from parents. As part of this development, peers become the centre of one's life, and can feel sup-portive or demonical.

Young patients bring into treatment visceral responses to Buffy mythology and to Buffy as heroine. Many patients feel overwhelmed in adolescent turmoil, but they identify with the victoriously attrac-tive, superhumanly powerful Buffy.

She has self-confidence and authority. She does not let anyone push her around and is unafraid of classmates knowing she is really friendly with a geek and a nerd. At the same time, patients identify with her awkward outcast friends, the nerd and the geek.

However, patients do have fears about unleashing sexual and destructive impulses, which they see Buffy doing. Patients worry about being omnipotent, but being out of control as a result. Seeing Buffy masterfully embody all of these qualities is empowering.

Teenagers wonder: will I alienate people if I show my prowess? If I reveal my true identity, will I endanger myself or people around me? Buffy's mantra might be her battle cry exclamation, "Don't kill my date!" She is very attracted to her date, but she warns herself about the dangers of aggressive intimacy.

Patients suffer from inhibitions or enactments, with varying symptomatology. For more disturbed patients, "shape shifting" indicates fluidity of body image. Furthermore, diverse monsters in Buffy mythology represent split-off sexual and aggressive inner worlds. For these people, primitive internal objects have not been thoroughly mentalized and integrated. Instead, they are projected on to vicious, non-human, part-object demons. For such non-integrated patients, "bad" monsters may function defensively: these patients do not want their inner worlds destroyed and may, in fact, be trying to repair them. Unfortunately, the attempts to safely distance themselves can leave them feeling alone, their inner worlds depleted. There is a profound sense of alienation, despite social contacts. Buffy is seen as someone with a unified self: a heroic accomplishment.

Facets of Buffy's conflicts contain patients' family romance fantasies such as: I live with a family that does not understand the real me, a family where I do not belong. I am actually a special "chosen one", and my true family would recognise my authentic, unique self. Patients are, in part, working on "Where do I fit in?" Like Buffy as a Slayer, their true identities are kept hidden.

Physical changes are critical in Buffy mythology, as well as in adolescence. What the television series refers to as the "crucial mystical upheaval coming" is puberty for adolescents. It is the shape-shifting of mythology. When the Watcher informs Buffy, "Testosterone is a great equaliser: it turns all men into animals", he did not add that sexuality is at least equally important for girls.

Sexuality and gender identity are unquestionably at the core of adolescents' lives. Much of the phenomena in Buffy refer to freeing these inner forces and wondering what to do then. Buffy (and patients) talk about "my maiden voyage" and boys wanting to know her "deep dark secrets".

Buffy and her friends are sexual virgins. Struggling to be free of her duties so that she can be a "normal" teenager and date, she "coincidentally" finds herself being pulled away from her dates. Thus, her ambivalence is displayed.

Adolescent patients ask: what will sexual intimacy be like? In *Buffy the Vampire Slayer*, the experience is typically suffused with sado-masochism. Like the goddess Earth Mother, Buffy emasculates and kills—propelling her body at monsters and attacking them with weapons. She also, like some goddesses, bonds with the people she saves. Buffy, who is sometimes called Joan, is comparable to Joan of Arc, sacrificing herself for her people.

Sexual and oral hunger can be found in the erotic tension of preda-tory vampire fangs penetrating tender flesh and sucking blood. Vampire and victim are intimately bound. Buffy's first sexual encounter and intense love is with a highly sexualised, aggressive male, ironically named Angel. Young girls invariably want to have such an outstandingly handsome and powerful boyfriend.

As it turns out, Angel is a several-hundred-years-old vampire. His curse is that his sexual and emotional joy with Buffy means he must revert to being a killer vampire. When he becomes vampiric, because he has sexually penetrated her, Buffy must penetrate him, with a phal-lic stake. Patients throb with their sweet angst.

Interestingly vampires, as well as mythological gods and goddesses, are referred to as "ancients". This implies that they repre-sent adults. Sexual attraction to ancients thus carries the threat of incestuous desires for parental figures. Clinicians know that children view their parents as gods. In addition to the threat of becoming aware of incestuous feelings for ancients, growing up embodies other frightening, though alluring, prospects. Becoming an adult means losing one's parents.

Buffy is a feminist and feminine heroine. Her femininity is not the caricature that Joan Riviere (1929) described. Although her appear-ance is that of a conventionally gendered young woman (Jowett, 2005, p. 14), she can undergo transformations. There are numerous instan-ces of gender fluidity. She is also fully committed to her work, which is traditionally thought of as a male attribute. Yet, like contemporary women, Buffy tries to balance her personal and professional life (Jowett, 2005, p. 24).

Another mythological aspect concerns Buffy's name. It suggests a mundane, even silly person. This corresponds to many patients' low self-esteem. Buffy's last name, Summers, connects to transformations associated with the goddess Persephone. Buffy and Persephone des-cended into Hell (Wilcox, 2005, p. 63), re-emerging as protagonists of mythic abilities, bringing summer and growth. Buffy is a heroine for many young females dealing with daunting obstacles. She eventually negotiates becoming a fully realised adult with an adult's pleasures and responsibilities.

Juno

This chapter looks briefly at one additional film: *Juno* (Cody, 2007). Named for the goddess Juno, patron of marriage, the teenage Juno defines herself as "non-conforming".

She lives with her father and stepmother. Juno's biological mother is out of the picture. (That union clearly did not last.) Juno has been trying to locate where she fits in.

Like a number of patients, she is poised at early pubescence, which can be quite androgynous. She recognises her own physical boyishness. Yet, she pursues a boy (also somewhat androgynous) whom she loves and who cares for her.

Their sexual encounter results in pregnancy, so her shape is very much shifted. Her changing body recalls the shape shifting at which the goddess Juno was an expert.

Juno struggles with this sudden plunge into an adult maternal role amid pressures from various people about what she should do. She turns what might be seen by some as a "victim role" into a powerful personal victory. Juno is plucky. An independent, strong girl, she deals with this life-changing event with clear-eyed mindfulness.

Patients view her as heroic in part because she works out her emerging identity and values. She becomes able to share her vulnerable feelings—her tender love for her unborn baby and for her boyfriend. She then expands her world of cherished object relationships to include an infertile adoptive single mother. (The woman's spouse had abandoned her, as Jupiter did so often to the goddess Juno, and as many patients' parents have abandoned them. The mother of the film's Juno had also emotionally abandoned her.)

She is heroic because she bravely takes authentic charge of her life. Juno faces down jeering classmates. She at first finds a loving couple to adopt the baby. Yes, she idealises the chosen couple, because she is also trying to find "an unbroken" family. Then the adoptive couple breaks up. Does nothing last?

Patients see Juno as a role model because she is ultimately able to feel much closer to answering the question of "Can I be loved forever, just for myself, no matter what shape I am in?" She sees the loving gleam in the adoptive mother's eyes, in her boyfriend's eyes, and in the eyes of her pieced-together nuclear family.

Juno is a heroine for young patients searching to individuate from parents (while maintaining her ties) and while yearning to make a new life and find new love. In the process, her identity as fully female is well on the way to being solidified.

Conclusion

Hushpuppy, Buffy, and Juno are mythological heroines for many contemporary girls. Resilient, resourceful, and spirited, they are seen as having out-of-the-ordinary, sometimes superhuman, strength in a world that poses dangers. Each pursues her individuality and gains a strong sense of self-agency. Ancient mythology and contemporary mythology share many important elements.

To varying degrees, contemporary heroines cope mightily with faulty parental attachment, looming perils, and waves of id and super-ego pressures. Their hard-won battles include many losses but they ultimately embrace their intellectual, sexual, and physical powers. They prevail and grow. Perhaps they have even out-distanced the goddesses of long-ago myths.

Notes

1. This also evokes many children's memories of playfully splashing in a bathtub as their mothers bathed them.
2. This can be seen as a pernicious variation of the father's describing the mother as "so pretty that she never even had to turn on the stove . . . she would just walk into the room and the burners would ignite".
3. Familiar farm animals suddenly become voracious and threatening in the film. Analogously, Hushpuppy's father can suddenly turn from nurturing to fiercely frightening.

References

Ainsworth, M. D. S., Blehar, M. C., Waters, E., & Wall, S. (1978). *Patterns of Attachment: A Psychological Study of the Strange Situation*. Hillsdale, NJ: Lawrence Erlbaum.

Alibar, L. (2013). *Juicy and Delicious* (Stageplay). New York: Dramatists Play Service.

Alibar, L., & Zeitlin, B. (2012). *Beasts of the Southern Wild* (film), B. Zeitlin (Director). Cinereach.

Cody, D. (2007). *Juno* (film), J. Reitman (Director). US. Producer: Mr. Mudd.

Hesiod (1988). *Theogony and Works and Days*, M. L. West (Trans.). Oxford: Oxford University Press.

Jowett, L. (2005). *Sex and the Slayer: A Gender Studies Primer for the "Buffy" Fan*. Middletown, CT: Wesleyan University Press.

Lefkowitz, M. R. (2007). *Women in Greek Myth*. Baltimore, MD: Johns Hopkins University Press.

Riviere, J. (1929). Womanliness as a masquerade. In: A. Hughes (Ed.), *The Inner World and Joan Riviere: Collected Papers 1920–1958* (pp. 90–101). London: Karnac.

Whedon, J. (1997). *Buffy the Vampire Slayer* (television series). Mutant Enemy Productions.

Wilcox, R. (2005). *Why Buffy Matters: The Art of Buffy the Vampire Slayer*. London: I. B. Tauris.

CHAPTER EIGHTEEN

Contributions Part V: implications for psychoanalytic psychotherapy

Arlene Kramer Richards and Lucille Spira

T his section comments on the contributions by John Ross and Ellen Sinkman, whose chapters show how fathers, male mentors, and the overall male power structure, help or impede the psychological and social development of young girls, teenagers, and women. Identifying with the father of power shores up the daughter's power; identifying with weak fathers like Hushpuppy's can lead to grandiosity. The implications for the psychoanalytic psychotherapist of conflicts particular to young girls, teenagers, and women are highlighted.

Beriosova and aggression

Ross's spicy paper brings up a very important issue in the analysis of women. Foremost is the issue of female aggression. Modern men complain about female aggression. Dr Ross does not ask whether females still complain about male aggression. Sexual aggression is still far more prevalent as male on female rape than the other way around. Verbal abuse, on the other hand, might well be more prevalent in a female on male pair. But Ross also complains about the ballet star Beriosova, who was not verbally aggressive enough at a dinner party.

Therein lies a female dilemma. How aggressive is aggressive enough? And how much is too much?

In some traditional societies, women could hardly confront this dilemma. Women were best off being as passive as possible. Passive was feminine, aggressive was masculine. For a female patient, the question of how aggressive is too aggressive is crucial. She says, "I worry that he will think I am a ball buster if I don't go along with his way", or "I just want to have my own time to do what I want. What is so bad about that?" or "How come I need to work all week and then clean the house on weekends when he doesn't do anything but watch sports and read the paper?" "Does complaining that it is not fair make me the mean one?", or "Am I a shrew?"

At a later time in her treatment, her questions are about not being sufficiently aggressive. She worries: "Am I a wimp?", or "Will I get to be the manager if I don't speak up enough?", or "Can I keep my marriage together if I don't give him an ultimatum about being home with the kids so we can all have dinner together?", or "Will I just have to accept being less important if I don't speak up?"

Addressing both sides of the dilemma with the patient is important because the decisions about behaviour will affect how others react to her and how she feels about herself. Lamenting the social conditions that make what is expected of the woman different from what was expected of women a generation or two earlier is a beginning in allowing the woman to understand that she is not responsible for the problem, but pushing beyond that to understand her choices now and relating her feelings to her choices is a uniquely analytic and helpful way to empower her.

The issue of female aggression links with the issue of masochism in that aggression turned inwards results in punishing oneself for the aggression of others. Turning anger inwards when one is hurt is triggered by the fear of harming the aggressor as well as fear of punishment from the person who is doing one harm. The film *Black Swan* by Darren Aronofsky is a very sad and very beautiful expression of this psychological outcome. The victim of aggression becomes an aggressor herself, but, in masochism, the aggression is directed against the self.

Returning to the anecdote about Beriosova, it is important to recognise that a prima ballerina has undergone rigorous training in following the ballet teacher's instructions. From early childhood she has been taught to move, not speak, to accept discipline from her mostly male teachers and later directors, to be the conduit for the choreographer's feelings and ideas, to subordinate herself to the demands of others. To expect her to speak up in a conversation among intellectual men is to expect her to be someone she has spent her life training not to be. This is important because Beriosova is only an extreme example of the training imposed on girls to make them into women who will meet the social demand for passive femininity. Where this passive femininity is adaptive, it is very difficult to change. Only when it clashes with a woman's own demand for expression of her aggression can it and should it become the focus of analytic work.

In sum, our purpose in doing analytic therapy is to help the woman find what works for her, the degree of aggressiveness and the degree of passivity that will work in her own particular life. Whether she marries, whether she chooses to have children, whether she chooses to be close to her extended family, how much time she spends on her own work is not our choice to make. What analysts can do for patients is help them see what makes them happiest at the moment and what will make them happy in the longer term.

Hushpuppy, Buffy, and Juno

Ellen Sinkman's commentary on *Beasts of the Southern Wild*, *Buffy the Vampire Slayer*, and *Juno* follows developmental sequence from the phallic–oedipal child to the early adolescent, to the late adolescent mother. Her comments on *Beasts of the Southern Wild* trace the stages of development of a little girl who is at once bereft of the support and nurturance of a mother and at the same time an oedipal winner in that she has her father to herself.

The film Sinkman is commenting on shows a girl named Hush-puppy who sees herself as all-powerful at the same time that she experiences herself as a tiny being trying to withstand the forces of nature. She has the idea that she must be strong and at the same time has the story of her mother, who was unable to be a mother because of her too strong sexual need. The message is that female sexuality is dangerous and destructive. It unfits a woman to be a mother. It leaves her child motherless.

Buffy the Vampire Slayer deals with similar conflicts at a later age. Now the young woman still has to save the world from terrible danger. She has more than adult responsibilities, yet she is still too young for sexual fulfilment. She struggles with the issue of how to be a world-saver and still experience sexual pleasure. The danger of sexual pleasure is clearly, as Sinkman tells us, the loss of her attention to her world-saving role. But who is the world-saver? The mother (Thomson-Salo; Turrini, this volume). Here again is the conflict between being a mother and being a sexual woman. Buffy's mother is not up to the role of world-saver, so Buffy, like Hushpuppy, must take it on herself.

Juno shows a young pregnant woman who has no mother. She decides to become a mother herself, but realises that she is too young and powerless to raise a child. Older and more experienced than Hushpuppy and Buffy, she knows that she cannot save the world. Instead, she chooses to save her foetus and give it life. She accepts her own limitations and appreciates her own strengths.

It is possible to see all of these heroines as parentified children. Deprived of the comfort and protection of a strong mother, each of these heroines manages her endangered life according to her developmental stage. Hushpuppy assumes superhuman powers, Buffy accepts the position her fate assigns her, Juno makes a realistic choice. The three heroines all achieve a kind of power. If Hushpuppy is omnipotent, Buffy is overcoming fear and accepting her responsibilities, and Juno is giving her child what she herself does not have: a competent mother.

Identifying with the father

Grown-up patients who were parentified children can be helped to deal with the scars left by the failure of their parents to protect and comfort them. It is often painful to allow oneself to see one's parents as flawed, weak, and dependent on their children. But recognising that one was overburdened as a child helps people to stop blaming themselves for not saving their parents, for not protecting their siblings from parental failure and inadequacies, and for having rescued themselves. One of the tag lines I use when patients suffer from guilt over rescuing themselves while being unable to rescue their family is: "On the aeroplanes they say, 'Fasten your own oxygen mask before helping others'."

PART VI

CHAPTER NINETEEN

Conclusion

Arlene Kramer Richards and Lucille Spira

F reud turned to myths to understand himself and his patients. His insistence on the Oedipus myth as central to the psychological development of both men and women led to a century of constricted thinking about both female and male development. Although modern psychoanalytic theory has expanded to include contributions by Horney, Klein, Mahler, Kohut, Winnicott, and others, myths still have a role to play. The powerful goddesses, heroines, literary and folk tale characters whom you have just read about highlight the connection between art and life—the boundaries are permeable. Psychoanalysts, classicists, and literary scholars believe that literature teaches us about the human condition. Our authors' contributions stimulated us to think about how an awareness of mighty women from the past empowers our women patients. As we examined the mythic stories about mighty women, the conflicts, both internal and external, that press upon the fictional and heroic characters presented are similar to those that women experience in the world.

The long ago past has an impact on the lives of contemporary women and the decisions they make. While myths might not enter the consulting room directly, we show how unconscious phantasies can be teased from the latent content of the narratives our women patients present. Making explicit the wishes and lessons encased in the myths and locating them in history allows for deeper understanding. The struggles and values that give rise to the conflicts that beset today's women, particularly ones that centre on being allowed a voice, justice, and power, can be examined to allow for working through.

Sex, aggression, revenge, and love, both for self and other, figure prominently as themes in this volume and in our lives. "Motherhood" and the fullness of what that concept and role means as portrayed in myths is discussed. For us, how to use these myths to empower women in the face of hardship and sleights, real or seemingly over-exaggerated, is an important goal. Trauma, loss, and mourning are also issues for the characters, as they are for all of us as we focus on how to use the underpinnings of myths as adjuncts to our psycho-analytic theory.

In therapy, we hear the hurt and pain of women who are rejected by their husbands or lose their spouses to death. Medea expresses her rage by murdering her husband's and her children; Inanna expresses her contempt by taking on the sole care of her children and her coun-try; and Meng Jiangnü expresses her sorrow and her anger by humil-iating the man responsible for her husband's death. Helen of Troy adapts to whichever man she is with: her first husband Menelaus, her second, Paris, her third, Paris' brother, and finally back to Menelaus. Pragmatic or opportunistic, she survives losses by choosing the most powerful man. Molly Bloom has lost her sexual relationship with her husband through a missed mourning for a child. Musing about the reawakened sexual feelings she felt with another man, she reaffirms her love and affection for her sometimes wandering husband.

All of these situations and resolutions are prototypes of adult women's choices when marriages go sour or are totally lost. The ther-apist's awareness of the multiplicity of choices in myths frees her to think of many choices in the therapy encounter. She may choose to keep silent about these choices or may actually tell the patient about the myths. However she uses them, the mythic solutions affect how the patient understands and reacts to her own choices. The openness supported by the encounter with myths and understanding the conse-quences of the choices one makes is ultimately what is important.

Mythic stories, with their archetypal characters, arouse powerful emotions and resonate with our deepest longings, wishful phantasies, fears, and aspirations. We hope our readers can connect with some aspect of a particular myth as they parallel women's lives. Envy, greed, vengeance, and the wish for magical powers are prominent themes in myths, as they are in life.

One of our main interests was to show how reason and careful strategising can overcome brute force and allow women more power in the world. Myths reinforce what we understand from psycho-analytic theory: we must temper our rage, draw boundaries around certain of our sexual wishes, and find outlets for our impulses, ones that do not stir unmanageable guilt or harm society. Real people are subject to real pain.

In the journey through psychoanalytic psychotherapy, many sources can be used to help the patient towards her solution to her individual quest. In our sections on the implications of myths for psychoanalytic psychotherapy, where we view the mythic stories through the lens of a wide range of psychoanalytic theory, we keep Meyers' (2010 and Epilogue, this volume) contribution in mind. She beautifully demonstrates how Freud's theory becomes richer as it draws upon the rich repertoire of analytic contributions available to today's analysts. While Freud asked, "What do women want?" we ask, "What does a woman need?" We answer, the right to control her body, mind, and the sense that she will be treated justly.

A tribute to Helen Meyers, MD

D r Helen Meyers was indeed a Mighty Woman. One story (among many) stands out in my memory: it was in the 1990s, at a conference for the American Psychoanalytic Association, and Helen was a discussant on a paper. A colleague in the audience asked her about the theoretical basis for the paper, and Helen said that she had a larger framework within which she could place the work, would the questioner like to hear it? Knowing of Helen's longstanding position at the helm of the Curriculum Committee at the Columbia Psychoanalytic Center, and her accomplished career as a highly respected teacher, thinker, and training analyst, the colleague, and the audience, responded with an eager "yes". Helen then proceeded, very modestly but with great mastery, to lay out the integrative framework that lay behind her teaching and practice, in which she could place all the post-Freudian approaches in a continuum, defined by, but not limited to, Freud's own theories. Ego psychology, object-relations theory, self psychology, Erikson, Jung, Adler, Klein, Winnicott, Lacan, Kohut, Mahler, Kernberg, Schafer, they all fell into place, part of a shimmering coherent matrix, not in conflict, but part of a beautiful integrative mosaic that Helen constructed before everyone's eyes. To her students and supervisees in the audience this was no surprise; her teaching and training were always rooted in rigorous logic and an encyclopaedic knowledge of psychoanalytic theory. But to all in the room this was a bit of magic, like a pedagogical Brigadoon in which all of a sudden the spectrum of wide-ranging, ostensibly contradictory analytic approaches all made sense as a family of intellectual siblings, integrated and available to be applied both alone and in concert. At the end of her ten-minute synthesis, there was a brief silence and then the stunned room erupted into several minutes of applause.

Helen was/is the smartest, most intellectually gifted woman I have ever known, who exhibited grit, grace, and generosity. For the first thirteen years of her life, she grew up in pre-war Vienna, a block away from Freud's home and office. In 1938, Hitler absorbed Austria in the *Anschluss* and her family prepared to leave. Fortunately, her father, Alfred Kestenbaum, a world-renowned pioneer in the newly emerging specialty of neuro-opthalmology and a professor at the Vienna University Medical School, had treated a number of government officials who, although they identified with the pro-Hitler National Socialism and its anti-Semitism, permitted his family to get an exit visa and leave Vienna for the USA. One of Alfred's American students immediately offered to sponsor his migration to the USA, whereupon, four months after Hitler entered Vienna, Alfred, his wife, Ada, herself a physician, Helen's older brother, William, and Helen embarked on the French luxury liner, the *Normandy*, with the small amount of money and other possessions they were allowed to take. Helen was permitted to visit first class during the voyage where she made some needed American currency giving English lessons to passengers—she spoke English and French as well as her native German.

Helen was an academic powerhouse and a true therapeutic craftsperson—an exceptional student, a gifted, generous teacher, and a highly regarded clinician. Blessed with a quick and omnivorous intelligence, Helen skipped grades in high school, finished Hunter College early, earning both Phi Beta Kappa and Cum Laude (despite frequently skipping class to bet on the races), attended NYU Medical School, followed by her residency at Bellevue, where she met me, her future husband. We both came to the Columbia Psychoanalytic Center, where we joined the faculty and became both supervising and training analysts. Helen served the Center for over fifty years as a popular and versatile teacher, sought-after supervising and training analyst, longest serving Curriculum Committee chair and Associate Director. She was also Education Director, Chair of the Progression Committee, and Chair of Supervising and Training Analyst Committee, among many other positions. If anyone can be said to be the symbol for intellectual ambition and clinical wisdom at the Center, it was Helen. She was a mentor to two generations of psychoanalysts, teaching the core theory class and supervising a large and loyal group of therapists who became like her children. While Helen's mighty intelligence could be intimidating to some, her easy warmth, sly humour, and generosity of spirit made her a popular and beloved mentor, colleague, and teacher. And her clinical virtuosity and commitment were well known; she was a sought-after therapist who had a full practice of dedicated patients well into her late seventies. Her patients continue to express their thanks to me to this day.

In the larger world of American and international psychoanalysis, Helen was also a mighty figure. There is only room here for some of her positions: locally, she was the Director of the Riverdale Mental Health Association. At the American Psychoanalytic Association, she was a Fellow of the Board of Professional Standards, Executive Council, Steering and Program Committee member, and Chair of the International Relations Committee. Internationally, Helen was a member of the Executive Committee and Vice-President of the International Psychoanalytic Association. Perhaps most relevant to this book, Helen was Chair of the American Psychoanalytic Association's COPE Study Group on Issues for Women Analysts, and the First National Travelling Women's Scholar, which led to her work for the IPA as North American Chair of the Committee on Women and Psychoanalysis (COWAP). It was her pioneering work on behalf of women in psychoanalysis that led to the creation of the Helen Meyers Travelling Women's Scholarship, a fitting honour for such an important trailblazer for women in the field.

So, it is fitting that the editors of this work on Mighty Women asked me, with my son's help, to write this dedication to Helen. She did not call herself a "feminist", perhaps because she came from a world in which she was expected to achieve and compete despite the barriers placed before women (as had her mother), perhaps because she felt that working harder for respect was just another challenge to knock down through the sheer force of will and intelligence (as had her father against anti-Semitism), or maybe she was just a little old-fashioned. But she was very proud to be a role model for women, both in the field and beyond, as she was for so many of our colleagues and for our granddaughters, Rennie and Maddie, two mighty young women themselves. And she was very committed to the success of COWAP and to advancing the role of women in psychotherapy. I believe that Helen would be honoured to be associated with this volume, and with both the myth and reality of the mighty woman.

Donald Meyers, MD, 18 January 2015, Bronx, New York, with the help of my son, Andrew Meyers.

Meyers has her say

Interview with Helen Meyers by Henry Schwartz

We agreed to do an interview for the Bulletin more than four years ago, in July 2005. Helen wanted to talk about an article on integrative psychoanalytic theory that Henry Smith (2005) had recently published. She had been discussing these ideas in her teaching at the centre for years, and she was at work on an article (or was it a book?) on the subject. Rather than wait for her to get it all down in writing, an interview seemed a more expeditious approach. We ended up doing two interviews, but were not satisfied with either. Now, as time passes, we both begin to find them more acceptable. Is Helen mellowing? Although her ailments cause her to attend fewer meetings than she once did, she is as feisty as ever, and her opinions are just as strong. I have no explanation for her change of heart regarding the interviews, and can only thank her for it. In this, the first of the two interviews, we talk about her own ideas regarding the Smith paper, and have the kind of tussles that always made working with Helen so frustrating as well as enlightening. However much I suffered in my supervision with her when I was a candidate, I always felt Helen's warmth and affection. As always, Helen slides in some zingers, and puts me in my place. I have left these in for the reader's amusement, as well as to reveal the robust mix of drive derivatives that are so characteristic of this remarkable educator.

Henry Schwartz

*   *   *

Henry Schwartz: [I started by introducing Smith's two main points: (1) conflict as a central organising principle in all psychoanalytic theories; (2) that the relationship between theory and practice is much looser than is usually claimed and that theoretical inconsistency can still make for proper practice.]

Helen Meyers: Number two is not a new idea of Smith's. Sandler has spoken of it, as has Pine. But Smith's point is not exactly the same as Pine's. Smith comes across as promoting the theory of Charles Brenner. In his 2003 paper Smith also spoke on this topic, comparing three ego psychologists with two relational theorists. Smith's point is that various theories can be differentiated and integrated yet have a lot more in common than they think. My thought is that they can all be integrated under one overarching theory. Probably nobody really agrees with me, but I think that it is very helpful to have an overarching theory to encompass, not all parts of the theories, but major aspects of the theories. This is why I think one has to know these theories inside out, so one doesn't have a hodge-podge, but sees where everything fits in the overarching theory. Now that's metapsychology, rather than sloppy theory. You can use all the different theories, but you don't have to be rigid about only one theory. You have to know where it came from and then you use it. You're bound to the overarching theory, but not to the smaller details.

HS: But then you are bound to the one overarching theory.

HM: Yes, but that includes all the different theories.

HS: Does it exclude anything?

HM: No. It excludes monopoly of detailed theory. Yes, Smith is saying that conflict is central, but that it's seen differently in different theories. I don't care about those differences. All that matters is that you have conflict, with a defence and a critical agency. What difference does it make what it's between? Smith compares the different theories beautifully. But I don't want to compare them only in terms of conflict. I want to compare them in terms of their view of reality, of development, of what is pathology, of what is the unconscious, of what is energy or motivation, of therapeutic action and therapeutic technique, of object relations; there are at least ten or twelve different dimensions on which to compare the theories. Conflict, for Smith, is a little more central than these other factors.

HS: But that's because all the theories can agree on the presence of conflict more than they can on those other factors.

HM: Yes, except that Kohut doesn't agree on the presence of conflict, though Smith gets around this in his paper. A psychoanalytic theory probably has to include conflict, unconscious motivation, unconscious fantasies, object relations, internal and external, and arrested development. Those are the basic elements of psychoanalysis. The different theories have different emphases, but you can include them all, provided you understand what you're doing. So I think it's a mistake to view everything only in terms of conflict. I am not happy with his [Smith's] total acceptance of Brenner, that is, to say that everything is a compromise, and that it is more experience-near to talk about a wish, defence, unpleasant affect, and a punishment. It doesn't help me to get rid of id, ego, and superego, because that's what they're talking about. Their complaint is that those terms are too reified. But you can also reify wish, defence, unpleasant affect, and punishment. The way I remember those four items is by id, ego, and superego. It's easier for me to give the baby a name, to have a mental structure to hang it on.

HS: You like the terms id, ego, and superego. Why?

HM: Because I think my modern version of ego psychology is the overarching theory. But it isn't drive based, limited to drive, defence, punishment, and an anxiety signal. It includes all of object relations theory, in Kernberg's version, meaning that the id, ego, and superego consist of clumps of self and object representation with an affect link between them. You put them all together and you can call it wish or drive or punishment or guilt, but the content really consists of internalised object relationships. You weren't born with the id, ego, and superego. You developed them, and their character was determined by these internalised object relations. Freud said the character of the ego consisted of the abandoned object cathexes. That's more or less a version of internalising external object relations. So the content of these agencies is completely determined by object relations theory. And I think the Kleinian addition of early fantasies is very helpful, that is, seeing fantasising as a way of thinking. And Dan Stern has a theory of even pre-fantasy thinking, which then develops into the kind of thing Isaacs was talking about.

HS: RIGs: Representations of interactions that are generalised?

HM: Yes. And then they also become Arlow's kind of unconscious, which includes conflict and compromise, wishes and defences. So you can include a lot of Klein in early development and fantasy, and I think her enormous stress on aggression is very helpful. Because I do think there's an enormous amount of aggression there . . . Whether it's inborn, or develops because you're always frustrated as a little child; when you are mistreated, or met unempathically, you develop reactive depression. And that brings in Klein and Kohut.

HS: Does it matter whether it's primary or secondary?

HM: I don't think so. Maybe theoretically, but not practically. I don't know if we can ever determine that, because from the word go you're met with frustration. Maybe I just don't like the idea that man is born with a killer instinct; your grandiose needs are frustrated from the very beginning. To go on to self psychology, the whole idea of a self fits in very nicely with a more current view of ego psychology, in that the ego is a self. It's not just the initiator of action, but it's also the whole person that's the initiator of action. Hartman wrote about the Self, with capital S, which is the exact same self as the one Kohut wrote about. He wrote about it with a little s as well. The total id, ego, and superego form the Self with a capital S. This is the person, as Schafer puts it, or the initiator of action, which is Kohut's bipolar self. Kohut's bipolar self is basically an id, ego, and superego, only he gives them different names to make a different point. The important point is the cohesion of the bipolar self.

HS: I'd be surprised if a self psychologist would accept what you're saying.

HM: No! They wouldn't accept it! Who said they would? But the only way you can really remember what Kohut was saying is if you remember it as id, ego, and superego. One end of the bipolar self is your needs and desires, or id, and at the other end is your idealised pole, the parental things, or superego. And in the middle you have the facilitator, which is the ego.

HS: That's a really good point. Is this your idea?

HM: Yeah. Actually I'm sure I've taken some things from other people, but not much. I am the only one who does these kinds of integrations. Others like to keep the theories separate, because they're afraid they would lose their essence, but I don't think so. You lose the exclusivity, but not the essence. Then if you go into some of the other theories, like relational, you find that it's not really a complete theory, not a metapsychology.

HS: It's a clinical theory.

HM: Right. And that then shifts beautifully into this overarching thing. Because nobody ever said—well, I certainly didn't—that ego psychology doesn't include the relationship, when you deal with patients. A big part of the therapeutic action, even as conceived by ego psychologists, has to do with the relationship. You are not vulnerable to the patient's anger, you are not critical, you are not some kind of automaton, but at the same time you don't impart a corrective experience. As the analyst you are a completely different person from the parents, in that you are non-judgemental. Like a regular person, you get turned on, but when upset you don't get hurt or destroyed.

HS: Now this is not shared by all the different theories.

HM: Well, aspects of the relationship are shared.

HS: I'd say the intersubjective camp wouldn't say you don't get hurt, you don't get turned on, or whatever.

HM: That is true, but intersubjectivity is not an analytic theory. It's a clinical stance.

HS: But we're talking now about the clinical differences.

HM: It's not as different as one might think. I do subscribe to a lot of intersubjective theory, because I do think you have an impact on the patient and the patient has an impact on you. Mostly that you have the whole baggage that you brought with you.

HS: And you can't know your own unconscious.

HM: Right. You see the patient through your baggage, just as the patient sees you through theirs. But there is a difference in the degree because it's the patient who is on view. The analyst isn't. The object of the exercise is to dissect the patient. So the analyst's subjectivity is not as potent an interference as the patient's, which is why I think transference is the most important thing in the analytic encounter. Yes, there's also transference from the analyst toward the patient, but it is quantitatively so different.

HS: But that's not the only way to look at it. What about Racker's view that you can never find a larger group of patients than at a meeting of analysts? As well as his question, why put a plaque on your door saying you're there to help people unless you feel you've done something wrong? He is suggesting the analyst needs patients so they will cure him.

HM: My view of Racker is that there's an enormous projective identification; the analyst responds and becomes the object or subject, depending on what is being projected by the patient. And projective counter-identification has also been written about: the idea that if one patient goes to seven analysts and each throws him out in a year, it's a matter of projective counter-identification. He projected it into them. If, on the other hand, you have several patients, and all of them you throw out after a year, it comes from your own unresolved counter-transference from your childhood. That is not projected, because it comes from you. Of course, it's both. When a patient projects something into you there has got to be something in you that is willing to respond that way. It can't be that there's absolutely nothing there.

HS: That's how it always is, all the time.

HM: Right. But the analyst is protected from too much counter-transference, because they're not the object of observation. They're not sitting there talking about themselves. They had a training analysis in which they worked out some of their problems. They have a theoretical background that gives them succour. You know what that is?

HS: It's who you never give an even break.

HM: Sustenance. Bob Michels wrote about how you need theory to hold your hand, and not feel alone, like having a friend to hold on to. So the analyst is a little more protected, even in intersubjectivity.

HS: You can be protected in some ways and not others; obtaining succour from your theory and at the same time responding as a person as well.

HM: Would you explain that?

HS: If my patient attacks me, I may be able to understand that attack in terms of my theory, and respond in a completely appropriate psychoanalytic manner, and yet have some clues within my response that could be picked up on by particularly receptive patients, who may then say something to me about my perfect clinical response. And then it's back in my court. How am I supposed to know if they are accurately perceiving something in me that I hadn't noticed, or if I was really precise and correct in my response? Now we're in a dimension where it's just between the two of us.

HM: That's true, but on the other hand you see many patients and so have some guidelines as to your own reactions and what you respond to emotionally and what not.

HS: I never feel I can overestimate my susceptibility to letting things slip out.

HM: It may be. And I do think we need to constantly re-examine ourselves. And like Hoffman says, you should always try to understand what the patient thinks is going on inside you. But that doesn't mean the patient knows better than you do. There is a quantitative difference in the subjectivity involved. Ogden's analytic third is a cute idea, one of the clinical things you can play with. But it's an example of how not everything clinical is related to a full metapsychological theory. His articles on de-centring are very interesting, but perfectly compatible with every theory. Clinically all these different techniques that belong to different theories should be used, not because you're sloppy, but because a different part of the elephant—or psyche—is under examination. You use the technique that goes with the therapeutic action concept that relates to the different theory, even though you don't say: "Now I'm going to use object relations theory."

HS: There must be incompatibilities in certain parts of the theories.

HM: Of course there are in some parts.

HS: So how does one choose between them?

HM: One throws out the incompatibilities.

HS: But that means you keep one and throw out another. Who decides which one is thrown out and which is kept?

HM: In my theory I do. In your theory you do. I don't think that's such a complicated question. For example, take the incompatibilities between Kohut and Kernberg, or Mahler. Kohut says that Mahler strives for separation–individuation, that is, separation, where what he's talking about is self-object connections. Well, he's just wrong, because Mahler never suggested it's only about separation, but rather that individuation makes it possible for people to relate better to each other. She's not striving for people to be unconnected individuals. She's talking about developing individuality so you can relate better. Kohut's view that it's splendid isolation is a misunderstanding of her concept. On the other hand, Mahler was wrong when she kept criticising Kohut for talking only about what others can do for you and not what you can do for them. The self-object function of the other is what Kohut talks about.

HS: There's a difference in the fundamental view of the human being, right?

HM: I don't think so.

HS: You're saying the Mahlerian view is not of the individual functioning autonomously, but of the individual as a social creature. I'm not so sure that's the way everyone else would interpret Mahler.

HM: Maybe not, but I worked with her a long time and I think it is. But you don't have to agree. Autonomy is different from isolation. I didn't say they're not autonomous, I said they're not in isolation, and Kohut said Mahler strives toward people being in splendid isolation. I'm saying she said it's toward autonomy, but autonomy to relate. So I leave everything in from the individual theories, but then I do take out what I feel enriches my basic framework, thus making it a much larger framework which includes all these different theories and also the development of cognition, and some neurology, and some other things.

HS: What if we look at a clinical example. A young woman in treatment has been unhappy in her marriage for years, wanting to leave her husband, but never able to do it. In the past she has said: "I could never leave him without there being another relationship there for me. I couldn't be out on my own alone." I have responded—she took it as an assertion, but I meant it as a question—by wondering whether that would be best for her; whether there was something to be said for doing one thing at a time, first separating from her husband so she has time to understand that that's really what she wants to do, before entering another relationship. So, three years into this discussion she starts having an affair, and now for the first time gets serious about getting a divorce. And we return to the question of whether that is because she's in this other relationship, and whether that's best for her. She says: "You just think waiting is the best thing for me because you think the ideal for what a person should be is an individual. That's a very male idea. I think people are meant to be together, and being off on my own for a while, and getting by on my own, is nothing to strive for. It is a good solution to go from marriage right into this other relationship." That raises the question of incompatibility between your Kohutian model and Mahlerian model.

HM: That's all very superficial stuff. You're both right, but that's external stuff. I would be thinking she wants you, but she can't have you, so she picks another guy. You want her to be out in the cold, but she doesn't—she wants you. And there's something about her mother and father in there, with her saying that women want relationships, and that's good, and men don't. That's a conscious idea that's based on something unconscious, something from culture, like the things Carol Gilligan wrote about. You have to figure out what her needs are and why, and what went on with her mother and her father. Did she get what she needed from her mother or didn't she give a damn? The wish to be in a relationship can be healthy, or it can be a neurotic wish. You say her need to be in a relationship is neurotic, and that may be, but she can't let go of you.

HS: No. I only posed the question as to whether that was the case, and she decided that's what I was saying.

HM: Yeah, well it could be. It could also be healthy that she wants to relate to somebody. But that's not the primary thing, because you're leaving yourself out. And that comes from somewhere before you. You were not the first man in her life. So whether she wants to be in a relationship or out is external—it's psychotherapy.

HS: Well, it is a psychotherapy.

HM: Well, that's what one does in psychotherapy. But it does not eliminate the deeper feelings. She needs to understand where it comes from. And yes, you're right, Kohut and Mahler would argue on that, but that's their most external aspect.

HS: So then are you saying that the difference between Kohut and Mahler is superficial?

HM: Yes I am. And I think that occurs all over the place, even if you go to somebody who's totally divergent, like the British modern Kleinians, Steiner and Britton. Steiner's idea of neurotic retreat is really about sicker patients. Even then it's not incompatible. He throws in an interpretation to fish them out. It doesn't matter if the interpretation has anything to do with what they're really struggling with. It's a lifeline—something that they can hold on to. It's very different from the kind of interpretation Freud talks about, where you point out something that really is there and the unconscious becomes conscious. For Steiner it's enough that the patient hears that the analyst is there for them and seems to know and understand something. Let me give you a clinical example. A woman felt there was a terrible emptiness, like a tunnel or a hole, that she was going to fall into. She was very traumatised as a child and did not trust her mother, who had stood by while she was being abused. At least that's how she perceived it. She couldn't work on anything because she was afraid she would fall into that pit. To deal with this I had to reassure her, which is totally unanalytic in the classical view. Reassure her that I was there and wasn't going to let her fall. I would reach out a hand and hold her. It got to the image of her standing on a little platform at the edge of the pit, and looked[*sic*] over the railing into the pit, and I was holding her hand and wouldn't let her fall in. After a while she decided she could trust me a little bit and go down a little. And as we got to the analytic stuff, slowly the pit started filling in until the pit got to be solid ground. I didn't have to hold her any more, because she couldn't fall in. There was a combination here of relationship and some totally unanalytic parameters, along with analysis of her background and why she felt there was a pit; why she didn't trust me when I was the bad mother, so how I could become the good mother? Then we could get to some of the real oedipal dynamics. And she did great. It took a long time to fill in the pit, and that is not classical analysis, but it led to undoing the developmental aspect of the emptiness. It was very much like Steiner's fishing them out.

HS: You were using suggestion. And it worked.

HM: Absolutely. I never claimed that I don't seduce. I think in a way that all good interpretations are seductions, because you appear to the patient that you have something to offer they didn't know about.

HS: Now I said suggestion, but you're saying seduction.

HM: Right. You say suggest, but I say seduce. It was a suggestion, but it was more than that. You didn't want to call it that because seduce is a dirty word. Suggestion wouldn't have been enough.

HS: Well you made her believe that you would protect her. I guess seduction is the best form of suggestion.

HM: OK. I don't do that in general, but all interpretations have an aspect of suggestion and seduction—but only an aspect. Who knows much is really there? Are you creating it, the way Schafer thinks, creating a dialogue in the narrative between you, or is it really there? Well, to some extent, something like this must be there, because patients don't respond to everything the same way. You can make an interpretation that has no impact, and another that does have an impact.

HS: This is the reverse of projective identification because it comes from the therapist. There may be a big part that's just about the therapist and a little part about the patient, or a little part about the therapist and a big part about the patient.

HM: Yeah. Sometimes you make an interpretation that's very upsetting. It may be that you've hit something that's there, or it may be that they're upset that you misunderstand them. Sometimes it works and they can move on, but incorrect interpretations can work too. But I do think there's got to be something there.

HS: So this is the Meyers clinical theory that goes along with the overarching general theory, the metapsychology.

HM: Right. We got into clinical theory in a very fragmented, topsy-turvy way. I was really talking about the theoretical interpretation, and pushing that because I think it's so needed, and so important; because people go around saying: "Oh my God, there's so much pluralism, what theory should I use?" They're confused by that notion when they don't think they can make their own integration. It can be very confusing. But I love pluralism, because I think it can all be used together.

HS: So the overarching theory is a theory every practising analyst has to come to on his or her own. It's not that you think everyone should follow your overarching theory.

HM: Well, it would be nice, but they don't have to. I think it's terribly logical, and very easy, and it's very satisfying, and it works. Obviously others may do it differently. This is just so ready-made and available. The problem is that people confuse ego psychology with Arlow and Brenner, and not with the present. They think it has to be drive, it has to be severe, it has to be limited. And all the other theories are what you get in your fourth year at New York. It's a pity when one doesn't integrate them.

HS: So you call it ego psychology because that's your home base. You could be an object relationist and say this is all encompassed within that.

HM: I could, but object relations alone wouldn't give me the compromise formation Brenner talks about. It wouldn't give me wish and defence and punishment.

   Those have to be in an agency, in a clump of certain types of psychic phenomena, such as punishment, wishes, and defences.

HS: But you can have compromises between the internal objects, between the arrays of self, object, and affect.

HM: But Kernberg believes in the structural theory. He did not say he was in conflict with it. Rather, he was adding to it. He never threw out id, ego, or superego. He didn't even throw out libido.

HS: But id, ego, and superego are there in object relations theory as well.

HM: That's a funny way to put it. It's object relations theory that fits into id, ego, and superego.

HS: So you feel that if you're talking id, ego, and superego, you're talking ego psychology.

HM: Yes, it invented them.

HS: No, ego psychology didn't do that, Freud did.

HM: Yes. But Freud developed structural theory which was elaborated into ego psychology, with more of a dominance of the ego. The ego psychologists developed it. But you can't say the object relationists invented it.

HS: That's the beauty of it, because nobody really owns it.

HM: They do own it. They invented it.

HS: If you think Freud was an ego psychologist I guess you would say that.

HM: I don't think of Freud as an ego psychologist. I think of Anna Freud, and Hartmann, and Kris and Lowenstein, even Arlow and Brenner, as ego psychologists. Freud was a structuralist.

HS: Melanie Klein used id, ego, and superego as well.

HM: Not really. Not as much, but to some extent. They all used Freud, but it's come a long way since Freud.

References

Smith, H. F. (2003). Can we interpret the diverse theories and practices of psychoanalysis? *Journal of the American Psychoanalytic Association, 51S*: 127–144.
Smith, H. F. (2005). Dialogues on conflict. *Journal of the American Psychoanalytic Association, 54*: 327–363.

INDEX